3

D1091631

Ben Jonson an...

The challenge to t.. .... comedies is usually seen as an extension of the provocative techniques of English Morality drama. In this lucid and penetrating study, Professor Duncan aims to supplement that view by suggesting a more sophisticated precedent for Jonson's methods in the practice of 'oblique teaching' which Erasmus and More developed out of their admiration for the Greek author Lucian.

Part One discusses the Lucianic tradition, the controversial status of Lucianism in the sixteenth century, and its possible impact on English drama up to Marlowe. Part Two argues that Jonson – especially in *Volpone, Epicoene, The Alchemist* and *Bartholomew Fair* – consciously adopted Lucianic strategies as a means of squaring his distrust of the 'strumpet' stage with his enjoyment of it and his sense of the opportunity it offered to reach the widest available audience.

Jonson shows that stage-comedy is not as incompatible with the techniques of 'Menippean' non-dramatic satire as has often been thought. More generally, what is called here his 'art of teasing' places him in the centre of a long line of Christian humanist writers – stretching from Erasmus and More to Milton and Swift – who used fiction to educate their public through devious processes of moral and intellectual testing.

Jacket illustrations. The two editions of Nicolas Perrot d'Ablancourt's French translation of Lucian, published in Paris in 1654 and in Amsterdam in 1697, contain frontispiece portraits of Lucian which differ markedly; in the earlier edition, Lucian the jester is pictured as a fiercely Juvenalian figure (front of jacket); in the later edition (back of jacket), as mildly Horatian – see p. 12. (Reproduced by permission of the Sterling Memorial Library, Yale University.) The jacket design is by Michael and Shirley Tucker.

.... the later years of Elizabeth into the more established conditions of Jacobean times. Part II shows the interaction of Jonson's work for the court with Shakespeare's for the popular stage. Part III outlines post-Shakespearean developments.

'. . . has an unrivalled sense of theatrical continuity . . . every page reveals her encyclopaedic knowledge and has some striking comment or suggestion thrown out – she has produced a superb book both for the scholar and the general reader.'
The Guardian

Issued in hard covers and as a paperback (both on its own and as part of a six-volume series)

Ben Jonson and
the Lucianic tradition

Ben Jonson and
the Lucianic tradition

Ben Jonson and
the Lucianic tradition

DOUGLAS DUNCAN

Professor of English, McMaster University
Hamilton, Ontario

CAMBRIDGE UNIVERSITY PRESS

CAMBRIDGE
LONDON · NEW YORK · MELBOURNE

Published by the Syndics of the Cambridge University Press
The Pitt Building, Trumpington Street, Cambridge CB2 1RP
Bentley House, 200 Euston Road, London NW1 2DB
32 East 57th Street, New York, NY 10022, USA
296 Beaconsfield Parade, Middle Park, Melbourne 3206, Australia

© Cambridge University Press 1979

First published 1979

Printed in Great Britain at the
University Press, Cambridge

Library of Congress cataloguing in publication data
Duncan, Douglas J. M.
Ben Jonson and the Lucianic tradition.
Includes bibliographical references and index.
1. Jonson, Ben, 1573?–1637 – Criticism and
interpretation.   2. Lucianus Samosatensis – Influence.
3. Satire – History and criticism.   I. Title.
PR2638.D78   822'.3   78-18093
ISBN 0 521 22359 8

HUGH STEPHENS LIBRARY
STEPHENS COLLEGE
COLUMBIA, MISSOURI

PR
2638
.D78

Contents

172256

Acknowledgments

Canada has been good to university teachers during the past ten years. I am especially grateful to my own university and to the Canada Council for enabling me to take leave during 1972–3.

I conceived this book as an exploratory essay, not a comprehensive dissertation. For that reason it seemed proper to document it lightly, though how much I owe to 'guides that went before' will be clear on every page. My most significant debts are to Leonard Dean's introduction to *The Praise of Folly*, which started me on my trail when I happened to read it in conjunction with *Bartholomew Fair;* to the writings of Craig Thompson on Lucian, Erasmus and More; to Walter Kaiser's *Praisers of Folly*; to the Herford and Simpson edition of Ben Jonson; and to the seminal Jonson criticism of Jonas Barish. From the many other scholars who have shaped my thinking I can only ask forgiveness if their names have not been duly recorded.

I have been helped by conversation with many of my colleagues, notably Sharon Adams, Thomas Cain and Ronald Vince. From my graduate students I have also learned much, and most from my first, Peter Hyland, whose book *Disguise and Role-Playing in Ben Jonson's Drama* (Salzburg, 1977) hardly owes more to our collaboration than this does. Barbara Fraser, Maurice Riordan and, especially, Jennifer Taylor contributed ideas which I am conscious of having used, and to the last-named I am further indebted for salutary criticisms and improvements of style. To Jayne Berland, and to Audrey Alexander for impeccable typing, my warm thanks are also due.

A pilot-article for this study appeared in *ARIEL*, 1.2 (1970) and a version of Chapter 7 in *Wascana Review*, 5.2. (1970). Acknowledgment is made to the proprietors of these journals

Acknowledgments

for permission to use that material. Some passages in Chapter 9 are taken from the introduction to my edition of *Bartholomew Fair* (Fountainwell Drama Texts, 1972).

Most of all I am grateful to my mother, for her faith that this book would appear, and to my wife Janet, whose wise refusal to read a word of it before it was finished has forced me to use my own judgement for better or worse.

D.D.

McMaster University, Hamilton, Ontario
1978

Jonson's art of teasing

Volpone, Epicoene, The Alchemist and *Bartholomew Fair* are by common consent Ben Jonson's most successful comedies. Acted or read, they succeed by being funny and at the same time serious, so that to explain their success one must be able to connect the laughter and the thought they provoke. They are also more 'ironic' than Jonson's earlier and later comedies, which makes it likely that this irony, whatever it may be, contributes to their success and their peculiar brand of serious humour. Irony, alas, is a fractious term which literary critics are struggling to put to bed after a long and exhausting day, one of several such terms which this study cannot hope to avoid. Its commonest application to drama, as we know, describes the situation when a playwright shares a secret with his audience at the expense of his characters; its pervasiveness then depends on how many of the characters are deluded for how much of the time, and its depth depends on the meaning to be drawn from their delusions. But in explaining the effects of Jonson's major comedies we have to deal also with another form of irony which is directed against us, as spectators or readers. Far from being invited to share its secret, we are challenged to see that it exists. Its meaning is to be found in our own responses, and its pervasiveness in the fact that we are, or should be, engaged all the time. If we fail to perceive it, it is we who are deluded; we become its victims.

Every writer is an ironist at the expense of his public when he bids for a response without drawing attention to what he is doing. That is to say that irony was implicit in the humanist notion of literature as rhetoric. Here are the second and third of our fractious and overwrought terms, both of which will be used in simple, traditional senses. Of all English dramatists

Introduction: Jonson's art of teasing

Jonson was the most fully a 'humanist' in being dominated by the urge to embody in his work what he had learned from his study of the Greek and Latin classics. A part of what he learned was that Aristotle and Cicero, still the recognized authorities on rhetoric in his day, had defined it as the art of effective communication by which an expert persuades or instructs the populace. Needless to say, the function of rhetoric was normally thought of as being carried out in an open and straightforward manner, as when Johnson himself distinguishes 'Poets' from 'Poetique elves' by their mastery of the rhetorical process:

> All that dable in the inke,
> And defile quills, are not those few, can thinke,
> Conceive, expresse, and steere the soules of men,
> As with a rudder, round thus, with their pen.
> He must be one that can instruct your youth,
> And keepe your *Acme* in the state of truth,
> Must enterprize this work.[1]

But more secret and devious uses of word-power were encouraged by the humanist assumption that the writer was wiser than his public, an assumption which Jonson was prone to accept, especially when addressing a theatre audience. This irony was not, of course, motivated by the diabolical purpose of misleading or making monkeys out of ignorant spectators, though it sometimes came dangerously close to that in practice. Properly used, what we shall call the 'art of teasing' was a process of educative testing, variously playful or hostile, whereby the moral intelligence of the public was to be trained by being subjected to attempts to undermine or confuse it. In drama, particularly, it took the form of alerting audiences to the moral anomalies which are apt to arise in the theatre when natural instincts and sympathies are allowed to respond freely to the authority, wit, glamour or eloquence of the actors on stage.

No doubt one reason why Jonson's plays can be seen in this light is that we have become accustomed to the hostility of writers and film-makers who exploit our eagerness to be entertained at all costs in order to shock us into forms of uncomfortable awareness, while at the same time exposure to commercial advertising has made us sensitive to the hidden persuaders of devious rhetoric. But our first and simplest reactions to the four major comedies make clear that we are not reading into them techniques of the twentieth century. Why, for instance, since Volpone is a monster of evil, are we encouraged to share his amusements and even to see his downfall as heroic? Why the trick-ending of *Epicoene?* What about the applause for Lovewit and Face? And if Quarlous in *Bartholomew Fair* becomes the mouthpiece of a plea for tolerance, why is he presented as a sharking opportunist?

The author we have to explain is a consistent moralist who assaults our powers of moral discrimination, a satirist who plays on our susceptibilities, an ironist who lures us into false or incomplete or compromising reactions to what passes on stage. He is a born dramatist, but one who came close to equating 'good theatre' with moral delusiveness, and wrote many of his best scenes when he did so. He is a master of farce, but typically used that medium to illumine a serious issue, simultaneously tempting us to laugh it out of mind. He is not, in short, an author who asks to be trusted or loved. Empathy with his characters is far from impossible – is indeed often forced on us – but is always perilous, since to feel for them naïvely and then complain of problems is to acknowledge the discomfort of a trap. This is not to suggest that the right way to experience a play like *The Alchemist* is with a worried frown of mental concentration, as though one were crossing Niagara on a tightrope or having one's soul examined. The essential is to recognize the nature of the game, which requires, above all, a sense of humour, but also the capacity to balance our laughter with awareness of its implications. It calls for total involvement, but of a moral and intellectual as well as an emotional kind. Jonson assures us that all can play and win who have 'the wit, or the honesty to thinke well of themselves';[2] anyone, that is, who can trust his own judgement or conscience. And a factor which makes playing more pleasant – though it clearly defeats Jonson's purpose – is that most of us enjoy measuring fiction by more rigorous standards of morality than we normally apply in real life.

It would be a mistake, however, to rush blindfold into the labyrinth of Jonson's comedies, questing for ironies, ambivalences and traps. If this study is to be useful, it should concentrate

3

less on uncovering particular moves than on finding out more about the nature of the game. What were its rules, and who had played it before? An answer to the first question will arm us with some critical terms, and the second may lead us to see our object more clearly in the context of a literary tradition.

Many have managed to explain Jonson's irony without recourse to the tradition studied here. Recently, after a period when criticism focussed mainly on his satiric vision and his language, there has been a return to emphasis on his satiric techniques – a revival of the question raised by L. C. Knights in 1937 when he wrote of the 'double attitude' which an audience must adopt toward Volpone.[3] It will be clear, for example, that Alan C. Dessen sees an author similar to the one just described:

> Jonson does not, in his best plays, resort to moral extremes... but offers his audience complex situations that challenge and perplex... *Bartholomew Fair* (or *Volpone* or *The Alchemist*) shows us the satiric manipulator forcing his audience into untenable positions and making them find their own way out. The laughter evoked by moral comedy is carefully controlled so that eventually it turns back on the laugher... Only by forcing the viewer to see himself in the glass of satire can moral comedy succeed.[4]

But Dessen writes this after applying to Jonson the approach which has been so fruitfully applied to renaissance drama in the past twenty years, seeing his comedy as a development of the popular tradition of Morality plays. Since we are dealing with a synthesizing author, the value of that approach does not need to be questioned. There is no doubt that the medieval Vice-figure, taunting and joking with his audience, forecast the insidious threats of Jonson's rogue heroes, and prepared his public to regard the theatre as an arena of temptation. It is certain, too, that Jonson's perplexing techniques worked often by upsetting the expectations of those who were familiar with Morality patterns. Thus the anticipated conflict of vice with virtue is replaced by a conflict of vices; figures who seem to be labelled Goodness or Justice turn out to be impotent or tarnished; wry epilogues subvert reliance on safe, homiletic conclusions, and so forth. But more explanation is needed of the spirit in which Jonson worked on those materials and the satiric mode which he followed. Parody and inversion are sophisticated ploys. It is probable that, in feeling his way toward a new style of comedy in *Volpone*, Jonson would not be content with the guidance of popular tradition alone but would seek to reinforce it from the example and authority of more learned writings.

A case used to be made in this connexion for the influence of Roman comedy, the witty slaves of which do indeed contribute to Jonson's early plays. Their role, however, had been assimilated earlier on the English stage with that of the Vice and was stereotyped by the 1590s. Apart from the licensing of social indecorum, common to most comedy, the Roman playwrights offered little precedent for close, critical engagement with an audience. We must look elsewhere to find 'learned' precedent for Jonson's practices, and not necessarily to drama at all. The terms which have been used to describe his procedures will have been familiar to all who have grappled with Swift. It seems reasonable, then, to direct our search to some of Swift's forerunners: particularly Lucian, Erasmus and More.

The immediate purpose of this book is to argue that the serio-comic balance and teasing rhetoric of Jonson's middle comedies mark a conscious adaptation to the stage of satiric techniques which are found in such works as *The Praise of Folly*, the *Colloquies*, and *Utopia*, and which Erasmus and More associated with their favourite Greek author, Lucian. More generally, however, we shall explore what can be learned about Jonson from reading him with those writers in mind. Since they are not in the minds of all students of drama, relevant aspects of them will be treated discursively in Part 1, which will also try to sketch the fortunes of 'Lucianism' between the early sixteenth and seventeenth centuries. Luckily, this background is neither difficult nor dull. Part 2, dealing directly with Jonson, will pursue the approaches and apply the terminology made familiar in Part 1. These later chapters presuppose knowledge of Jonson's plays and are not meant as comprehensive critical accounts of them.

Limiting our study for the most part to a very few writers may make the tradition described seem narrower than it actually was. Lucian was not the only model for humanist *joco-serium*, nor were Erasmus and More its only practitioners. Jonson did not give these authors undivided attention, as might seem to be suggested, nor was his art of teasing an isolated phenomenon. Since the term *joco-serium* (Greek *spoudogeloion*) was associated with Menippus, our subject will be seen to impinge on the history of 'Menippean' fiction. Also, since the term is paradoxical, we shall skirt the field of humanist paradox so boldly charted by Rosalie Colie.[5] And recalling Donne's description of paradoxes as 'alarums to truth to arme her'[6] – as helpful obstacles on the roundabout climb to Truth's summit – we shall recognize that Jonson's placing of obstacles in the way of his audience is related to that process of educating the reader by 'intanglement' which is now being widely discovered in renaissance literature, following Stanley E. Fish's approach to *Paradise Lost*.[7] This book may contribute a little to the study of that process. Essentially, however, it draws on Jonson's comedy to build on the conclusions of H. A. Mason[8] by arguing that it was Jonson who renewed and transmitted to English writing the most vital achievement of sixteenth-century literary humanism, the engaged and engaging irony of Erasmus and More. In pursuit of that aim, these pages will not hesitate to suggest rather more than they can prove, rating stimulus to discussion above fear of rash judgement or of heresies in method. Donne also wrote of paradoxes that 'if they make you to find better reasons against them they do their office'.[9] It is in the belief that there is room for that spirit in literary criticism that the following study is offered.

PART ONE

Lucian and Lucianism

Est hoc nimirum sanctissimum fallendi genus, per imposturam dare beneficium

Erasmus, *De Utilitate Colloquiorum* (*LB*, I, 901F)

Lucian

From the late fifteenth century until well into the nineteenth, Lucian held his place among the most widely translated and imitated of Greek authors. He later came to be banished from the pantheon of nineteenth-century Hellenism, partly because he was a 'silver' Greek – or rather not a Greek at all but a Syrian of the second century A.D. who had copied the styles of an earlier age – but mainly because of his ambiguous attitude toward the nobler ideals of Attic culture. His status today typically reflects the split between the scholar and the general reader of ancient literature which the decline of classical education has brought about. The object of recondite and forbidding monographs on the shelves of university libraries, he also appeals directly, with his agile and mocking wit, to a larger public which encounters selections of his work in attractive contemporary versions.[1] There is need for a scholarly study of Lucian which would unite the interests of his readers in a common focus on his satiric art, and also provide a basis for a thorough assessment of his impact on European literature. Neither of these functions can be attempted here, but even a sketch may indicate the perils of ignoring him altogether. Although his influence on master-satirists, from Erasmus and More to Fielding and Voltaire, has often been noted and in some cases analysed in detail, it remains true that the average student of literature uses his name less often and less confidently than those of Horace and Juvenal.

Explicit acknowledgments of debt to Lucian, and precise definitions of his character as a satirist, are not as common in the highways of literature as a writer on this subject might wish. Had they been more common, the subject would have been long ago exhausted. In fact, as will later be shown, educated people

Lucian and Lucianism

in the sixteenth and following centuries had a clear idea of the general characteristics of 'Lucianism', though they disagreed about its moral usefulness and rarely analysed its methods. Lucian's influence is readily detectable by those who have read him, especially (though not necessarily) if they can share with earlier ages an appreciation of his beautifully light, lucid and flexible Greek. And a likely reason why it was not more often openly acknowledged is that writers assumed that it would always be recognized as clearly and intuitively as it was in their day. Many a witty ghost such as Swift's has been vexed as a result of that assumption. But if we ask why renaissance criticism transmitted no image of Lucian as vivid or definite as those of the Roman verse-satirists, we must look for an explanation to the varied, and in one sense anonymous, nature of his work.

The writings attributed to Lucian are numerous but short, and were printed by his earliest editors in a single Folio. (The beautiful *editio princeps* of Lascaris appeared at Florence in 1496, that of Aldus at Venice in 1503.) The renaissance critic, trained to classify authors in terms of genre, was faced with a baffling diversity of pieces, ranging from various forms of rhetorical display through narrative, biography and epistle to several distinct types of dialogue. In his influential *De Satyra Graecorum Poesi atque Romanorum Satira* (1605), Isaac Casaubon classed Lucian as a 'Menippean' or 'Varronian' satirist because a mixture of prose and verse is found occasionally in his dialogues and because Menippus himself, the Cynic philosopher, appears in a few of them. Another factor which led to that classification was Lucian's claim to have invented the Comic Dialogue by uniting the serious connotations of philosophical dialectic with the wit and fantasy of Aristophanic comedy, a claim which Casaubon associated with Strabo's description of Menippus as *spoudogeloios* and Cicero's somewhat similar characterization of the writings of Varro.[2] Properly defined, the concept of *spoudogeloion*, or *joco-serium*, is distinctly relevant to Lucian, but without close definition it could fit other satirists equally well, and since the intermixture of verse in Lucian's prose is almost always by way of parodic quotation, little but confusion could result from linking him in that respect, as Casaubon did, with such different writers as Petronius, Martianus Capella and Boethius. 'Menippean/Varronian' was probably the best single label that a classifying critic could stick on Lucian, and it has been endorsed by Northrop Frye in *The Anatomy of Criticism*. But its clarity and usefulness are diminished by the fact that the satires of Menippus and Varro have almost totally perished; nor is it applicable to many of Lucian's unless we interpret it, as Frye does, very broadly indeed. To read all of Lucian is to perceive the first reason why he has never been definitively typed in terms of genre. The immediate impression he gives is of dazzling variety, and such constant factors as are present throughout his work resist analysis in formal neo-Aristotelian terms. They are of a kind which renaissance authors were better able to imitate than to define critically.

One of these constant factors, the evasiveness of his personality, provides the second and more important reason for the failure of critics to clarify Lucian's image. We are taught that the images which Horace and Juvenal present of themselves in their satires were carefully-modelled *personae* which ought not to be mistaken for autobiography. None the less, the masks are so memorable – in Juvenal's case so forceful and in Horace's so subtle – that the temptation to treat them as self-portraits has always been irresistible. This is less true of Lucian, and not solely because of his fondness for the dramatic method. Ultimately it makes little difference to the character of a Lucianic piece whether the author presents himself in it or not, and whether in the first person or in the third, but it is worth noting for a start that he does, in fact, present himself often. Thus, to take random examples, there are *The Dream, or Lucian's Career* and *To one who said 'You're a Prometheus in words'* in which he uses the first person to tell of his choice of career and his invention of the Comic Dialogue respectively; there are pieces which he introduces as Lucian (*Nigrinus*) or in which he refers to himself as Lucian (*A True Story*); and there are many dialogues such as *Hermotimus, The Double Indictment* and *The Dead Come to Life, or The Fisherman* where he disguises himself thinly as Lycinus, the Syrian, or 'Frankness'. He shows no reluctance to talk about himself and his concerns. What is meant, then, by referring to a quality of 'anonymity' in his work?

We can approach an answer to that question by noting the difficulties experienced by seventeenth-century interpreters in trying to decide what kind of a man they were dealing with. Two editions of Nicolas Perrot d'Ablancourt's French version of Lucian, published respectively at Paris in 1654 and at Amsterdam in 1697, are each prefaced by a portrait, the second being clearly a reworking of the first. A jester in cap and bells, with a bauble in one hand and holding a mask in front of his face with the other, stands on a platform and addresses an audience below. But the figures of the satirist are totally different: the one masculine and burly, the other short and effeminate. There is no correspondence at all between the faces behind the masks; the first is stern and angry, the second is delicate and smiling; the components of *joco-serium* have been separated. What has happened is that Lucian has been interpreted in terms of the more familiar and more easily visualized characters of Juvenal and Horace. The vivid way in which the Roman satirists stamped themselves on the seventeenth-century imagination is best illustrated by the astonishing substratum of sexual metaphor in Dryden's famous comparison, to which the portraits of Lucian provide a good gloss:

The delight which Horace gives me, is but languishing...He may ravish other men; but I am too stupid and insensible to be tickled. Where he barely grins himself, and, as Scaliger says, only shows his white teeth, he cannot provoke me to any laughter. His urbanity, that is, his good manners, are to be commended, but his wit is faint; and his salt, if I may dare to say so, almost insipid. Juvenal is of a more vigorous and masculine wit, he gives me as much pleasure as I can bear; he fully satisfies my expectation; he treats his subject home: his spleen is raised, and he raises mine:...and when he is at the end of his way I willingly stop with him.[3]

By contrast, it is Dryden's inability to muster any kind of intimate response which makes his *Life of Lucian* (written three years later) so flat. His perfunctory comments on Lucian's wit might suggest that, like the artists, he saw no distinctive face behind the mask at all: 'for the most part, he rather laughs like Horace, than bites like Juvenal. Indeed his genius was of kin to both, but more nearly related to the former.'[4] The *Life of*

Lucian

Lucian sometimes reads like an exercise in writing upon nothing, yet it is not altogether imperceptive, and Dryden's failure to bring his subject to life stems rather from the fact that the face which he did see was inscrutable. Lucian's genius, he declares, 'whose image we may clearly see in the glass which he holds before us', was that of a Sceptic who

doubted of every thing; weighed all opinions, and adhered to none of them; only used them as they served his occasion for the present Dialogue, and perhaps rejected them in the next...never constant to himself in any scheme of divinity, unless it be in despising his gentile gods.[5]

The Sceptic is essentially faceless, though as a Protean artist he may wear any number of masks. The near relation which Dryden saw between Lucian and Horace was in part that between the Sceptic and the Eclectic, but the latter builds a positive identity where the former does not. And in noting an affinity between Lucian and his own times ('all knowing ages being naturally Skeptick, and not at all bigotted') Dryden was well aware that uncommitted knowingness could involve some loss of 'humanity'. When we assess the effect of the numerous personal appearances of Lucian in his work, it is true that the total picture is of a kind of thinker and a kind of artist – the contexts always present him in one role or the other – rather than of a recognizable individual human being.

Where the Roman satirists use the *persona* to establish a persuasively human and authoritative character through whom to launch their attacks, Lucian uses it more flexibly as a means of making witty points in a variety of ways. Normally it will be Lucian or Lycinus who is used when a precise attitude is to be adopted on a philosophic or artistic issue, but as Dryden noted their attitudes may vary from one piece to the next, and they can also have the laugh turned against them, as when Lucian becomes the foolish narrator of *A True Story* or Lycinus is overwhelmed in *The Cynic*. On specific issues with which Lucian was not professionally concerned, such as the social position of hired writers or the cult of athleticism, the mouthpiece is likely to be anonymous (*On Salaried Posts in Great Houses*) or else an invented character (Tychiades, for instance, who explodes superstitions in *The Lover of Lies* but also becomes a victim of

13

ingenious special pleading in *The Parasite*). When the object of satire is more general, the mouthpiece will be a character from history or myth: Menippus surveying life as a comic chaos or Charon observing the vanity of human wishes. But a large number of Lucian's most characteristic dialogues do not employ a mouthpiece character at all. The short *Dialogues of the Courtesans*, *Dialogues of the Gods*, *Dialogues of the Sea-gods* and *Dialogues of the Dead* are fragments of 'overheard' conversation in which the satiric point has to be deduced by the reader from the unconscious self-revelation of the speakers. Lucian's touch is of the lightest, and many of these pieces are no more than witty embroideries on well-known literary situations, but the technique has obvious possibilities for the theatre. The best example to cite in a book on Jonson is the ninth *Dialogue of the Dead*, where old Polystratus, newly arrived in Hades, recounts with bland satisfaction to an equally cynical acquaintance how he had pitted legacy-hunters against each other by making separate promises to each and finally left his money to 'ennoble' a handsome young slave. The effectiveness of such dialogues depends absolutely on the non-expression of the author's viewpoint. Corruption and cynicism are made to appear as the norm, endorsed from beyond the grave.

But even when the characters are objectively conceived in this way, they have no function beyond enabling the author to make his point, either obliquely (as in the case just cited) or more directly. This is why the presence or absence of a mouthpiece makes no essential difference to the nature of a Lucianic dialogue. The subordination of character and plot to intellectual play is the key factor in Northrop Frye's broad categorization of 'Menippean' fiction, distinguished from other forms in which character and plot have greater independent value.[6] Most of us first become aware of this distinction after falling down in the attempt to read *Gulliver's Travels* 'straight'. We note that the story-line subserves the making of satiric points; that Gulliver is not so much a consistent character as a multi-functional mechanism for implicating the reader; and that Swift does not mean us to reconcile our responses to the creatures he shows us – the Brobdingnagians, for instance, being physically repellent and politically admirable in something like separate compartments. It is certain that Lucian did not invent this uncomfortable mode of fiction, but the accident of survival made him the main starting-point for its later development. With regard to its effect on drama, its tendency to relegate character, as Frye says, to the expression of 'mental attitudes' points an obvious affinity to Roman comedy's representative types and to Jonson's 'humours'. The theatre, however, resists the mode to the degree that an actor cannot help imposing a single, consistent identity on the character he portrays.

Intellectual play, teasing impersonality, a glittering and superficial virtuosity over the whole range of classical prose-forms – the very factors which made it difficult for the Renaissance to feel at home with Lucian as a man made it easy to recognize him as a type of the uncommitted thinker and the artist dedicated only to his art. Historical criticism of the past hundred years has attempted to unearth the 'real' Lucian, to trace his career as a rhetorician and lecturer around the Mediterranean, to relate his culture to that of the Second Sophistic period, to examine the genres to which his various pieces belong and the purposes for which they were written. There is no reason to suppose that the Renaissance knew nothing of these matters, since most of the evidence is present in Lucian's writings, and it is likely that Erasmus and More were able to draw some historical analogies between Lucian's cultural position and their own. None the less, if his place in the mental landscape of sixteenth-century writers is to be properly understood, it is not the historical Lucian that we must study, but rather the dominant concepts which spring from his work, and especially the dominant metaphors which the renaissance imagination was quick to apprehend.

The unifying concept is detachment and the key metaphor is that of the detached observer, or *kataskopos*.[7] The viewpoint of the 'down-looker' or 'over-viewer', who belittles human concerns by seeing them from a great height, was a favourite commonplace of the Cynics. That it was especially associated with Menippus is implied by Lucian's dialogue *Icaromenippus*, where the philosopher, seeking eternal verities, harnesses himself to the right wing of an eagle and the left wing of a vulture and launches himself from Olympus on a flight to the Throne of Zeus. He pauses *en route* on the moon, from which, with a little help from Empedocles, he obtains insights into the activities of men, swarming below like ants in ant-hills.[8] This passage, though it has many analogues, was to become the *locus classicus* for the ironic world-view of the *kataskopos*. For Lucian the figure meant much more than a Cynic device to be parodied; it keeps recurring in various guises as the *leitmotiv* of his art and thought. All his writings reflect in some way the search for a detached point of vantage, a rejection of prior commitments, a compulsion to get out in order to look in. Even as a professional educator he kept his public at a distance. In *The Dream, or Lucian's Career* (15) the first reward he receives from Paideia (Education), after choosing her service, is to be taken for a sky-ride in her chariot:

I was carried up into the heights and went from the East to the very West, surveying cities and nations and peoples, sowing something broadcast over the earth like Triptolemus. I do not now remember what it was that I sowed; only that men, looking up from below, applauded, and all those above whom I passed in my flight sped me on my way with words of praise.

Probably that is what it feels like to make a successful lecture-tour, which most of Lucian's life seems to have been. Not for him the image of the teacher *agonistes*, sweating it out with his students in the classroom day after day. He is the travelling performer wafted to the airport on waves of applause. Above all, he is the actor *kataskopos* (on a podium, as in the portraits) who recollects an endless succession of upturned admiring faces more clearly than the message he has tried to convey.

Lucian is always to some degree sceptical about the substance of what he writes, except where the substance is scepticism itself. Failing to perceive this, earnest critics often used to assume that a writer whose main stock-in-trade was philosophy ought himself to be judged as a philosopher, and so proceeded gravely to fault him on the score of inconsistency or lack of commitment. Since *Nigrinus* pays tribute to a Platonist, *The Cynic* to Cynicism, and *Alexander the False Prophet* to Epicurus, sympathetic attempts were even made to salve Lucian's reputation for sincerity by arguing a chronological progression from one allegiance to another. Nowadays it is generally agreed that Lucian's intellectual positions are almost infinitely variable, depending on the subject in hand, so that the exposure of a sham prophet, for example, was appropriately conducted under the mantle of Epicurus, the chief enemy of credulity. For Lucian's true position, in so far as it matters, one looks to *Hermotimus*, which certainly seems – one can say no more – to be the philosophical dialogue with the least infusion of *jocus* in its *serium*. It favours scepticism on the ground that no choice of a philosophy can be valid unless based on full experience of all, for which life is too short. The farcical complement to *Hermotimus*, and much more typical of Lucian's tone in such matters, is *Philosophies for Sale*, in which representatives of the different sects are paraded for auction. The last to be auctioned is the Pyrrhonian, or Sceptic. Reduced to worm-like inconsequence by being sure about nothing, he tries to balance arguments equally on a pair of scales until any kind of preference becomes impossible. His standpoint is caricatured as wittily and incisively as those of the others, yet is conspicuously close to the underlying assumption of the dialogue itself that all creeds are equally prone to absurdity, especially when valued by the common-sense norms of the market-place.

Defending *Philosophies for Sale* in its sequel, *The Dead Come to Life, or The Fisherman*, Lucian's spokesman wins acquittal on the charge of insulting philosophy by advancing the stock argument that he has ridiculed abuses and perversions rather than the founders of the great schools themselves. But the sparkling comedy of the trial-scene is persuasive evidence that Lucian should always be read as a satiric artist and not as a thinker. It is in fact in relation to art that his cult of detachment is most interesting. He enjoys the idea that the creator of the universe must have stood outside it (*Icaromenippus*, 8), and at a more practical level he is scornful of artists who sell themselves to patrons (*On Salaried Posts in Great Houses*). But he is also concerned about the extent to which aesthetic distance is desirable. When Charon the ferryman comes up from Hades to investigate for himself the human scene which his clients are always so reluctant to leave, Hermes proposes a high point of vantage with a good view in all directions (*Charon, or The Inspectors*, 2). Piling Pelion on Ossa, and Oeta and Parnassus on top of both, they achieve a kataskopic survey of the earth. Charon objects, however (6), that he is now too high up to see anything plainly. 'What I wanted was not just to look at cities and mountains as in a picture, but to observe men themselves, what they are doing and what they are saying.' The details of human behaviour are as important to the satirist as the total picture. Charon is classed as an *idiotes* (4), a term regularly applied by Lucian to the uninitiated and the unenlightened.[9] His problem is solved for him by Hermes, the divine wit, who endows him with the necessary bi-focal vision by reciting a charm out of Homer. Only the highest art, Lucian would seem to be saying, has the power to reconcile close observation with large-scale perspective.

A more technical account of a similar problem is found in *The Dance*. The art-form discussed here (*orchesis*) was the dramatic representation of myth by a dancer and a speaking actor, supported by chorus and musicians. Lucian's concern is with the balance between detachment and involvement to be achieved in the performers' role-playing, which in turn determines the degree to which the audience will identify with the spectacle. The ultimate aim is to effect in the audience a sort of *katharsis*, which Lucian appears to interpret as the inducement of mental equilibrium, a cure for disturbed emotions: 'If a lover enters the theatre, he is restored to his right mind by seeing all the evil consequences of love; and one who is in the clutch of grief leaves the theatre in brighter mood, as if he had taken some potion that brings forgetfulness' (79). But this can only be achieved if the audience is persuaded to identify with the performer: 'The praise that he gets from the spectators will be consummate when each of those who behold him recognises his own traits, or rather sees in the dancer as in a mirror his very self, with his customary feelings and actions' (81). Thus drama enables the audience to fulfil the Delphic injunction, Know Thyself, 'and when they go away from the theatre they have learned what they should choose and what avoid, and have been taught what they did not know before' (81). That is the ideal. Typically, however,

Lucian

Lucian concentrates on what is apt to go wrong. An incompetent performer will fail to involve the audience at all. Even more disastrous will be one who enters too fully into his role and causes the audience to forget itself by identifying to excess. Lucian gives an amusing sketch of a dancer who ran amok in 'The Madness of Ajax', almost brained the actor playing Odysseus, and fetched up in the front row of the stalls, to the consternation of the senators who feared he would mistake them for the sheep which Ajax traditionally slew. Though the 'polite' and 'understanding' sector of the audience was embarrassed by the performance, its effect on the unenlightened (*idiotai*) was to make them throw off their clothes and behave as wildly as the performer. This is to 'debauch the histrionic art' (84) by confusing mimesis with reality. The decorum of the theatre requires from both performer and spectator that emotional involvement should be controlled by the detached intelligence.

The vision of the detached observer led Lucian to large, simplifying metaphors of human life. Though inevitably shared with many other writers, these are so characteristic of Lucian that some of them should be described. 'Ants in ant-hills' has already been mentioned – another good one is bubbles at the foot of a waterfall (*Charon*, 19) – but most are taken from the theatre. The main impression derived by Menippus looking down from the moon is of life as a discordant chorus:

It is as if one should put on the stage a company of singers...and then should order each singer to abandon harmony and sing a tune of his own; with each one full of emulation and carrying his own tune and striving to outdo his neighbour in loudness of voice...Such is the discord that makes up the life of men. Not only do they sing different tunes, but they are unlike in costume and move at cross-purposes in the dance and agree in nothing until the manager drives each of them off the stage, saying that he has no further use for him. After that, however, they are all quiet alike, no longer singing that unrhythmical medley of theirs. But there in the play-house itself, full of variety and shifting spectacles, everything that took place was truly laughable (*Icaromenippus*, 17).

The emphasis here is on competitive chaos, with the implication that the chorus ought to be working as an ensemble, though it would be less amusing if it did. In *Menippus, or The Descent into Hades* (16) the grim figure of the Manager becomes more prominent and is identified as Fortune, dressing the actors for roles in her pageant. The following reflections are suggested to Menippus by the sight of heaps of indistinguishable skeletons on the Acherusian plain:

So as I looked at them it seemed to me that human life is like a long pageant, and that all its trappings are supplied and distributed by Fortune, who arrays the participants in various costumes of many colours. Taking one person, it may be, she attires him royally, placing a tiara upon his head, giving him body-guards, and encircling his brow with the diadem; but upon another she puts the costume of a slave. Again, she makes up one person so that he is handsome, but causes another to be ugly and ridiculous. I suppose that the show must needs be diversified. And often, in the very middle of the pageant, she exchanges the costumes of several players; instead of allowing them to finish the pageant in the parts that had been assigned to them, she re-apparels them, forcing Croesus to assume the dress of a slave and a captive, and shifting Maeandrius, who formerly paraded among the servants, into the imperial habit of Polycrates. For a brief space she lets them use their costumes, but when the time of the pageant is over, each gives back the properties and lays off the costume along with his body, becoming what he was before his birth, no different from his neighbour.

Such metaphors have their force but are somewhat simply fatalistic. Lucian's *kataskopoi* are expert at pointing to the vanity and absurdity of the human spectacle, but they rarely offer a more positive response. In Greek tradition the observer could respond in one of two ways: he could look on and laugh with Democritus, or look on and weep with Heraclitus. We shall therefore not be surprised to find the figure of Democritus, the laughing philosopher of Abdera, intimately linked with renaissance Lucianism. He does appear also in Horace, and presides memorably over Juvenal's Tenth Satire, a kataskopic survey of the vanity of human wishes in which Juvenal stands unusually far back from his material. But the mask of irresponsible, disembodied laughter was not one which Horace wore for himself, and Juvenal's poem does not fail to end by urging a life of virtuous action and praying for Stoic firmness of mind to resist the paralysing concept of Fortune. Lucian only once shows the world-stage metaphor inducing an active response. His Nigrinus sees Roman life at least in part as a moral challenge:

Seating myself, as it were, high up in a theatre full of untold thousands, I look down on what takes place, which is of a quality sometimes to afford laughter

Lucian

and amusement, sometimes to prove a man's true steadfastness...Don't suppose that there is any better school for virtue or any truer test of the soul than this city and the life here; it is no small matter to make a stand against so many desires, so many sights and sounds that lay rival hands on a man and pull him in every direction. One must simply imitate Odysseus and sail past them; not, however, with his hands bound (for that would be cowardly) nor with his ears stopped with wax, but with ears open and body free, and in a spirit of genuine contempt (*Nigrinus*, 18–19).

But even the Platonist prefers to turn to the comic aspect of the scene. We soon learn not to expect Lucian's characters to run for the immortal garland or welcome the dust and heat of the arena. Instead we note that the strenuous Stoic, toiling incessantly up the steep hill of virtue, was a favourite mark for his wit (*A True Story*, II.18).

Compulsive detachment can also be seen reflected in some of his commonest fictional devices: most obviously, in the dialogue-form itself. Lucian's speakers tend to be far removed from the battle. His mythological characters talk like men but belong to a timeless world. His Gods comment on life from above, his Dead from below, and even his Courtesans gossip off-duty. Perspective is variously achieved. In *The Dream, or The Cock*, for instance, it comes from the bird's remarkable capacity to remember its previous lives; and in *A True Story* we find the opposite device of the appropriate after-life, when Lucian journeys to the Elysian Fields and sees how well-known figures from the past are spending eternity.

A True Story – always Lucian's most popular piece and effectively the source of that fertile genre, the Imaginary Voyage – also provides the most spectacular indication of how much he worked through literary allusion. His tale will be enjoyed, he says,

not only for the novelty of its subject, for the humour of its plan and because I tell all kinds of lies in a plausible and specious way, but also because everything in my story is a more or less comical parody of one or another of the poets, historians and philosophers of old, who have written much that smacks of miracles and fables. I would cite them by name, were it not that you yourself will recognise them from your reading (I.2).

Lucian is always fundamentally the cultural gamesman, holding the whole of Greek culture at his finger-tips and requiring his readers to be able to do the same. What he says to the philosophers in *The Dead Come to Life, or The Fisherman* (6) can well be more widely applied:

> I have always consistently admired philosophy and extolled you and lived on intimate terms with the writings you have left behind. These very phrases that I utter – where else but from you did I get them? Culling them like a bee, I make my show with them before men, who applaud and recognize where and from whom and how I gathered each flower; and although ostensibly it is I whom they admire for the bouquet, as a matter of fact it is you and your garden, because you have put forth such blossoms, so gay and varied in their hues – if one but knows how to select and interweave and combine them so that they will not be out of harmony with one another.

Not only his ideas but his art and his humour are highly esoteric. He makes most of his points and gets most of his laughs by turning a story on its head, playing on the recorded quirks of his characters, juggling with myth, punning on etymologies, quoting from Homer or Herodotus or Plato in incongruous contexts. Editors are constantly acknowledging that many of Lucian's jokes are lost to us through the disappearance of his sources, and although his sense of the ridiculous is universal enough to attract readers who share little of his background, it inevitably appeals most to those who share his background most fully. Even by classical standards, Lucian carried the practice of literary allusion to quite extraordinary lengths. Concluding an exhaustive study of this subject, the French scholar J. Bompaire asserts that Lucian's main claim to originality lies in the extent of his imitation.[10] Thus an important part of his appeal in the Renaissance was to humanist scholars who enjoyed pitting their newly-acquired knowledge of Greek literature against his. Those who were clever enough to understand his game were far from repelled by his bookishness. An Asiatic who had out-Greeked the Greeks, a writer of the Christian era who had brought a thousand years of Greek culture to life as though it were contemporary, he was an example of what still might be done.

Did Lucian's joking really have a serious purpose? In the following chapters we shall be concerned with conflicting answers to this question that were offered in the sixteenth century. Here we may note his own suggestions on the matter, which, though they need not be accepted at face value, did provide a basis for later assessments.

There is first of all the defence of the preserver and popularizer, the custodian of the Greek garden who kept it open to the public. We have been visualizing an élitist who wrote for the initiated and scorned the *idiotai*, but Lucian would have denied that he lacked an educative purpose. He makes clear that his invention of the Comic Dialogue was a popularizing gambit. In his defence of it he begins by identifying his own type of public epideictic oratory ('we...who come before a crowd and offer our lectures'), and then proceeds to a series of flippant analogies between himself and Prometheus as inventors.[11] The serious analogy which demands to be drawn, though he is too witty to make it explicit, is that he, like Prometheus, has applied his invention to the good of mankind. His claim to have made philosophy attractive by 'farcing' the Platonic dialogue with Aristophanic ingredients could be read as an extension of the well-known Promethean claim of Socrates to have brought down philosophy from heaven to earth.[12] Thus, although his 'invention' is now generally seen as only a small step in the movement to popularize philosophy which had already been going on in his day for hundreds of years, one can readily understand how his claim could establish him in sympathetic eyes as a responsible educator, one who had cleverly made use of a popular medium to disseminate ideas, along with high standards of wit and polish, to a wide audience.

Lucian also parades as a serious critic of contemporary abuses. The remoteness of his satiric standpoint and the element of literary pastiche in his writings do not prevent him from giving us a detailed picture of life and manners in the second century A.D. Even when his themes are stock subjects of satire, such as funerals or sacrifices or the parasites and legacy-hunters who haunt the rich, his treatment of them is clearly enlivened by personal observation. He does not always confine himself to general ridicule of the human comedy; many of his shafts are aimed quite precisely at specialists who traded on ignorance and folly, bogus men-of-learning who imposed on the public and thus trod on his professional toes: pretentious jargon-mongers

Lucian and Lucianism

(*Lexiphanes*), meretricious lecturers (*A Professor of Public Speaking*), and sham philosophers of all sects (*passim*). Two pieces which came to be particularly admired as attacks on the exploitation of ignorance are *The Passing of Peregrinus* (on the well-advertised suicide of a religious maniac) and *Alexander, or The False Prophet* (a caustic account of an all-round charlatan). In most of Lucian's writings the values upheld are honesty and common-sense, not wit or learning, with the result that there is frequent disparity between the simple norms which he states and those which he implies through his highly sophisticated manner. Readers more influenced by the latter might well suspect that he took nothing seriously at all except his art, but the unimpeachable safeness of the norms through which he sought to make contact with his public could always be accepted as evidence to the contrary.

For posterity, however, the most significant of Lucian's claims to seriousness lay in the hints he gave about the value of literary play. The concept of *lusus* is widely recognized as among the most influential which the ancient world bequeathed to the Renaissance. Used by Virgil to describe his pastorals, and by Horace of his slighter odes, the term was an expression of conventional self-depreciation (*eironeia*) about work done in unpretentious literary genres. It was often associated with the idea of 'playing' on traditional materials, as in our word 'allusive'. Lucian's writings qualified as *lusus* by their modest scope and parodic method as well as by being generally light-hearted. Essentially, of course, the term was a metaphor from the school-room, so that literary play meant relaxation from ambitious intellectual labours and strenuous didactic intent. No humanist who knew the consummate works of art which Virgil and Horace had classified as *lusus* would use the term disparagingly, and although opinions certainly differed about the value of Lucian's contribution in the field, we shall find it significant that the first sentence of *A True Story*, his best-known work, had provided a classic statement in defence of it. Just as athletes regard relaxation as the most important part of their training, so (says Lucian) nothing is more important for students, to refresh their minds and prepare them for further

Lucian

labours, than the right kind of light reading. As we have seen, the particular form of *lusus* which Lucian had in mind in *A True Story* was no simple rest-cure but a teasing literary puzzle. Following the example of Odysseus, who had 'humbugged the illiterate Phaeacians' (*idiotas*) with a sequence of tall stories, Lucian will tell a tissue of 'plausible and specious' lies, under a misleading title, and challenge his readers to do better than the Phaeacians by spotting his parodies from poets, historians and philosophers. Here, in essential form, is the defence of *lusus* on which Lucian's renaissance imitators were to build. It is a diversion in which the writer not only displays his own wit but also tests and invigorates the wit of his readers.

There is always a danger of reading into an ancient author the motives of those who imitated his art in a later age. This applies particularly in trying to assess the seriousness of an author's wit, and we can be thankful that we do not have to make a final judgement on the relative importance of *jocus* and *serium* in Lucian. As early as the fourth century, Eunapius destroyed the balance of *joco-serium* and loaded the scales in favour of irresponsibility by describing Lucian as 'a man who made serious efforts to be funny'.[13] Most classical scholars today would accept this morally dismissive view. It was not, however, the view of Erasmus and More.

CHAPTER 2

Erasmus

In the sixteenth century the names of Erasmus and More were inevitably linked with Lucian's.[1] They came to be recognized as his leading interpreters to the humanist world, partly because their Latin translations of more than thirty of his pieces were the medium through which he was most commonly read, and partly because of the stimulus they were seen to have drawn from him in their works of serio-comic wit. They were thus assured of a place at the centre of the Lucianic controversy which alternately raged and smouldered throughout the century, as will be described in Chapter 4. Their stated attitudes toward Lucian were remarkably similar, and were closely bound up with the shared literary ideals of their early friendship. What we call their Lucianism was a joint creation: each struck sparks from the other as well as from the author they admired. It will be useful, however, to focus separately on the different contributions each made to the later development of the art of teasing. This will mean studying Erasmus's example mainly in terms of his satiric theory and art, and More's mainly in terms of the *persona* which he created for himself in his writings and which was fostered by biographical tradition.

The first reason for Lucian's popularity among humanist scholars at the start of the century was the suitability of his language as a guide for those who were eager to teach themselves Greek. 'The true learning that you seek is acknowledged by all to be enshrined in the wisdom of the Greeks. Your toil will become light and amusing, and your progress sure, if only you will read a little Lucian every day.'[2] So Thomas Linacre, writing to encourage Greek studies at Oxford, typified the estimate of Lucian as a purveyor of Greek without tears, and it was undoubtedly in that spirit that Erasmus and More first turned to him. As well as the purity of his Attic style, the idiomatic vivacity of his dialogues commended him for peda- gogical purposes. Greek was rarely taught as a spoken language, but the age-old habit of teaching elementary Latin through dialogue was naturally carried over into the teaching of ele- mentary Greek. Lucian was much used in the sixteenth century for both purposes, sometimes in editions which printed the original Greek and a Latin translation in parallel columns. While it is always difficult to assess the creative influence exerted by school-books, the probability that Lucian's matter and manner impressed themselves on children's minds must be very high indeed. There is a strong likelihood that Ben Jonson, at Westminster in the 1580s, encountered Lucian in the course of being introduced to both the classical tongues.[3]

Erasmus appreciated this aspect of Lucian's usefulness, but from the start pitched higher claims for his content and literary art. Many of these claims occur in dedicatory letters prefixed to his translations of single dialogues and addressed to distin- guished men. For example, the dedication of *Toxaris, or Friend- ship* (1506) to Richard Foxe, Bishop of Winchester, includes some purely literary comment, drawing attention to the de- corum of characterization observed by Lucian in distinguishing his interlocutors by their style of speech, a distinction which Erasmus as translator says he had tried to preserve. The style of the Greek Mnesippus is said to be distinctively Grecian ('comis', 'facetus', 'festivus'), while that of Toxaris has the qualities appropriate to a Scythian ('simplex', 'incondita', 'aspera', 'sedula', 'seria', 'fortis').[4] The first set of adjectives introduces us to a large family of terms denoting polished wit and sophisticated good humour which Erasmus and More persistently apply to Lucian himself, indicating the side of his appeal which they responded to most intimately. One should not, therefore, assume that Bishop Foxe's recommendation of Lucian in his founding statutes for Corpus Christi College, Oxford, was solely based on his usefulness for teaching the language of the New Testament. In fact, though Erasmus always makes the conventional claim that his author offers an equal measure of profit and pleasure, his early remarks imply that at that stage in his career he appreciated Lucian with a mainly aesthetic relish as the author who, more than any other, had introduced him to the ideals of intellectual poise and gracefully-carried sophistication which he associated with Greek culture. He was not slow, of course, when occasion offered, to make a case for Lucian's contemporary relevance, as in sending to the Bishop of Chartres a version of *Alexander*:

that dreadful scoundrel, who, however, gives us an object-lesson for detecting and refuting the impostures of those who even to-day pull wool over the eyes of the mob with their hocus-pocus miracles, false relics, bogus pardons, and such-like trickery.[5]

But the tone of that dedication denies a zealous motive. The bishop is praised as a man 'naris emunctissimae' ('of extremely well-blown nostril', hence 'of keen discernment') who is expected to respond to Alexander's outrages as Lucian and Erasmus had done, 'summa cum voluptate'. He is one who can lay aside sterner studies to embrace 'the more elegant Muses' and find time for this sort of *lusus*. All Erasmus's prefaces to the Lucian translations stress that he and his reader are engaged in a form of relaxation, yet suggest that it is the mark of a cultivated man to be able to relax so intelligently. 'These are nothings, of course', he confesses to the Archbishop of Canterbury, 'but civilized nothings' ('nugas sane, sed literatas').[6]

To justify this predilection, however, Erasmus had also to assert the moral usefulness of his author as a satirist. The fullest and most influential of his attempts to do so is found in his dedication of *The Dream, or The Cock* to Christopher Urswick, which opens with playful aestheticism and works its way toward a bold evaluative conclusion:

As I approached the home of the Greek Muses – for even in winter the Muses' gardens are green – I saw at once this little flower of Lucian's smiling at me with a charm surpassing that of all the many other flowers there. Not with my nail but with my pen I plucked it, and send it to you for the sake of its delightful freshness, its many-coloured beauty, its fragrant scent, and also for the instant health-giving properties of its sap. Horace tells us that the author who combines improvement with entertainment wins every vote, and none in my opinion has achieved this better than Lucian. Reviving the sharpness of Old Comedy, while stopping short of its abusiveness, he shows amazing artistry and finesse in his wide-ranging criticisms, turning up his nose at the

Erasmus

whole world, rubbing the salt of his wit into every pore and always ready with a nasty crack on any topic that crosses his path. He is particularly strong against philosophers, against the Pythagoreans especially and the delusive claims of the Platonists, and also against the Stoics, whose intolerable arrogance he belabours savagely with every sort of weapon. And he is right to do so, since there is nothing more hateful, nothing we should less endure, than vice masquerading under a show of virtue. But that is how he got the name of 'blasphemer', which means slanderer, and got it (of course) from those whom he had touched on the raw. He takes the same freedom in merrily carving up the gods, whence his second name of 'atheist' – actually rather a complimentary title, considering the superstitious paganism of the religion in question. They say he lived around the time of Trajan, but surely he deserves better than to be classed with the sophists of that period. He has so many good qualities: a graceful style, a sure imaginative touch, pleasant humour, biting shrewdness, teasing allusiveness. He has a way of mixing gravity with his nonsense and nonsense with his gravity, of laughing and telling the truth at one and the same time. He can draw the moods and passions of his characters as vividly as with a painter's brush, so that you don't so much read about them as see them exhibited plainly before your eyes. And the result is that, for profit and pleasure combined, I know of no stage-comedy or satire which can be compared with this man's dialogues.[7]

The early humanists conventionally built their critical edifices out of phrases used in other contexts by authors such as Cicero, Horace or Quintilian, sometimes giving cause for the objection that they were more interested in writing idiomatic critical prose than in expressing what they saw and thought. Erasmus has used several such phrases here, notably Horace's famous defence of his raillery, 'what stops a joker from telling the truth?' ('ridentem dicere verum / quid vetat?'). But this passage was evidently written with the eye on the object; any weakness it has as criticism stems rather from an excess of personal enthu- siasm. The crucial and understandable renaissance complaints about Lucian, that he was a compulsive mocker and flippantly anti-religious, are cleverly side-stepped in a manner that was destined to carry little weight with graver critics. It is a revealing sign of Erasmus's involvement with his subject that the qualities he praises in Lucian's satire became even more apparent in his own. With regard to content, we have only to substitute theologians for philosophers to be reminded of Erasmus's campaign to undermine by ridicule the scholastic establishment of his day, his attacks on the vain masquerades of those who were entrusted with teaching the simple truths of religion. His admiration for the effectiveness of Lucian's dialogue-method as combining the best features of verse-satire and stage-comedy – the pungency of the one with the communicative immediacy of the other – was to find expression in the long series of his *Colloquies*. And equally fruitful was his appreciation of Lucian's tone. The Aristophanic sting without the Aristophanic rudeness – 'priscae Comoediae dicacitatem, sed citra petulantiam referens' – this was the urbane alternative to muck-raking which in Erasmus's view was to make satire viable for cultivated Christians.

There is no reason to doubt that he meant what he said in exalting Lucian above the writers of comedy (Aristophanes, Plautus, Terence) and the satirists (Horace, Persius, Juvenal). If the judgement seems extraordinary, *The Praise of Folly*, written three years later, does much to justify and explain it. Dedicating this work to More, in whose house it was written in 1509, Erasmus relates that the original idea had come to him as he journeyed north from Italy, cherishing the memory of their collaboration during his previous visit to England (1505–6), the period of most of the Lucian translations. What he describes as his 'lusus ingenii' ('play or game of wit') sprang from recollection of a friendship which he looked forward to renewing, one in which enjoyment of Lucian had played a major role. His preface pays tribute to More's sense of humour in language which echoes his earlier tribute to Lucian's, and elsewhere he associates his gift with the recipient's 'particular delight in Lucian'.[8] *The Praise of Folly* is a much-studied work, the subject of excellent and accessible criticism which need not be duplicated here.[9] We must, however, attempt to summarize the nature of its debt to Lucian and the relationship of this to the techniques of humanist *joco-serium* which it pioneered.

The limits of that debt should be clarified first. No one will miss that Erasmus's work is vastly more complex, challenging and profound than anything Lucian ever wrote. Whatever he found in him has been radically transformed. Mention in the preface of Lucian's *The Fly* and *The Parasite* among a large number of ancient precedents in the tradition of the mock-

encomium does not mean that these relatively slight exercises
in the genre were particularly influential. The numerous
passages where Erasmus alludes to Lucian often show him
altering his original significantly. Thus Leonard Dean used
Erasmus's treatment of the world-stage metaphors of Lucian's
kataskopoi to demonstrate the greater depth and wisdom of the
later writer, showing how the simple ironic viewpoint of
Menippus becomes more intellectually interesting when the
ironist's name is Folly.[10] We find ourselves brought much closer
to reality than we ever were in Lucian when Erasmus's observer
points out that as actors in the play we have no option but to
join in. Even with regard to satiric techniques, we must be ready
to acknowledge that some of Erasmus's most dazzling
achievements, like his manipulation of paradox and the
changing *persona* of Folly, lie far beyond Lucian's range.

Where Lucian was decisively important for Erasmus was as
the main classical inspiration and authority for his theories of
lusus. That term infallibly recurs, in one form or another,
whenever Erasmus discusses or defends his work. He seems to
have considered it in three closely-related aspects. The first of
these is the surface quality of the game, the display of wit, which
he regards as mainly responsible for producing *voluptas* or
pleasure. The second is the serious content or implication of the
game, embodying *utilitas* or profit. The third aspect, which no
author who made use of the printing-press could responsibly
ignore, however little he may have wished to say about it, is the
rhetorical method involved, the intended impact of the game
on the reader as participant. This raised the problem of how
to justify the presentation of truth through baffling and devious
means.

Since even Lucian's detractors have always been willing to
concede his brilliant showmanship, no difficulty arises on the
first of these topics in tracing back to him the delight in verbal
and intellectual display revealed by *The Praise of Folly* and later
by Rabelais and the Swift of *A Tale of a Tub*. The notion of
a work of literature being conceived out of a desire to show off
may be offensive to modern readers but was firmly legitimized
by the classical tradition of epideictic oratory, to which many

of Lucian's pieces, and all mock-encomia, belonged. According to Aristotle, the purpose of such writing was not to win the public's consent to an argument but simply to give it the pleasure that came from testing and admiring the performer's skill.[11] This authority would have enabled Erasmus to defend *The Praise of Folly* as *lusus* in the simple sense of a *jeu d'esprit* that made no more pretence to usefulness than Lucian's praise of the fly. Although he never relied on that line of defence alone, it served to justify the coruscating display of *allusiones* (a word covering not only 'allusions' but all forms of literary play: puns, parodies, paradoxes and so on) which gives *The Praise of Folly* so much of its character. He called this 'erudite joking'. In his *Adagia*, illustrating the proverb *Ollas ostentare* ('to parade one's kitchenware'), he discusses the writing of mock-encomia as the verbal embellishment of mundane objects. Such a game, he says, echoing Lucian's defence of *A True Story*, can be played as a useful form of mental exercise or relaxation ('vel exercendi, vel laxandi ingenii gratia'). But he adds the proviso that the joking should be conducted in a learned manner ('modo jocus sit eruditus').[12] So learned are the jokes of *The Praise of Folly* that in 1515 he instigated the publication of an elaborate commentary to explain them, which appeared under the name of his pupil, Gerard Lijster.

'There is no greater proof of intelligence', Lijster claimed, 'than erudite joking.'[13] For the humanists *lusus ingenii* was always, at least in part, a virtuoso performance. Through the medium of the printed book, Erasmus in *The Praise of Folly* courted a reputation for brilliance of wit much as Lucian had done through his public lectures, and with the same motive as scholars on the European university-circuit had for centuries been vying for recognition through the medium of learned declamation or debate. Significantly, it was by means of a parody of the traditional learned oration that Erasmus put his new standards of wit on display. Even as he pokes fun at the rhetorical flourishes, the accumulation of proofs, the parading of authorities that had marked the performance of his predecessors, we realize that his genius for sustained parody is being exercised in a spirit not wholly dissimilar. The joking manner which ostensibly depreciates the worth of the performance is in reality an almost arrogant assertion of a new kind of intelligence. One need not try to separate the element of exhibitionism in *The Praise of Folly* from responsible didactic purpose or the self-delighting play of the liberated mind. The important thing is to recognize how all three elements are held in balance in a manner that gives a persuasive guarantee, indeed a deliberate demonstration, of intellectual control. Sensing this balance in Erasmus's work, we are better able to detect the achievement of something similar by authors who learned from his example. Even works like Sidney's *Defence of Poetry* or Jonson's major comedies, which belong less openly to the epideictic mode, have a similar *éclat* which derives in part from the conscious way in which the authors parade their dexterity.

If present-day readers are not always equipped to enjoy Erasmus's virtuosity, they make up for this by fully appreciating his seriousness. His modest claim to have praised folly not altogether foolishly has been upheld and amplified by modern criticism, which is usually willing to allow seriousness to the operations of a first-class mind on any subject, particularly if the mode of operation is irony. The seriousness of *The Praise of Folly* is generally located in its complex and sympathetic understanding of the limits of rationality in human life, and it has been most commonly demonstrated by analysis of the ironic procedures through which the paradox of *homo sapiens et insipiens* is illuminated. Though he wrote several defences of his work, Erasmus in common with all the great renaissance ironists offered no detailed account of his procedures and indeed never used the term *eironeia* except in the proper Socratic sense of self-depreciation and the pretence of ignorance by the principal speaker in a dialogue. The modern critic can therefore be excused for finding Erasmus's statements about *The Praise of Folly* rather unhelpful. They were written in answer to what now strike us as crass and irrelevant objections. But in the late sixteenth century such objections were still to be heard, and Erasmus's defences require our attention because it was in terms of them that his work continued to be discussed.

The simplest of the moral lines of defence was to say that

joking provided an attractive means of introducing serious ideas. Scholars, like any other class of men, should be allowed their *lusus*, 'especially if frivolity leads on to serious matters'.[14] This is essentially the defence of the merry tale or fable used to introduce points of doctrine in pulpit oratory. It can be applied to *The Praise of Folly* in the sense that its subject-matter shows some sequential advance from *jocus* to *serium*, from the flippant mythologizing of the early pages through the longer passages of contemporary satire to the Christian truths embedded in the final sections. But Erasmus's erudite joking pervades the whole piece and was not meant merely to soften up the reader and prepare him for doctrine. In fact he makes clear that the profit as well as the pleasure provided by jokes depends on the way they are handled: their moral function coincides with their humorous appeal. He allows *lusus*

provided the jokes are so treated that a reader who is not utterly thick-headed can get more profit from them than from the forbidding and pretentious arguments of certain persons...As nothing is more trivial than to treat serious matters with triviality, so nothing is more truly entertaining than to treat trivial matters in such a way that you appear anything but trivial.[15]

This recalls his praise for the mixture of nonsense and gravity in Lucian, where it was not a progression from one to the other that he had admired but the ability to laugh and tell truth simultaneously. Nothing, he says, is more 'festivus'. This word is translated here as 'truly entertaining' in an attempt to restore the faint but distinct moral colouring which it had for the early humanists. Suggesting a kind of merriment that is morally and intellectually sanctioned, its primal literary associations were with the philosophical mirth of Plato's *Symposium* and thence with the long tradition of 'festive' philosophical dialogues, often called *convivia* or 'feasts', which descended from that source. It was Erasmus's favourite label for Lucian, and by applying it also to his own work he brought both into association with the highest humanist ideal of intelligent and profitable amusement.

Such an ideal was necessarily threatened in *The Praise of Folly* by the infusion of vigorous satire, directed against every class and profession of men from princes and popes downward. Thus each apology Erasmus made for his work involved him in an apology for satire itself. The arguments he used were not original, but his formulation of them was influential, and it was to his words that Jonson was to turn for support at the beginning and end of the main period of his involvement with ironic comedy.[16] There are times when Erasmus's anxiety to present satire as a proper occupation for a civilized Christian scholar makes him seem to slur over the essential satiric ingredient of hostility. 'This liberty has always been permitted to men of wit, that in their jests they may poke fun at [*luderent*] the general manners of men with impunity, so long as their licence does not extend to outrage.'[17] *Ludere* seems a mild verb to describe Erasmus's treatment of the monks, for example, which might well have appeared as outrageous. But he never denied that his *lusus* could be sharp. His main concern was to vindicate his satire from charges of personal abuse and crude sensationalism. On the first score he repeats St Jerome's opinion that general satire is monitory rather than insulting;[18] he points out that he has not named names as Jerome sometimes did; and he says that anyone who complains of being libelled betrays his bad conscience or at least his fear.[19] Those who object to his satire are probably the kind of people who read Juvenal to find material for abusive diatribes, so becoming teachers of smut.[20] But he himself has refrained from 'stirring up the cesspool of obscure vices after the manner of Juvenal'; he has preferred to focus on the ludicrous rather than the foul; and his aim has been to give pleasure rather than to bite.[21] At one place in his preface Erasmus envisages that compulsive wranglers ('vitilitigatores') will charge him with having reintroduced the biting invective 'of the Old Comedy or Lucian'. His point here, which More is to understand, is that ignorant critics will fail to distinguish between these two precedents. Erasmus's defence of his satire has plainly coincided with his praise of Lucian for 'reviving the sharpness of Old Comedy, while stopping short of its abusiveness'. It was the standard of trenchant but morally innocent wit which, in Erasmus's view, distinguished Lucian from Aristophanes, and it is this also which leads Erasmus to dissociate his own work so pointedly from that of Juvenal, since, as Lijster mentions in a note, Old Comedy was thought to have found its successors among the Roman satirists.[22]

Several shades of meaning in the term *lusus* as applied by

Erasmus to *The Praise of Folly* have now become apparent, ranging from the recreational exercise of wit (with undertones of competitive display) to the satiric use of wit (with undertones of monitory didacticism). The application which probably best fits our experience of the book is the one which carries undertones of *festivitas*, signifying a civilized game of wit in which *jocus* and *serium* are equally balanced and fused. For all these senses of the term, as we have seen, Erasmus found support in Lucian. There remains, however, a further sense in which he used it, a derogatory one which paradoxically led to the most ambitious moral justification. Granted that the most profitable kind of writing is the straightforward exposition of Christian truth, any form of *lusus* will be inferior and relatively harmful. Recognition of this fundamental objection occurs, as one might expect, not in the original preface but in the later defences written when the work had come under moral condemnation, and whether Erasmus was troubled by it at the time of writing may well be doubted. But the 1515 defences, equating *serium* with truth, show willingness to downgrade *jocus* to the level of justifiable falsehood and deception. In *Ollas ostentare* the joker is a pimp (*leno*) operating on truth's behalf. Using a serpent-image significantly more appropriate to the devil's party, Erasmus says that 'truth may insinuate herself [*irrepat*] pleasantly and inoffensively into the minds of men when made to appear attractive by such pimping [*lenociniis*]'. Here we have a suggestion that the practitioner of *lusus* uses foul means to achieve fair ends.

This line of thinking gives unequal weight to the components of *joco-serium* and produces a version in which joking is the falsely-attractive, meretricious exterior that contains and conceals a kernel of serious truth. Though much more morally austere than the 'festive' version, this too refers back to Platonic thought and the *Symposium* in particular. Since only the truth is beautiful, the attractions of *lusus* are morally speaking ugly. But Erasmus could turn this difficulty to advantage by analogy with that favourite passage in the *Symposium* where Socrates is likened by Alcibiades to the statuettes of Silenus. As he explained in the 1515 edition of the *Adagia*, the proverb *Sileni Alcibiadis* is used

36

either with reference to a thing which in appearance (at first blush, as they say) seems ridiculous and contemptible, but on closer and deeper examination proves to be admirable, or else with reference to a person whose looks and dress do not correspond at all to what he conceals in his soul. For it seems that the Sileni were small images divided in half, and so constructed that they could be opened out and displayed; when closed they represented some ridiculous, ugly flute-player, but when opened they suddenly revealed the figure of a god, so that the amusing deception would show off the art of the carver.[23]

Expanding the reference to Socrates, Erasmus stresses how

his eternal jesting gave him the air of a clown...But once you have opened out this Silenus, absurd as it is, you find a god rather than a man, a great, lofty and truly philosophic soul...So it was not unjust that, in a time when philosophers abounded, this jester alone should have been declared by the oracle to be wise, and to know more – he who said he knew nothing – than those who prided themselves on knowing everything.[24]

He goes on, in a passage that has often been related to the last section of *The Praise of Folly*, to describe Christ and his followers as Sileni, unimpressive externally when judged by worldly standards. 'The very Scriptures themselves have their own Sileni. If you remain on the surface, a thing may sometimes appear absurd; if you pierce through to the spiritual meaning, you will adore the divine wisdom.'[25] Having mentioned Holy Writ, Erasmus could hardly appropriate the metaphor to his own jesting in *Folly*, but the analogy was there to be drawn. Not only does 'the amusing deception...show off the art of the carver'; it also offers a profitable lesson, if – and this is the crucial condition – the observer is clever enough to see that the Silenus can be turned inside out.

We note, then, that another shade of meaning in *lusus* for Erasmus comes close to what we now call irony: a game with a deceptive surface which the reader is challenged to penetrate. This is clearly the sense of the most often-quoted defence, the following passage from the *Epistola Apologetica ad Martinum Dorpium* (also 1515):

The aim of my *Folly* was exactly the same as that of my other writings, though I used a different approach. In my *Christian's Handbook (Enchiridion)* I taught the pattern of a Christian life unambiguously. My *Prince* gives straightforward advice on how a prince should be trained. Here in *The Praise of Folly*, though pretending to write an encomium, I make the same points obliquely which in those works were made quite openly. *Folly* covers the same ground as the *Handbook* but in the guise of a game [*sub specie lusus*].[26]

Lucian and Lucianism

We are relieved to find Erasmus at last making a clear acknowledgment of the ironic or oblique method, and the passage is commonly interpreted as a painfully explicit statement of 'what ought to have been obvious' to the dunderhead Dorp. Yet it is also a disingenuous piece of simplification, as anyone will discover who tries to reconstruct the *Handbook* by turning *Folly* inside out. Erasmian irony is rarely so simple. What the Fowler brothers wrote about Lucian is more notoriously true of his successor: 'you cannot tell when you are to reverse him, only that you will have sometimes to do so'.[27] In each of his defences he offered as a clue to the proper reading of his work a reminder of *decorum personae* – that it is Folly who speaks, not Erasmus – but the simple reversal of Folly's statements on the ground that they are foolish brings us very little closer to the author's wisdom than the acceptance of them at face value. To dissociate oneself automatically from all that Folly says would lead one to deny one's humanity in the first place and ultimately one's claim to be a Christian. It is likely that the Silenus analogy helped to make *The Praise of Folly* the supremely exhilarating work that it is, emboldening Erasmus to feel that in the satyr's mask he could drop all inhibitions, and that *sub specie lusus* no holds need be barred, no subject need be sacred. None the less, as a moral justification of this particular game it was more plausible than fair, since one does not arrive at its beautiful seriousness by peeling off layers of jest. A metaphor appropriate to the allegorical 'opening up' of obscene stories in the Old Testament is less appropriate to the holding in balance of conflicting facets of truth which Erasmian irony usually requires.

Folly is not a good advertisement for *decorum personae*. She is neither consistent nor even (as some have maintained) consistently inconsistent in accordance with her nature. Rather she is a 'Menippean' character as defined in the previous chapter, a flexible mouthpiece through which the author can turn his wit in whatever direction he chooses. Like the teller of Swift's *Tale*, she is deliberately unrealized in order that the reader may be kept on the edge of his seat and denied the comfort of being able to sum up the speaker by seeing her in settled perspective.

Erasmus

One of Erasmus's comments on *decorum personae* makes an analogy with dialogue which suggests that he thought of Folly as wearing more than a single mask. He complains that his critics

> are not giving full weight to something which is very important in a dialogue, the fitness of the speech to the speaker; and they imagine it is Erasmus speaking, not Folly. It is just as if one were to write a dialogue between a pagan and a Christian, and be told it was sacrilegious to make the pagan say anything against Christian doctrine.[28]

Certainly Folly's speech demands the response that is proper to a dialogue. She is not one speaker but several, and the reader's task is to distinguish her voices, sorting out the varying degrees of speciousness and validity in her arguments. Outwardly a monologue, *The Praise of Folly* is essentially a dialogue projected into the reader's mind.

In that connexion one recalls that Lucian's *The Parasite*, cited as a mock-encomium in the preface to *Folly*, had indeed been cast in dialogue-form. It illustrates by contrast, however, the much greater intentness with which Erasmus plays with his reader. Though there is irony in the way the parasite's speeches in praise of his art are allowed to persuade the other speaker, it is not the kind of irony which implicates the reader; nor could one mistake the whole dialogue for anything more than a clever exercise in parody and special pleading. As imitators of genius, Erasmus and More were inclined to remake Lucian in their own image. Just as we suspect that they exaggerated the serious element in his *festivitas* – 'Lucian', according to the former, 'produced almost nothing that is trivial'[29] – so it is certain that they developed the art of teasing far beyond the hints which Lucian provided. But the hints were unquestionably there. As well as *The Parasite* one could instance *Alexander*, which Erasmus called *lusus* presumably in recognition of the way the reader is wheedled into enjoying the exploits of a crook; or we could remember how the readers of *A True Story* were challenged to detect the author's 'plausible and specious' lies.

Why were the humanists attracted to this art? Text-books of rhetoric did not recognize it. Not even the theory of epideictic oratory, which encouraged the speaker to dazzle his public and freed him from the obligation to persuade, went so far as to countenance the intention to perplex and confuse. The readiness of the humanists to practise beneficent deception was a result of the age-old procedures of scholastic logic. Training his pupils to detect fallacies or deceitful arguments (thirteen types of which had been listed by Aristotle in *The Sophistical Elenchi*), the master of logic had himself to be expert in their use.[30] In the disputations which were carried on in universities for centuries both before and after Erasmus, the opponent or examiner had licence to employ false or ambiguous reasoning in an effort to trap the answerer into admitting the reverse of his thesis.[31] Such deception was sanctioned by the Church, within the confines of the schools, as a means of preparing the theologian to defend his doctrines against heresy. It was a widespread and serious academic game, obviously susceptible to parody, and it helps to explain why the inquisitorial instinct was stronger in Erasmus than in Lucian. Erasmus altered the direction of the test, challenging his reader not so much to distinguish heresy from dogma, the false from the true, as to recognize the complexity of truth, to face the paradoxes and moral dilemmas which arise in the pursuit of truth, and to see that these cannot be simply resolved without loss of wisdom. Like the posing of paradoxes, the whole exercise was a dangerous one which could be harmful unless restricted to its proper function of sharpening the advanced intelligence. One of the main arguments of this book is that Jonson, in mid-career, loosed this dangerous cat from its bag by applying the art of teasing to the widest of available audiences. Erasmus could hardly have foreseen such an eventuality. He originally wrote *The Praise of Folly* for an audience of one, the wisest and wittiest man of his acquaintance, 'whose extraordinary keenness of mind leads him to differ from the crowd very sharply'.[32] Even when he came to publish it he must have envisaged a small circle of readers whose scholarly pretensions ought, at least, to have enabled them to cope with its deceptive methods. It is significantly an academic audience that Folly addresses. Haggard faces light up at her approach, and the values she is made to uphold – natural energy, cheerfulness, sociability, tolerance, even Christian humility – would seem to have been chosen with the needs of the academic profession particularly in mind.

Erasmus could not foresee *Bartholomew Fair*; he could not even, in 1511, foresee the consequences of handing over his erudite joke to the printer. But the consequences had already begun to embarrass him four years later, as the solemn defences and the annotated edition of 1515 imply.

There is much in this book [Lijster insists complacently] which cannot possibly be grasped except by an erudite and alert reader. This is partly because of the widespread use of Greek words, partly because of the frequency of concealed allusions, and partly because the joking is so subtle that only men of the keenest discernment can perceive its force. For there is no greater proof of intelligence than erudite joking.[33]

The appeal to an intellectual élite (the well-blown nostrils once again) was not well calculated to pacify a sincerely scandalized opposition. Though Erasmus had meant *The Praise of Folly* to separate sheep from goats in the humanist world, it proved far more seriously divisive than he had anticipated, and only once in his later writings did he permit himself a similar exercise of mischief.[34] This was again in a work addressed to the learned world, the dialogue *Ciceronianus* (1528). Since sacred matters were less closely involved on this occasion Erasmus's conscience may have been relieved. But he can hardly have expected to arouse less controversy.

Ciceronianus was famous throughout Europe for as long as the principle of literary imitation and the writing of Latin prose remained matters of central concern. Though still read by literary historians, its satiric methods have not been much studied.[35] It employs the common Lucianic device of ridiculing an abuse through the self-revelation of the principal speaker, and it exemplifies *lusus* of the kind we have just been considering in that the author manoeuvres his intended victims into almost hopeless perplexity. The abuse in question was the cultivation of an exclusively Ciceronian diction and style for all literary purposes, as recommended by Bembo and his followers in Italy. Erasmus disapproved of this policy because it emphasized words over matter, forcing every kind of matter into a single linguistic mould instead of allowing style to be determined by content.

It ran counter to his view that classical models should be adapted to fit modern requirements, and in particular that various models should be used for various purposes. He regarded the puristic pedantry of the Italians as a plague which was spreading northward, likely to prevent Latin from becoming a medium sufficiently flexible for the dissemination of a broad Christian humanist culture. And he suspected, not without reason, that Cicero was closer than Christ to the hearts of his devotees.

The dialogue is in three parts. The first builds up an amusing caricature of the Ciceronian Nosoponus. His name (parodying a common dialogue-name for the scholar, Philoponus, 'lover of toil') suggests one whose toil has become a disease or a sick obsession. He pines with longing to be recognized as a Ciceronian by the Italians, an honour which he thinks will rank higher than canonization in the eyes of posterity. The other speakers naughtily feign sympathy in order to draw out the details of his illness. For seven years he has read and dreamed nothing but Cicero, and he has compiled three vast dictionaries of Ciceronian usage – one of words, one of phrases, one of rhythmical patterns – to ensure that everything he writes or speaks will have the master's authority. In the second part of the dialogue, the satiric baiting of Nosoponus gives place to the reasoned refutation of his basic assumptions. The main authorial spokesman, Bule-phorus ('counsellor'), advances Erasmus's pleas for a balanced view of Cicero and a more liberal concept of imitation. This is the argumentative core of the dialogue. There is plenty of incidental wit – a Ciceronian version of the Christian creed expressed in terms of Roman religion is notably funny – but the general drift is clear and unambiguous, so that by the end of the second section Ciceronianism has been demolished by argument as well as by caricature. It is the third part that courts trouble. Nosoponus is invited to measure the great masters of Latin prose by his Ciceronian yardstick. Beginning with the Romans themselves he works his way through the ages and finally arrives at Erasmus's contemporaries. As name after name among these is proposed to him, he appraises the right of each to be ranked as Ciceronian. Another change of tone in the dialogue, and a deceptive shift in the presentation of the principal speaker, have now taken place. The long tribunal is conducted solemnly in the language of learned compliment and mutual congratulation so enjoyed by the humanists, and the speeches of Nosoponus cease to be crankish and assume a semblance of judicial authority. Thus conditioned, Europe's great scholars anxiously read on to find what is said about them in Erasmus's work. Strictly in terms of the dialogue as a whole, their satisfaction or dissatisfaction with what they find will register the extent to which they accept the criteria of Nosoponus, earlier thoroughly discredited. But what scholar would not hope to be publicly praised by Erasmus for writing as well as Cicero, or would be pleased to have his failure to do so publicly noted?

The dialogue caused acute consternation, especially among the Italians and French, and its chief victim was Budé, the recognized leader of the humanists in Paris. The very casualness and brevity of the reference to Budé would seem to have been a calculated stroke, since the point on which he took offence was that his name had been slipped in for consideration amid a number of smaller fry. When asked if he will allow Budé the title of Ciceronian, Nosoponus merely responds, 'Why should I grant what he does not strive for and would not recognize if I should?'[36] A gross insult to French scholarship was drawn from the implication that its leader could not write like Cicero. Erasmus could, and did, respond that the words were spoken by the foolish Nosoponus. He also could, and did, defend the passage as a compliment paid by himself, since it was indeed complimentary to say that Budé would have no truck with the affected Ciceronianism attacked in the dialogue. The contradictory nature of the two explanations, found side by side in the same letter,[37] is a clear sign of the game Erasmus was playing. 'I am astonished', his friend Vives wrote to him, 'that Budé or any other, *knowing the art of dialogues*, has been offended at what you have said.'[38]

It was not altogether so astonishing. Like *The Praise of Folly*, *Ciceronianus* probes academic pride at a vulnerable point and is essentially a test of humour: the only 'right' response is to laugh in the spirit of the author and recognize the nature of his game. But the later work singles out individuals, and those who objected to it did so not because they misunderstood the nature of the game but because they disapproved of it. The heated rejoinders of J. C. Scaliger and Etienne Dolet attacked Erasmus as a Lucianist.[39] Moreover, comparison of the two satires reminds us how much the Lucianic method depends on the appearance of total objectivity; it is wrecked if the author shows his own hand; it is coarsened if the suspicion arises that he is paying off scores. It is better fitted for the virtuoso expression of free-ranging wit than for voicing the earnest concerns and vested interests of a sixty-year-old. Though Erasmus's concern to avert a decadence in the use of Latin was certainly altruistic, his interest in his fellow-scholars was not. His jealousy of Budé's reputation, his resentment over lack of recognition by the Italians, were widely suspected. The last section of *Ciceronianus* was a supremely clever challenge to his contemporaries, forcing them individually to consider where they stood in relation to the issue discussed, but it also gave Erasmus an irresistible opportunity to play God under a visor and bring the whole learned world to his judgement-seat. In probing the vanity of his victims he indulged his own; and those who responded without humour can be excused for declining to play a game so wholly conceived on the author's own terms.

These two satires represent Erasmus's furthest extension of Lucianic irony and, in particular, his most hostile development of *lusus* as a game which can be turned against the reader. But if an Elizabethan schoolboy had been asked to draw a parallel between Lucian and Erasmus, he would have pointed, not to those works, but to the *Colloquies* (*Colloquia Familiaria*) which were widely prescribed either along with, or in place of, Latin versions of Lucian's dialogues in the second form of grammar schools.[40] Meant to be broadly educative for the general reader and especially for the young, these 'informal conversations' could hardly make the sort of mischief which Erasmus felt to be justifiable in a gladiatorial combat of wit among scholars. None the less, they do in a milder way exemplify *lusus* as a means of provoking and implicating the reader, and probably, merely by being less erudite and more accessible, formed a wider channel through which Lucianism could come to influence the drama. Later chapters will contain examination of several colloquies in different connexions. Here we may restrict ourselves to some comment on their aims and methods.

Since there are more than fifty of them, various in character and published over a space of fifteen years between 1518 and 1533, they resist generalization and should not be glibly dubbed Lucianic. *Charon* is conspicuously so: in it we find a Lucianic character and situation adapted to the expression of a Christian viewpoint on an urgent contemporary reality, the spread of war. But its mythological setting is untypical of Erasmus, and to support the widely-shared view that the *Colloquies* generically owe much to Lucian we do not need to listen for precise echoes. Better evidence is the critical language in which they were discussed. Here is a late but representative humanist, Daniel Heinsius:

> In this wittiest of books Erasmus plays the part of a doctor, not grave or morose, but festive and genial. The subject of his game is essentially life, and his purpose is curative...He shows himself a very Proteus, ready to assume any shape and speak in any character, yet always himself, that is, straightforward and candid...But he was also well aware of the use made in the old days of Dialogue, which Plato and other sages had consecrated to Philosophy, which the writers of Old Comedy had applied to stage-poetry, and which Lucian had adapted for witty jesting in prose. In ancient Dialogue all values are relative; anything could be said on the spur of the moment; any opportunity for wit could be taken. And there was no shortage of opportunity, since in those days the specialists in this game had skeletal notions of piety and religion. Now that such opportunities are restricted, Dialogue can be devoted to the service of spiritual truth.[41]

This attributes to the *Colloquies* 'festive' morality, *lusus* made relevant to life, Lucianic *jocus* infused with Christian *serium*. Beside it we may put Erasmus's best-known claim for these writings:

> Socrates brought philosophy down from heaven to earth: I have brought it even into games, informal conversations, and drinking parties. For the very amusements of a Christian ought to have a philosophical flavor.[42]

Several colloquies describe feasts (*convivia*) and one, *The Godly Feast*, deliberately sets forth an idealized Christian version of classical *festivitas*: the enjoyment in pleasant surroundings of good company, good fare, good manners, good wit, good learning, good doctrine. But in the main Erasmus seems conscious of having carried a stage further Lucian's work of bringing 'philosophy' to the people; his speakers, his situations, his subject-matter are in general more homely and closer to the concerns of ordinary men and women than Lucian's. *Colloquia familiaria* are pitched lower than *dialogi*, just as the Lucianic dialogue was lower than the Platonic; they are scaled down to show ordinary representative people discussing commonplace issues, sometimes practical, usually controversial, in an informal way. In this declension Erasmus was not rejecting Lucian but applying him to a new set of circumstances, using his methods to encourage the play of mind in an unsophisticated audience.

Though a modern editor still finds it necessary to apologize for their 'obviously didactic intention',[43] it was for creating moral confusion that the *Colloquies* were attacked in their day. In 1526 a censure-motion was carried at the Sorbonne which listed sixty-nine passages as 'erroneous or as tending to corrupt youthful morals'.[44] Erasmus's response, *De Utilitate Colloquiorum*, is a diplomatic essay which was chiefly designed to bolster the respectability of the *Colloquies* in the eyes of the public for which they were intended; it takes no account of the basic objection of the ecclesiastical authorities. This was, of course, that the author had made satiric capital out of abuses among the religious orders and had hawked in the market-place controversial topics which ought to have been debated *intra muros*. On the laity's right to think for itself about ecclesiastical matters the *De Utilitate* has nothing to say, though the success of the *Colloquies* was one of the major assertions of that right in the early sixteenth century. Instead Erasmus bases his defence on the educative value of *lusus*. 'Nothing is better learned than what is learned as a game [*quam quod ludendo discitur*].'[45] Applied to the *Colloquies*, the defence of *lusus* amounts to a defence of the usefulness of fiction. Sensing that this was the point on which parents and schoolmasters were most likely to require reassurance, Erasmus makes his clearest reference to the idea of beneficent deception, the useful lie. 'This, surely, is the most easily sanctioned form of deception [*sanctissimum fallendi genus*], to do good by trickery [*per imposturam dare beneficium*].' As in *Ollas ostentare*, he presents himself as doing God's work with the devil's methods, 'hooking the young on an attractive bait', 'creeping like a serpent into their minds'.[46]

Lusus-as-fiction not only succeeds in capturing the attention; it can also give better schooling than life itself:

> It is a common-sense precaution to get to know the stupid motives and silly notions of the masses; and I believe that children can learn these things better from my little book than from experience, which trains up fools.[47]

This reminds us that the *Colloquies* were imitations of life first, dialectical approaches to the truth second. While Erasmus could, in the *De Utilitate*, summarize the moral points to be drawn from each colloquy ('in this I teach...' – 'in this I denounce...'), he took care that his reader should not be asked to accept those morals without first having been made to involve himself in a complex, life-like experience. In order to teach the way of Christ, he had first to describe the way of the world.

His techniques of doing so go far beyond the simple juxta-position of conflicting viewpoints which dialogue requires. In the first place, he almost invariably disguises his argumentative pattern in the interest of *vraisemblance*. One way of achieving this was through deliberately casual structure: a conversation may open in mid-flow, stray into irrelevance, or end in apparent pointlessness. Newcomers to the *Colloquies* often complain of this waywardness, like newcomers to the Joycean short story, and need to be shown that they must focus for themselves on the moments of greatest significance. Fictional overlay is sometimes so complete as to be positively distracting: *The Shipwreck*, for instance, can easily be read for its narrative interest alone. It also provides an interesting example of the decoy moral. A simple reader could be forgiven for locating its point in the opening and closing speeches on the theme of 'don't go to sea', and might have to be persuaded that more serious interest lay in the various reactions of the passengers to the threat of death, in such questions as how to pray and to whom, how to reconcile reliance on prayer with the need for practical action, or the instinct for self-preservation with concern for the safety of others. *The Shipwreck* is a casebook of emergency behaviour-patterns, bristling with 'points for discussion'. The speakers present their material in a way that constantly provokes moral interpretation without actually providing it. Even the option of an allegorical reading is delicately kept open.

Another technique which helps to complicate the moral pattern is to cast doubt on the authority of the main spokesman. In *The Girl With No Interest in Marriage* the excellent and undoubtedly Erasmian arguments by which Eubulus ('good counsel') seeks to dissuade the girl from her hasty decision to enter a convent are coloured from the start by his revelation that he wishes to marry her. The point is not made strongly enough to compromise the force of his arguments, but it is a point which the reader is unlikely to overlook and it sets Erasmus's admonitions in the context of a difficult and no doubt common human predicament. Again, in a dialogue which we shall later consider more closely, *The New Mother*, one may wonder why Erasmus allows his simple view that a mother should breast-feed her own child to be expressed in terms of blatant sophistry by an impertinent young painter. Characters who voice a 'true' comment on a particular situation are often as imperfect in their own way as the antagonists they criticize. Cocles, of *The Pursuit of Benefices*, is an ignorant, stay-at-home, 'one-eyed' character who meets an old friend Pamphagus ('all-devourer') returning from twenty years of unsuccessful benefice-seeking in Rome. When the latter compares himself to Odysseus, Cocles is totally baffled by the reference, but Pamphagus, in explaining the parallel, also gets the story wrong. Between abject ignorance and the flaunting of superficial knowledge there is little to choose. The only factor which enables Cocles to serve as a valid critic of benefice-hunting is that by staying at home he seems to have acquired a measure of stability which the other lacks, and especially a surer sense of humour. It is he who conducts the extraordinary digression on noses which inspired Sterne. To extract *serium* from *jocus* in this odd little dialogue would be a ticklish exercise, but one which Erasmus presumably expected his reader to undertake.

In the art of teasing, very little separates the intentional blurring of moral outline from a positive intention to mislead, and there are moments when Erasmus steps over the boundary, in spite of what Heinsius says of his straightforward candour. The *Well-to-do Beggars* could be cited in this connexion. The opening of the dialogue, where two Franciscans are refused shelter for the night by a parson and an innkeeper and are denounced as wolves in sheep's clothing, gives every indication that Erasmus is about to add to the literature of anti-mendicant satire. There can be little doubt that he deliberately encourages this supposition, and at least one modern editor has accepted it.[48] We have to wait until the end of the dialogue to be shown that the adjective 'well-to-do' in the title – 'rich' would be a better translation – is meant, not satirically, but in a spiritual sense.[49] The point is that these particular friars face the full barrage of conventional criticism of their order, but survive the ordeal with patient good humour. The emphasis on clothing which is maintained throughout the dialogue is ultimately used to turn the satire back against the critically-minded innkeeper and show that a refusal to judge by appearances has its own pitfalls. Readers whose satiric sense has been stimulated are reminded, along with the innkeeper, that sheep's clothing may, after all, contain a sheep.

The *Colloquies* do indeed foster the critical spirit, but also insist on awareness of the perils that attend it. They raise many more questions than they answer, rarely if ever leave the feeling that a subject has been settled, and constantly undermine any kind of simplistic or dogmatic certainty. Cornelia's harangue on women's rights in *The Council of Women* explodes in all directions like a splinter-bomb, and compels our attention, but if we try to pin down the author's attitude to each of her arguments, all we can be sure of is that he finds her fanaticism ridiculous. By contrast, an ideal exercise of critical reasoning is shown in *The Godly Feast*. There, the guests at the banquet consider a thorny text from St Paul. They examine the problems it poses and discuss alternative solutions. No 'right' solution is offered, but the host comments: 'One who can put questions thus doesn't need someone else to answer them. You've expressed your doubt in such a way that I myself am in doubt no longer.'[50] This is the response that the *Colloquies* as a whole seek to elicit. Play of mind is never an end in itself; it is the stimulus which should enable the reader to form his own judgement in silence, a judgement which can then be carried over into the crucial sphere of Christian action.

Clearly such features as the open-ended conclusion and the avoidance of black-and-white patterning are common to almost all the more intelligent modes of moral fiction. What marks out Erasmus's 'Menippean' mode is a basic distrust of fiction *per se*. For him, the imitation of life was still less an end in itself than the play of mind. His characters and their actions are never essentially more than counters in the intellectual game he plays with his readers, and when they do begin to take on independent life, when fiction asserts its power to 'convince', this is usually a sign that the game is being made more difficult in order to take account of life's failure to conform to simple moral and intellectual patterns. It would be absurd to suggest that Erasmus took no delight in fiction, almost as absurd as to make the same suggestion about Jonson or Swift. None the less, it is true that for the 'Menippean' writer the value of fiction stems from distrust of the lie and depends on the power of the lie to stimulate moral discrimination. It requires the response of a detached mind, and is thus distinct from the commoner kind of moral fiction – which it often deceptively pretends to be – which builds on the reader's emotional involvement in the story and his trust that the author will make the meaning clear.

Stimulus to right thought and action was, of course, the hinge on which Erasmus's interpretation of Lucian turned. Lucian, for the humanists, was the great non-affirmer, 'one of the Pyrrhonists', as Gilbert Cousin, Erasmus's pupil, remarks, 'who affirm nothing, but leave all doubtful issues unresolved'.[51] Non-affirmation is integral to Erasmian *lusus* in all its various facets: as fiction, as satire, as irony, as the display of wit in the author and as the testing of wit in the reader. But any teaching that employs such a basis can only be, in Erasmus's word, 'oblique'; and the teacher who avoids commitment himself must work to encourage it in his pupils. Between Lucian and

Erasmus there were many affinities which had nothing to do with didactic purpose: both, for example, were fastidious verbal artists; both delighted in the ridiculous for its own sake; both enjoyed exploiting their mastery of an older civilization; both had a vision of society that was wide rather than searching; and in both, most significantly, detachment and evasiveness were inescapable facts of personality. But the Lucian whom Erasmus allowed himself to approve was a long way removed from the clever, cynical relativist who horrified Luther and appealed to Voltaire. He was a teacher whose moral responsibility was not impaired by being deviously exercised, a writer whose genius for evasion enabled him to get under the guard of his public. A modern historian of satire, Ronald Paulson, writes of Lucian's purpose of 'discomfiting his reader, shaking up his cherished values, disrupting his orthodoxy' and describes him as 'the epitome of the satirist who writes at what he takes to be a time of extreme stodginess and reaction, when values have become standardized and rigid'.[52] Such a view locates the significance of Lucian's satire less in terms of its immediate objects than in terms of its general strategy against the reader. Whether or not it is true of the historical Lucian, it is certainly true of the Lucian whom Erasmus tried to recreate for the Renaissance.

CHAPTER 3

More

===

And so was he by Master Lieutenant brought out of the Tower, and from thence led towards the place of execution. Where, going up the scaffold, which was so weak that it was ready to fall, he said merrily to Master Lieutenant, 'I pray you, Master Lieutenant, see me safe up, and for my coming down let me shift for myself.'

Then desired he all the people thereabout to pray for him, and to bear witness with him that he should now suffer death in and for the faith of the Holy Catholic Church. Which done, he knelt down, and after his prayers said, turned to the executioner and with a cheerful countenance spake thus to him: 'Pluck up thy spirits, man, and be not afraid to do thine office; my neck is very short; take heed therefore thou strike not awry, for saving of thine honesty.'

So passed Sir Thomas More out of this world to God.[1]

A remarkable aspect of that famous passage is that neither William Roper who wrote it, nor Nicholas Harpsfield who used it *verbatim*, saw fit to make any apology for its close intermixture of solemn and jocular elements. The reason may be that More's habit of joking on serious occasions had already been established by that stage in their narratives; or it may be that his jests on the scaffold were so well known that no comment was felt to be needed. There could even be truth in the theory that the passage was meant to be implicitly analogous to the death-scene of that other wise jester, Socrates, as recorded by Plato and celebrated by Erasmus in *Sileni Alcibiadis*. Whatever the explanation, it has been quoted here as an early reminder that More's *joco-serium* has always been part of the legend surrounding him as a man, and has only to a lesser degree been associated with the techniques of wit employed in his writings.

This must be our pretext for altering the approach of the previous chapter. If we were mainly concerned to trace the development of Lucianism in More's work, we could follow it, as in the case of Erasmus, from its root in the early translations to its complex flowering in a single masterpiece, and then show how it was later modified by the demands of a wider audience and a more direct purpose. That process will require some attention, since we can be sure that Ben Jonson, as an intelligent sixteenth-century reader of *Utopia*, was well able to appreciate its debt to Lucian and its kinship with the motives and methods of Erasmian *lusus* that have just been described. But the same requirement of viewing our subject through sixteenth-century eyes makes it advisable to shelve the Lucianic approach for the moment and come to More, as Jonson himself must have come to him initially, through available contemporary images of the man.

These were, of course, partly to be found in the writings, since More was not only fond of self-dramatization, usually under a partial disguise, but also had the gift of transmitting his personality to almost everything he wrote. Educated readers were also able to derive an impression of More from the Latin tributes paid to him by fellow-humanists, notably Erasmus, whose Letter to Ulrich von Hutten gave international currency to an encomiastic but circumstantial account of his character and habits. Thomas Stapleton's biography, in *Tres Thomae*, was published at Douai in 1588 and Jonson owned a copy of it.[2] Known to have been circulating among English Catholics during the latter part of the century were manuscript copies of Roper's *Life* and other memoirs based on it – those of Harpsfield and a certain Ro. Ba. have survived – material which Jonson may have had access to from the date of his conversion to Catholicism in 1598, if not earlier. Easily accessible, also, were hostile sketches contained in Protestant works such as Hall's *Chronicle* and Foxe's *Book of Martyrs*. Finally, it can be assumed that every Elizabethan Londoner was familiar from childhood with orally-transmitted versions of the More legend, made all the more intriguing by the taint of official disapproval.

The play known as *The Book of Sir Thomas More*, written by various hands including Shakespeare's in the 1590s, draws much from written sources but also provides evidence of the popular image of More which it clearly set out to exploit. It exaggerates his humble birth and types him as a man of the people who rises to the highest councils of state. Instead of turning his back on his origins, he uses his position to reconcile the nobility and the populace, becoming 'the best friend that the poor ere had' (line 1648).[3] Not even his erudition deprives him of the common touch; he is 'a wise and learned gentleman, and in especial favour with the people' (402–3). The play shows plainly that it was More's sense of humour which had made him a favourite with the crowd. His recorded addiction to merry tales and practical jokes had fathered on him a host of anecdotes. Without sinking to the buffoonery of Greene's Roger Bacon, the playbook More similarly reflects the popular habit of humanizing 'great clerks' by turning them into figures of fun. Particular attention is paid to the prank in which Sheriff More does a deal with a cutpurse, setting him to rob a colleague on the bench as a means of teaching the latter a lesson. The piquant morality of that episode, also recounted by Stapleton, may explain why it lingered in Jonson's mind;[4] certainly it highlights the image of More as the offbeat doer of justice, the presiding genius of the 'merry magistrate' tradition so beloved by Elizabethan dramatists. Other exploits point to what may have been a traditional association between More and the theatre: his practical joking takes the form of disguise or role-playing. One of the commonest of stage-tricks is assigned to him when he changes clothes with his man Randall in order to test whether 'great Erasmus' – here presented as a comparatively wooden figurehead of learning – 'can distinguish merit and outward ceremony' (750–1). And Roper's story of how More as a boy in Cardinal Morton's household would 'at Christmas-tide suddenly sometimes step in among the players, and never studying for the matter, make a part of his own there presently among them'[5] is adapted and dramatized at length in a scene which seems specifically intended to emphasize his friendliness to the players and his enjoyment of their art.

The final scenes leading up to the execution intensify one's impression of the play as a *cento* desperately committed to working in as many anecdotes as possible. The hero's jests, first at the expense of grieving sympathizers and then on the path to the block, are awkwardly strung together and given disproportionate emphasis. Yet, in spite of the undistinguished quality of the writing, More's dignity in these scenes is not altogether lost. Foxe had included a version of five jests on the scaffold to point the moral that More was 'a scoffer unto his death',[6] and Hall, whom Foxe was following, had ended his account with the disapproving comment 'Thus with a mock he ended his life.'[7] The play, by contrast, ends in a spirit much closer to Roper's 'So passed Sir Thomas More out of this world to God.' Some attempt is made to match the mysterious blending of piety and homely wit which Roper communicates. One could reasonably infer from this that the authors felt that such a treatment of More's death would be generally acceptable to their public, and that respect for his spiritual stature had to some degree survived the influence of Foxe and the rabid Protestantism of the era. It is certainly clear that More's legendary character made him a tempting subject for popular dramatists. The downfall of a great statesman was convention-ally tragic; as a merry magistrate he was intrinsically comic; and as a champion of the citizenry he was well fitted for the type of chronicle play that could give an outlet to contemporary discontents.[8] More fundamentally, he had the appeal of a great Englishman of international renown whom the people persistently regarded as one of themselves. The play clearly tried to make capital out of all these factors; and such unity as it has derives less from any imposed concept of genre than from the traditional character of the hero himself, especially his distinc-tive combination of humour and moral seriousness.

For modern readers the play is a disappointment, as any Elizabethan play on the subject was bound to be, because the climax of the hero's life-story was too controversial to be treated at all. Elizabeth's implacable hostility toward More's memory – not even *Utopia* could be printed or sold in England during her reign – stemmed from his having opposed her father's claim to be head of the Church, but was reinforced by the use which continued to be made of him by Catholic propagandists. He remained what Foxe had called him in 1563, 'a great arch-pillar of all our English papists'.[9] *The Book of Sir Thomas More* makes no mention of his Catholicism and offers no explanation of the 'articles' which he died for refusing to subscribe. We are simply, and very suddenly, told that his conscience forbids him in an unspecified matter to obey the king, and that he must therefore die. The official line of the play is, as David Bevington says, 'staunchly orthodox, in that it absolutely forbids any compromising of duty toward the state'.[10] None the less, an audience would have been well able to fill in the blank which the authors left: a possible reason why (as seems likely) the play was never performed. Even on the point where it was obliged to say least, it provides an eloquent reminder that More was remembered best of all as a man who had followed his conscience to the grave. Whether he was to be condemned for disloyalty to his sovereign or admired for refusing to accommodate his principles to political expediency was a familiar and controversial question which any dramatization of his death would necessarily revive and throw open.

Compromising of principle was to become a central issue in Jonsonian drama, and it will be argued that More helped to bring it into focus not only by the example of his death but by the whole balance of *jocus* and *serium* in his life and writings. We must turn first to consider the terms in which that balance was explicitly presented by More and his biographers. As in the Erasmian interpretation of *lusus*, joking is made to seem defensible on two main counts, as mental relaxation and as mental exercise ('laxandi vel exercendi ingenii gratia'). On each count, old arguments are dressed in a garb that is very much More's own.

Since a compassionate interest in human limitations was one of the permanent characteristics of his thought, it is not surprising that we find his fullest discussion of jesting as a necessary refreshment for the spirit in one of his last, most serious, and most deeply personal works, *A Dialogue of Comfort Against Tribulation*, composed during his imprisonment in the Tower. In this he attempts to objectify his troubled state of mind at that time, and to prepare himself and his family for his expected ordeal, through a thin dramatic fiction in which Anthony and Vincent, an old man and a young, anticipate persecution at the hands of the Turks. Vincent complains that

More

the old man's rejection of all worldly sources of comfort 'seemeth somewhat hard':

For a merry tale with a friend refresheth a man much, and without any harm lighteth his mind and amendeth his courage and his stomach, so that it seemeth but well done to take such recreation. And Solomon saith, I trow, that men should in heaviness give the sorry man wine to make him forget his sorrow. And Saint Thomas saith that proper pleasant talking, which is called [εὐτραπελία], is a good virtue serving to refresh the mind and make it quick and lusty to labour and study again; where continual fatigation would make it dull and deadly.

Anthony replies that he had thought it unnecessary and indeed inadvisable to make this point since

folk are prone enough to such fantasies of their own mind. You may see this by ourself which, coming now together to talk of as earnest sad matter as men can devise, were fallen yet even at the first into wanton idle tales. And of truth, cousin, as you know very well, myself am of nature even half a giglot and more. I would I could as easily mend my fault as I well know it; but scant can I refrain it, as old a fool as I am.

His penitence for this 'fault' is an instance of More's habitual use of *eironeia* to express a bemused admission of his own and everyman's failure to live up to earnest ideals. 'Some are there of nature or of evil custom come to that point that a worse thing sometime more steadeth them than a better.' It is unfortunately true that a congregation which falls asleep during a sermon on the joys of heaven can be instantly roused by the promise of a funny story.

He that cannot long endure to hold up his head and hear talking of heaven, except he be now and then between (as though heaven were heaviness) refreshed with a merry foolish tale, there is none other remedy but you must let him have it. Better would I wish it, but I cannot help it.[11]

The literary design of *A Dialogue of Comfort* itself takes account of this regrettable human weakness, and with its wealth of merry tales strikingly exemplifies the practice of deliberately alternating *jocus* and *serium*. Curtius has argued that this technique, probably stemming from the *spoudogeloion* of Menippus in the third century B.C., had been recognized in Roman, and especially in medieval, literature, where the ability to pass from earnest to jest and back again could be admired in much the same way as it could be admired in a well-balanced individual; and he sees this as an explanation of the presence in much solemn medieval writing of ludicrous elements which a strict Aristotelean sense of decorum would find inappropriate.[12] For More, as the last passage quoted suggests, the practice seems rather to have been associated with the use of humorous *exempla* common in late medieval preaching. But a feature of subsidiary interest in the *Dialogue* is its reference back to the ancient concept of *spoudogeloion* through the medium of Boethius' *The Consolation of Philosophy*. That dialogue of comfort, also written in prison under the threat of death, must certainly have been the model closest to More's mind as he wrote. Formally linked to the Menippean tradition by its alternation of prose and verse, it repeatedly connects verse with refreshment and prose with stern medicinal instruction. More, while preserving the alternation of instruction and refreshment, departed from his predecessor's practice by substituting merry tales for verse, and thus consciously or otherwise restored the element of *geloion* which had been almost totally absent from Boethius' work.[13]

'Comic relief', though the phrase is overworn, was undoubtedly a concept which the sixteenth century understood. It was cherished especially by popular writers as a pretext for loading the market with trivia. The opening sentence of the jest-book *Howleglas* (version of ?1528) – 'This fable is not but only to renew the minds of men or women of all degrees from the use of sadness'[14] – typifies a stock justification of that sort of material which could easily be extended to farcical scenes in tragedy. But More reminds us that among serious writers the provision of comic relief was itself a comment on the reader's need to be relieved, a wry recognition that (in Eliot's words) 'human kind cannot bear very much reality'. As we have seen in relation to Erasmus, the polarity of earnest and jest continued in the Renaissance to reflect something of the old polarities between the sacred and the profane, between spiritual realities and worldly fiction. For Anthony merry tales are 'fantasies'. Milton was to make a comparable gesture of indulgence in *Lycidas*, playing off the delicate unreality of the pastoral *lusus* against the real implications of the storm-tossed corpse:

More

For so to interpose a little ease,
Let our frail thoughts dally with false surmise.

And a similar condescension to human frailty, though conceived in a more sardonic spirit, came to inform Ben Jonson's approach to popular comedy.

Thus, even in the version of More's *joco-serium* which we have so far considered, where the two ingredients appear to be used separately and alternately, a touch of gravity can be detected in the jesting through the implied reflection on man's incapacity to 'hold up his head and hear talking of heaven'. It will be clear, however, that this sense of *joco-serium*, though it may come close to that of the original Menippean *spoudogeloion*, differs markedly from the sense in which we are primarily using the term to convey a fusion, baffling and paradoxical, of its ingredient factors. But here, too, More's personal example is notoriously relevant. It was for his skill in 'pleasant dissembling, when we speak one thing merrily, and think another earnestly' that he was chiefly commended by Thomas Wilson in *The Art of Rhetoric* (1553) as one 'whose wit even at this hour is a wonder to all the world, and shall be undoubtedly even unto the world's end'.[15] In *The Dialogue Concerning Heresies*, where 'More' is the principal speaker, the Messenger says to him:

You use...to look so sadly when you mean so merrily, that many times men doubt whether you speak in sport, when you mean good earnest.[16]

The same point is made repeatedly in Stapleton's biography (1588):

But as in most serious matters he tried always to be pleasant and humorous, so in the midst of his jokes he kept so grave a face, and even when all those around were laughing heartily, looked so solemn, that neither his wife nor any other member of the family could tell from his countenance whether he was speaking seriously or in jest, but had to judge from the subject-matter or the circumstances.[17]

More has always been recognized as the grand master of poker-face jesting, and many of his recorded remarks take on an extra dimension when we imagine the consternation they must have caused among the simple or literal-minded. Most are examples of affectionate family teasing, but his devastating *mot* in the Privy Council, when he had opposed Wolsey and been called a fool – 'Thanks be to God that the King's Majesty has but one fool in his Council'[18] – shows that he would also use the deadpan technique in dangerous circumstances as a forensic weapon. Neither he nor his early admirers seems to have felt that this trait of behaviour needed any moral justification, though it plainly lay open to attack as flippant or obscurantist or as a mark of intellectual pride. To furnish a morally respectable defence of it one would have to resort to the defence of paradox – 'ingenii exercendi gratia' – taking this to mean that the hearer's wit is to be exercised as well as the speaker's. The challenge of ironic speech is that it forces the hearer to gauge sense and implication by intellectual tact, by a matching of minds with the speaker, taking clues 'from the subject-matter or the circumstances' and without relying on the normal guidance of facial expression and tone of voice.

The literary use to which More put this baffling mode of *joco-serium* will shortly be illustrated, but we should meantime take note of the contribution made by Erasmus to the legend of his friend's sense of humour. First, even in the formal portrait of the Letter to Hutten, we can trace recognition of its almost obsessive nature and also of its dramatic and combative tendencies:

From boyhood he took such delight in joking that it could appear to be the whole object of his existence, though he balked at scurrility and never cared to be abusive. As a youth he wrote little comedies and acted them. Anything wittily spoken would attract him, even remarks at his own expense, and his enjoyment of sharp, intelligent repartee continues even now. This explains why in his early years he amused himself writing epigrams. It also explains his special fondness for Lucian, as well as the fact that it was he who impelled me to write *The Praise of Folly*, training a camel to dance, so to speak. But the satisfaction of this instinct is a thing which he pursues on all possible occasions, even the most serious. In learned and intellectual company he finds it in the play of mind; among the ignorant and foolish he finds it in their folly. Not even clowns upset him, since his amazing adaptability enables him to get the most out of everyone. With womenfolk generally, even with his wife, he is forever up to his little tricks and japes. You could call him another Democritus.[19]

The wit which turned to ironic teasing in simpler company had demanded the stimulus of adequate competition. It was to ensure that his powers were stretched to the utmost that More as a young man had proposed to Erasmus that they should compete in the rhetorical exercise of framing replies to Lucian's declamation, *The Tyrannicide*.[20] In his earliest tribute to More (1506), Erasmus described that exercise as 'a bout in the wrestling-school of wit' conducted in friendly rivalry with one who shared his enjoyment of mixing *seria* and *ludicra*.[21] It was a private training-session, with no hostile purpose, but Erasmus was surely right in seeing that More's early taste for Lucian, like his fondness for writing epigrams, sprang from a sense of humour which was essentially provocative and satiric. It is Lucian's capacity to sting, to get under the skin of his readers, that More stresses in his formal commendation of the Greek author:

He everywhere notes and censures the defects of mortals; and does this so adroitly and effectively that, although no satirist pricks more deeply, no fair-minded readers are unwilling to admit that they are stung.[22]

The forensic instinct to make an opponent wince was from the start much stronger in More than in Erasmus; his competitiveness was to find a congenial outlet in his savage duelling with Luther, while Erasmus in controversy would increasingly withdraw into querulous complaint. Erasmus repeatedly acknowledged that it was More who had instigated his writing of *Folly*, and he allows us to conclude that it was More's natural bent for satire which had initially liberated his own, with Lucian serving as the main literary medium in the katalytic process. There may be some historical inaccuracy in the common picture of the Dutch 'camel' being taught to 'dance' by an Englishman boisterously addicted to merry tales and mischievous pranks, but it is a picture which Erasmus himself was willing enough to encourage.

The impression left on him by the taste for somewhat outrageous jesting in More's learned and pious household seems to find expression in his colloquy *Exorcism*. Seems, one is forced to say, since More's connexion with that cruelly funny piece can only be inferred, but in view of his reputation as a *farceur* in the sixteenth century the inference was probably easier to draw then than now. Polus, the hero of the episode recounted in the dialogue, is a gentleman with a house outside London who shares with his son-in-law a 'festive' wit and a bold taste for practical joking. His name being Greek for a young horse, this character has been convincingly identified as More's father-in-law, John Colt.[23] Erasmus's story may well have originated in an anecdote told by More in which Colt figured. One suspects, however, that the promotion of Polus to the central role was a blinding tactic by the author, and that the real inspiration for the story lay in Erasmus's recollection of More's own satiric sense, which is to be seen as being embodied in the figures of both son-in-law and father. By 1524, the date of the colloquy, Erasmus would hardly have wished to embarrass More, a member of the King's Privy Council and Speaker of Parliament, by any closer identification.

The story describes the baiting and exposure of a superstitious parish priest. Like Lucian's *The Lover of Lies*, a dialogue which More had translated and singled out as one of his favourites,[24] its attack is directed not so much against ignorant credulity as against the indulgence in superstition of those who ought to know better. Lucian's sceptical spokesman Tychiades had shown what More described as Socratic irony in his responses to tall tales of the supernatural told by a gathering of supposedly distinguished philosophers. In Erasmus's story the ironic response expands into punitive action. His plot is too detailed to be told in full and in summary loses much of its comic appeal, which depends on hectic accumulation of farcical incident, but a partial account will suffice for our present purpose. Throughout, the narrator compares the action to a five-act comedy written and produced by the principal actor. Polus is described as 'et auctor, et actor hujus fabulae' and also as 'choragus'.[25] He also contributes the prologue by starting a rumour among the peasants that a spectre has been seen and heard howling horribly on a briar-patch on his estate. His nature, we are told, is to enjoy playing this sort of trick on the people's stupidity: 'sic est hominis ingenium. Gaudet hujusmodi commentis ludere stultitiam populi'.[26] By way of illustration, a subsidiary tale is told of how, on a journey to Richmond, he had pretended so convincingly to see a fiery dragon in the sky that one after another his companions had claimed to see it too. For Act I of the main drama he selects as his antagonist Faunus, a priest with a high opinion of his skill in divinity, who has already accepted the truth of the rumoured spectre. Inviting him to investigate it for himself, and if possible to free the poor soul from its torment, Polus conceals himself in the briar-patch and makes mournful noises by blowing into an earthenware jar. He later listens to the priest's exaggerated account of the incident, keeping a perfectly straight face ('Vultum habet in manu. Dixisses rem serio agi').[27] Acts II and III consist of various *grand guignol* attempts at exorcism. Polus hands over the role of spectre to his son-in-law and himself assumes that of the devil, vying with Faunus for possession of the spectre's soul. One of his manoeuvres is to seek to disqualify his opponent by accusing him of fornication, a shot in the dark which forces Faunus to retire to confession. A variant of this technique is practised by the spectre who, by announcing that he too is called Faunus, plants the idea that he represents the priest's *alter ego*. The spectre declares that he has acquired a sum of money by fraudulent means and cannot be freed until full restitution has been made. The news that the sum is a large one is 'bonum atque commodum' to the priest, who gladly offers to dig up the treasure and devote it to pious uses. Act IV shows him becoming obsessed by the thought of the treasure to the point of insanity, making himself a laughing-stock in the district. Polus and his son-in-law then bring the action to a finely ironic close by allowing the priest to find a letter on his altar, written by the spirit in heaven, telling him that God has rewarded his good intentions and that he need not worry about the treasure any more. He now carries this letter around with him and displays it as an object of veneration, believing it to have been delivered by an angel. This, as the interlocutor remarks, was not to cure the man of his madness but to substitute one form of madness for another – 'istud non est liberasse hominem insania, sed mutasse insaniae genus'.[28]

Reading this 'drama' one constantly imagines what Jonson might have made of it by tightening its plot, trimming its ragged edges and sharpening its satiric focus. Features of it even as it stands point forward to Jonson's formulae for rogue-comedy, as in *The Alchemist*; but more important here, when we think ahead to *Epicoene*, is to notice how Erasmus's manipulators and practical jokers bear no relation whatever to the intriguing slaves of Roman comedy, much less to medieval Vices, but are firmly identified as intelligent and enlightened gentlemen. While one might well suspect that Erasmus felt that their treatment of Faunus bordered on cruelty, nothing is written into the text itself to enforce such a suspicion; on the contrary, the 'festivity' of Polus is the unchallenged norm· of the colloquy. One might similarly read between the lines of the Letter to Hutten and suspect that Erasmus had reservations about More's compulsive jesting, yet that could not be proved either. As so often with Erasmus, a suspension of judgement or even the semblance of a favourable judgement is intended to provoke the reader into forming his own. What does seem clear is that *Exorcism* was Erasmus's attempt to give heightened imaginative expression to his friend's extraordinary instincts for drama and satiric teasing. If that is so, it could place the young More near the head of the English dramatic tradition of teasing gentleman wits which was to run through Jonson's Truewit to the long line of his Restoration successors.

How were these instincts reflected in More's published writings? His dramatic sense is everywhere evident in the Dialogues already referred to. Teasing, too, is a regular mark of his style in controversy, though on matters of heresy it tended to broaden into ridicule or sarcasm. It took on a subtler guise in Latin writings intended for a select audience, especially around 1515–16. In those years More's literary development would seem to have reached a stage roughly comparable to that of Erasmus when he wrote *Folly*. In his late thirties – Erasmus had in fact been forty-three – the first flush of public recognition gave him the confidence to 'play' in the learned arena in a manner which his later responsibilities, as well as the changing political climate, were to make impossible. An excellent example is the opening of his Letter to Martin Dorp, who had twice publicly attacked Erasmus not only for *Folly* but also for his projected edition of the Greek New Testament. More begins with a conspicuous show of charity, refusing to believe the nasty things that are being said about Dorp, insisting that his jeering second letter must have been published without his knowledge, assuming that the real Dorp (whom he has never had the great joy of meeting) must be the Dorp whom he and Erasmus believe in, and so forth. This Socratic pretence of charity and naïveté has a devastatingly offensive purpose. The maintained fiction that all parties in the 'misunderstanding' still love each other dearly serves only to emphasize how badly Dorp has betrayed the humanist camp, especially by lapsing from its high standards of wit and intelligence. The following extract in Elizabeth Rogers's translation is fairly representative:

As for your second letter, now widely read with unhappy consequences, I am inclined to believe it was no deliberate action of yours but merely an accident that it reached the public. I am forced to this point of view especially because in this letter there are some things which I am fully convinced you would have changed had you wished to publish it, as they are not quite the sort of thing to be written either to him or by you. You would not have written such harsh words to so important a friend, or in such an off-hand fashion to a man as learned as he; as a matter of fact, I am positive you would have written in a more kindly vein, in keeping with your temperate character, and with greater care, in keeping with your extraordinary learning. Furthermore, as for the jests and jeers with which your whole letter abounds immoderately, I have no doubt you would have employed them much more sparingly, or at least, my dear Dorp, more cleverly. I do not make much of the fact that you attack the *Folly*, that you inveigh against the Poets, that you deride all the Grammarians, that you do not approve of the Annotations on Holy Scripture, that you are of the opinion a thorough knowledge of Greek literature is not pertinent – all of these points I do not make much of, since they are views each man is free to hold without offending anybody; and they have been discussed by you up to now in such a fashion that I do not have any doubt that several answers, which ought to be given to your objections, will occur to anyone reading them. Besides, by no means do I think you have said too much against any one of these points; and in certain instances even I miss many points with which I should have liked to have seen your letter better equipped as it advanced against Erasmus, so that he could have a finer opportunity to fortify his camp with more powerful siege works to oppose you.[29]

The satiric method here is fundamentally akin to that of Erasmus's baiting of Budé in *Ciceronianus*, but is superior in execution. When we find More politely expressing a wish that Dorp had put forward further (stupid) arguments against Erasmus so that Erasmus might have more ammunition for his reply, we recognize that the passage has been primarily a test of humour, conducted for the benefit of an amused élite, to whom copies of the letter were shown, at the expense of an individual who had proclaimed his humourlessness by demanding that Erasmus should recant *The Praise of Folly* by writing a Praise of Wisdom. Assumed to be incapable of disarming the satire by enjoying the joke, Dorp is to be seen as being trapped between two other responses, both of them ridiculous. Either he will fulfil the conventional role of the Socratic victim by failing to detect that the flattering tone of the passage is insincere, or, much more likely, he will detect the irony and be incensed by the implication that he was thought to be too stupid to do so.

The Letter soon abandons irony and proceeds to a reasoned refutation of Dorp's views, because More did in fact care deeply about their wrongness. But the spirit of mischief apparent at the start provides a good lead to the greater and more playful work on which More was then engaged, one which, in Lucianic fashion, set out to affirm nothing and to call everything into question. In the rhetorical strategy of *Utopia* the temptation to misinterpret was a primary gambit, and evidence of its success is not confined to the twentieth century. Tales quickly spread of those who supposed that Utopia was a real place. Thus Harpsfield:

Many great learned men, as Budaeus and Johannes Paludinus, seemed to take the same story as a true story. And Paludinus upon a fervent zeal wished that some excellent divines might be sent thither to preach Christ's Gospel; yea, then were here among us at home sundry good men and learned divines very desirous to take that voyage.[30]

Another kind of confusion resulted from failure to appreciate 'the art of dialogues' and the use of *persona*. Beatus Rhenanus reports in 1518 that

when the *Utopia* was mentioned here recently at a certain gathering of a few responsible men and when I praised it, a certain dolt insisted that no more thanks were due to More than to any recording secretary who merely records the opinions of others at a council, sitting in after the fashion of an 'extra' as they say, and without expressing any opinions of his own, in that all More said was taken from the mouth of Hythloday and merely written down by More...And there were some present who approved the fellow's opinion as that of a man of very sound perception. Do you not, then, welcome this elegant wit of More, who can impose upon such men as these, no ordinary men, but widely respected and theologians at that?[31]

More

The last sentence recognizes that *Utopia*, like *The Praise of Folly*, was essentially an 'imposture', a trap for learned fools. That it was also much more than that is of course proved by the stimulus and inspiration which its political and social ideas have offered over the centuries to intellectually distinguished readers, not all of whom have supposed that More was idealistically presenting 'the best state of a commonwealth'. It differs from Erasmus's work in its much more positive approach to the problems it raises, the far greater concern which it communicates about the possibility of effecting practical improvements on existing systems. So Sidney, who was fully alive to the deceptive nature of *Folly*, could none the less appear to accept that *Utopia* was literally intended as a perfect pattern.[32] It remains true, however, that *Utopia* and *Folly* start out from the same base as examples of provocative *lusus*, challenging every reader to exercise a mind as acute, flexible and untrammelled as those of their authors.

About the influence of Lucian on *Utopia* there is a surprising lack of unanimity. The Yale editors play it down. Father Surtz concedes only that the tone of More's work *may* owe something to the 'wit and pleasantry' of Lucian by which the Utopians are said to be captivated,[33] while for J. H. Hexter, Lucian's name is not even worth mentioning.[34] The reason for this is that students of *Utopia* quickly become preoccupied with its controversial ideas, as More certainly intended, and consequently show less interest in his methods than in determining his attitude to questions of capital punishment, euthanasia, community of property, pleasure as the supreme good, and so on. The questions are so perennially urgent, and are raised so sharply, that so-called 'relativist' critics who suggest that More need not have had fixed opinions on any of them are liable to be accused of trivializing their author. In a work so original, moreover, the matter of sources rouses very little interest. However, as in the case of *Folly*, one can distinguish between the vast range of heterogeneous reading which is casually reflected in the content of Utopia and the comparatively precise debt owed to Lucian by its form and rhetorical method. And again it must be stressed that Lucianic detachment, as interpreted by More and Erasmus, had none of the connotations of irresponsible disengagement or cynicism which it later acquired.

The fear of branding More as a mere witty relativist is what ultimately mars the main attempt that has so far been made to establish the Lucianism of *Utopia*.[35] T. S. Dorsch was right in his contention that, in 1517, its two books would have been recognized – one should perhaps say were *meant* to be recognized – as deriving their form and tone from a Lucianic dialogue and *A True Story* successively. Book 1 is closer to Lucian than to Plato in its blend of verisimilitude with hints of nonsense, in its comic anecdotes, in its introduction of the author under his own name, and especially in its scathing emphasis on contemporary abuses. Even more obviously, Lucian's fantastic shadow falls between the *Republic* and Book 2. Lucian had warned readers of *A True Story* that he was telling a pack of lies, but had none the less made his narrative 'plausible and specious' with a mass of circumstantial details and had thrown out the challenge of discerning his literary parodies. More disguises his lie more secretively, substitutes strange philosophical notions for Lucian's ridiculous travelogue, and offers a puzzle which is not so much literary as intellectual, but he also provides a vital clue to the right reading of *Utopia* through his use, plainly imitated from Lucian, of absurd compound proper names. Dorsch reminds us that the Greek derivations of all the names in Book 2, and of several in Book 1, carry suggestions of nonsense which undermine attempts to take the narrative seriously: Utopia means 'no-place' with a possible pun on 'good-place'; its capital Amaurotum means a dim place which baffles the sight; its river Anydrus means 'waterless'; Hythloday, the philosopher–explorer who describes and praises Utopia, means 'expert in nonsense'. But the most significant aspect of this clue is that its availability depended on knowledge of Greek. It was More's means of baffling the remnant of Greekless *idiotai* in humanist circles, and at the same time of alerting 'understanders' to the nature of the game being played.

Greek joke-names, fictional mystification, and the hide-and-seek use of *persona*, are already familiar to us as trade-

More

marks of Erasmian *lusus,* and most of what was written on that subject in the previous chapter can be applied to *Utopia* with little alteration. In particular, we should recall that the purpose of the 'oblique' method of teaching was not to test perception of a 'true' point of view so much as to enforce awareness of difficulty, to highlight problems of belief and paradoxes of experience which are incapable of dogmatic solution and require to be weighed in a sophisticated intellectual balance. By coaxing rigid minds out of their reliance on scholastic formulae, and persuading them to welcome complexity in a spirit of witty and liberal inquiry, Erasmus and More were working to encourage a wiser exercise of moral judgement, most certainly not its suspension. This is where Dorsch's account of *Utopia*'s Lucianism miscarries. Hindered by assuming that More must have either approved or disapproved of the Utopians, he concludes somewhat harshly that More found their systems not only 'ridiculous' and 'absurd' but also 'odious', 'pernicious', and 'repellent'. Book 2 must be read, he tells us, 'in reverse, as we read Lucian – and Swift'.[36] But do we, or should we, read Lucian and Swift in that way? We know what appalling simplifications result from trying to understand Lucian, or *Gulliver's Travels,* or *The Praise of Folly,* by simply reversing their apparent emphasis. The procedure leads to a sad neglect of wit, as when Dorsch brackets Lucian and More and Swift as 'intensely serious and intensely moral writers'. Admittedly, the opposite tendency of making them sound excessively flippant must also be resisted. C. S. Lewis's appraisal of *Utopia* as 'a holiday work, a spontaneous overflow of intellectual high spirits, a revel of debate, paradox, comedy and (above all) of invention, which starts many hares and kills none'[37] is almost as misleading as Dorsch's retort that More 'kills stone dead every hare that he starts'. But it should not be necessary for a critic of *Utopia* to elevate either *jocus* or *serium* at the expense of the other. The point where they reach equilibrium and fuse is in confrontation with the reader. More does not shoot the hares himself because he did not see it as his function to do so. Rather he was the hound which starts the hares gaily and drives them hard toward the hunters.

Lucian and Lucianism

The problematic question underlying all others in *Utopia* is how far Christian principles may be accommodated to the way of the world. It is a question on which the thinking of More and Erasmus has always been seen to overlap, and their treatment of it concerns us here because (in a manner foreshadowing Jonson's) it associates the polarity of *jocus* and *serium* with that of the flesh and the spirit, of expediency and moral idealism. Among various guises in which the question was raised, the one which has received most attention is the startling attempt made in *Utopia* and later in Erasmus's colloquy *Epicurus* to reconcile the Epicurean standard of pleasure-seeking with traditional Christian asceticism and *contemptus mundi*. But more directly relevant to our theme is the opposition exploited by both writers between absolutist philosophy and the play of life. On this topic Erasmus was the earlier contributor. It will be remembered that one of Lucian's world-stage metaphors had shown the philosopher Nigrinus choosing a seat high up in the theatre with a distant but comprehensive view of the arena. Lucian's Nigrinus had no thought of accommodating himself to the action, but had regarded the spectacle as a source of amusement and as a means of confirming his lofty principles. In answer to this, Erasmus's Folly condemns the wise man's non-participation as a denial of the only reality we have. To reject the play in the name of truth, to insist on stripping the masks from the actors, destroys the illusions which make life bearable. It is wiser, in Folly's opinion, to accept the limitations of human wisdom and stray along with the herd. Since this well-known passage will prove crucial in a later chapter, it should be quoted at length:

If someone should unmask the actors in the middle of a scene on the stage and show their real faces to the audience, would he not spoil the whole play? And would not everyone think he deserved to be driven out of the theater with brickbats as a crazy man? For at once a new order of things would suddenly arise. He who played the woman is now seen to be a man; the juvenile revealed to be old; he who a little before was a king is suddenly a slave; and he who was a god now appears as a little man. Truly, to destroy the illusion is to upset the whole play. The masks and costumes are precisely what hold the eyes of the spectators. Now what else is our whole life but a kind of stage play through which men pass in various disguises, each one going on to play his part until he is led off by the director? And often the same actor

70

is ordered back in a different costume, so that he who played the king in purple, now acts the slave in rags. Thus everything is pretense; yet this play is performed in no other way.

What if some wise man, dropped from heaven, should suddenly...exclaim that the person whom everyone has looked up to as a god and ruler is not even a man, because he is led sheeplike by his passions; that he is the meanest slave because he voluntarily serves so many and such foul masters? Or what if this wise man should instruct someone mourning his parent's death to laugh, on the grounds that the parent had at last really begun to live – our life here being in one way nothing but a kind of death? And what if he should entitle another who was glorying in ancestry, ignoble and illegitimate, because he was so far from virtue, the only source of nobility? And what if he should speak of all others in the same way? What, I ask, would he gain by it except to be regarded as dangerously insane by everyone?...He is indeed perverse who does not accommodate himself to the way of the world, who will not follow the crowd, who does not at least remember the rule of good fellowship, drink or begone, and who demands that the play shall no longer be a play. True prudence, on the contrary, consists in not desiring more wisdom than is proper to mortals, and in being willing to wink at the doings of the crowd or to go along with it sociably.[38]

'Comiter errare', which Leonard Dean has here translated 'to go along sociably', is a delicately ambiguous phrase with the secondary sense of 'to sin obligingly': a reminder, if any were needed, that the speaker is Folly. Typically, the joking fool makes a plausible case for accepting life and human nature as they unalterably are, while the voice of the serious moralist can be heard in the background protesting the uncomfortable truths and orthodox ideals of Christian teaching.

The dialogue thus covertly projected by Erasmus into the reader's mind receives openly dramatic expression in Book 1 of *Utopia*, where the focus of debate is narrowed to the role of the moral philosopher in politics. Hythloday declines to offer his services to a prince, arguing that in a context of *realpolitik* any counsellor who refuses to compromise his notions of truth will certainly be ineffective and will either be corrupted himself or will serve as a screen for the corruption of others. In an equally famous passage, equally central to later discussion, the 'accommodating' case is put by the speaker called 'More'. He says to Hythloday:

'In the private conversation of close friends this academic philosophy [*scholastica*] is not without its charm, but in the councils of kings, where great matters are debated with great authority, there is no room for these

Lucian and Lucianism

notions...But there is another philosophy, more practical for statesmen [*civilior*], which knows its stage, adapts itself to the play in hand, and performs its role neatly and appropriately. This is the philosophy which you must employ. Otherwise we have the situation in which a comedy of Plautus is being performed and the household slaves are making trivial jokes at one another and then you come on the stage in a philosopher's attire and recite the passage from the *Octavia* where Seneca is disputing with Nero. Would it not have been preferable to take a part without words than by reciting something inappropriate to make a hodgepodge of comedy and tragedy? You would have spoiled and upset the actual play by bringing in irrelevant matter – even if your contribution would have been superior in itself. Whatever play is being performed, perform it as best you can, and do not upset it all simply because you think of another which has more interest.

'So it is in the commonwealth. So it is in the deliberations of monarchs. If you cannot pluck up wrongheaded opinions by the root, if you cannot cure according to your heart's desire vices of long standing, yet you must not on that account desert the commonwealth. You must not abandon the ship in a storm because you cannot control the winds.

'On the other hand, you must not force upon people new and strange ideas which you realize will carry no weight with persons of opposite conviction. On the contrary, by the indirect approach you must seek and strive to the best of your power to handle matters tactfully. What you cannot turn to good you must make as little bad as you can. For it is impossible that all should be well unless all men were good, a situation which I do not expect for a great many years to come!'[39]

In view of More's known political career it would be useless to discourage the question of whether the attitude expressed here represented his real thinking in 1516. Still, it is probably more important to perceive that the *persona* he adopts is a comic extension of the character publicly conferred on him by Erasmus in the preface to *Folly*: 'one who is good at, and enjoys, being all things to all men, a man for all seasons'.[40] Further, the best-remembered facet of Erasmus's dedication was its pun on More's name, being Greek for 'fool'. It is therefore no accident that More attributes to himself a temporizing attitude akin to Folly's. Because his speech is politically oriented, and lays stress on acting in the public interest, it may appear more responsible than Folly's wholesale and cynical accommodation to human frailty. As a programme for the philosopher–statesman its intelligent seriousness is not to be doubted, yet it is placed, in its dialectical context, as the expression of a worldly point of view, which Hythloday rejects outright with a reminder that

72

Christ had commanded his disciples to preach truth from the housetops. We are shown that to sanction flexible role-playing against the strictures of the moralist is to adopt an essentially 'comic' posture, defending not only 'the play' but also, more specifically, Plautine *jocus* against untimely inroads of tragic *serium*. The whole provocative debate of *Utopia* is thus framed by the contrast between two types of fool, one comic and one tragic in the senses defined: 'Morus', whose folly is worldly wisdom, and 'Hythlodaeus', whose strenuous idealism corresponds to the Christian folly, worldly nonsense, described by St Paul and Erasmus. The contrast is reaffirmed in the book's open-ended conclusion. The worldliness of 'More' shies away from Utopian communism which 'utterly overthrows all the nobility, magnificence, splendor, and majesty which are, in the estimation of the common people, the true glories and ornaments of the commonwealth'; while at the same time his temporizing, 'tactful' instinct leads him to suppress this objection, doubting whether Hythloday 'could brook any opposition to his views'.[41]

The 'indirect approach' advocated in the last long quotation has its parallel in the rhetorical method of *Utopia* itself. 'What you cannot turn to good you must make as little bad as you can' coincides with a justification of *lusus* which we have noted in both More and Erasmus, that oblique teaching through pleasurable fiction and joking was (human nature being what it is) a better-than-nothing substitute for straight exhortation. But we have also seen that More's willingness to endorse merry tales for the purpose of keeping a congregation awake or comforting a man in tribulation was necessarily tinged with irony. To perceive that irony, to weigh against each other the positions of Hythloday and 'More', was the primary challenge of *Utopia*. Only when he had faced it was the reader in position to weigh the conventional attitudes of his day against the strange ideologies and customs which Hythloday recounts. There can be no doubt that More practised the art of teasing in making that challenge as difficult as possible. Much more subtly and insidiously than the *vraisemblance* of his traveller's tale, his deceptive use of *persona* encouraged the drawing of false

Lucian and Lucianism

conclusions about the nature of his book and the making of hasty assumptions about his own beliefs.

More's writings are never more deeply characteristic of their author than when they dramatize the accommodation issue, and usually they employ the play-metaphor in doing so. Toward vulnerable people, whose role in life obliges them to accommodate, he shows a delicate blend of sympathy and irony. We see this when he describes the 'mockish election' of Richard III and traces the thought-processes by which the common people make up their minds to do what is expected of them by Gloucester and Buckingham:

Men must sometime for the manner sake not be aknowen what they know...And in a stage play all the people know right well that he that playeth the sowdaine [sultan] is percase a sowter [shoemaker]. Yet if one should can so little good [have so little sense] to show out of season what acquaintance he hath with him and call him by his own name while he standeth in his majesty, one of his tormentors might hap to break his head, and worthy, for marring of the play. And so they said that these matters be kings' games, as it were, stage plays, and for the more part played upon scaffolds, in which poor men be but the lookers-on. And they that wise be will meddle no farther. For they that sometime step up and play with them, when they cannot play their parts, they disorder the play and do themself no good.[42]

So far from daring to expose the play, the poor take refuge in the pretence that they have no part to play in it. But since they see through the fraud, ought they to acquiesce in it? Though More indulgently omits to press the question, the key-point to emerge from the *History* as a whole is that people who recognize fraud and usurpation none the less accommodate them through weakness. More makes sad comedy of this frailty, wry comedy from Gloucester's ability to exploit it. His vision could be comic because he inherited the medieval view of sin as essentially foolish. Every willed act of disobedience to God, every neglect of conscience and principle, foolishly imperils the immortal soul and goes against the long-term interests of the sinner.

In line with the indulgence he shows toward the poor, More could also make the temporizing of sophisticated actors appear justified by consciousness of the comic parts they play. There is the story in *A Dialogue of Comfort* (which Harpsfield relates of More and Wolsey) of the guest at a banquet who had the

misfortune to be required to speak last in flattering his host's
oration:

> When he saw that he could find no words of praise that would pass all that
> had been spoken before already, the wily fox would speak never a word. But
> as he that were ravished unto heavenward with the wonder of the wisdom
> and eloquence that my lord's grace had uttered in that oration, he set a long
> sigh with an 'Oh!' from the bottom of his breast. [He] held up both his hands,
> and lift up his head, and cast up his eyes into the welkin and wept.[43]

Here, Harpsfield remarks, 'Sir Thomas More was in a manner
forced...to play a part to accommodate himself somewhat to
the players in this foolish, fond stage play.'[44] Such temporizing
was less easy to condone in those who had a responsibility for
the great man's soul, but even there could be viewed with
understanding. *A Dialogue of Comfort* tells elsewhere of priests
and chaplains who, 'to make fair weather withal', give the great
man 'fair words':

> And in such wise deal they with him as the mother doth sometime with her
> child...when the little boy will not rise in time for her but lie still abed and
> slug. And when he is up, [he] weepeth because he hath lien so long, fearing
> to be beaten at school for his late coming thither. She telleth him then that
> it is but early days, and he shall come time enough, and biddeth him: 'Go,
> good son, I warrant thee, I have sent to thy master myself; take thy bread
> and butter with thee, thou shalt not be beaten at all.' And thus, so she may
> send him merry forth at the door that he weep not in her sight at home, she
> studieth not much upon the matter though he be taken truly and beaten when
> he cometh to school.[45]

In that beautiful passage, gently satiric in reducing the great
man to a spoiled child and the problems of counsellors to those
of ordinary mortals, we see how More's compassion could
operate even when his moral disapproval was plain. At the heart
of human failure he saw the compulsion to turn *serium* into *jocus*,
to evade the tragic confrontation with absolute realities and to
cherish instead the comfort of short-term illusions.

But in matters of personal conscience, where the salvation of
a soul is directly at stake, there must be no playing of dishonest
roles, no accommodation with worldly folly, no bargaining with
God. Anthony stresses this in a great climactic passage of the
Dialogue of Comfort, but More's firmness on the point was put
beyond doubt for posterity by the stand on conscience which

resulted in his death. Erasmus had shown from the start that the 'flexible' More was complemented by the More 'whose extraordinary keenness of mind leads him to differ from the crowd very sharply'. Already in his lifetime he was seen as a paradoxical figure. We shall find little hard evidence that Ben Jonson made literary use of More in the way that we can prove that he used Erasmus. But More's traditional character clearly embodied conflicts which were central to Jonson's art and thought. It united extremes of willingness and refusal to bend to the ways of the world. It carried the free play of wit as far as it could morally go and no further, producing the astonishing paradox of a Lucianic martyr. Equally important for Jonson, it bridged the isolating gulf between the learned humanist and unlettered humanity. There were other facets of More's *persona* which Jonson may also have recalled. 'The best friend that the poor ere had' had been induced by principle to support the burning of heretics; the incorruptible magistrate was remembered as one who had played merry pranks with the law. Such anomalies could well have intrigued the author of *Bartholomew Fair*. Finally, if More was indeed a meaningful figure for Jonson, we can assume that he was never more so than in his frequent discussions of the stage and the morality of acting. How far, and in precisely what sense, the moralist could approve of the dramatic medium was for Jonson a question of abiding concern. More, we have seen, viewed flexible role-playing as a mark of man's comic imperfection. Jonson was to set out to justify his medium by using it to demonstrate, in both comedy and tragedy, man's primary duty to be constant to his better self. Here, too, More's example was singularly relevant. His final progress to martyrdom would not have appeared to Jonson as a rejection of 'the play' in the name of 'sincerity', since neither made an absolute distinction between acting and being oneself. What mattered was whose game one played. Jonson would have recognized that More's undeniably theatrical behaviour on the scaffold resulted from a determination to play, not the King's game or anyone else's, but God's and his own.

CHAPTER 4

Images of Lucian

Clever but harmless and undeniably light-weight, the Lucian we know today accords oddly with the Lucian who was fought over in the sixteenth century. Like Machiavelli, he ceased to be his writings and became a symbol of dispute in the century's attempts to reconcile theology and secular wit. Enlisted, as we have seen, by Erasmus and More as a 'festive' example of the liberated intellect which could be turned to the service of God, he offended the Reformers as an epitome of the worldliness which they felt must be rejected in their classical inheritance if God were to be served at all.

Since there are times when even Erasmus and More seem more worldly than spiritual in imitating Lucian, it is hardly surprising that others who imitated him did so with less discretion. The numerous translations of his work which appeared across Europe in the early years of the century have always been linked to the extraordinary outbreak of satiric energy which occurred in those years, typified by the vogue of the mock-encomium and the *Epistles of Obscure Men* and later to culminate in Rabelais and Aretino. Much of the early enjoyment of Lucian was frankly pagan. Thus in 1515, the year when Erasmus was already feeling qualms about the wisdom of having published *Folly*, Othmar Nachtgall (Luscinius) brought out a translation of Lucian's naughtiest work, the *Dialogues of the Gods*. He dismissed objections to their sexual immorality on the ground that the Old Testament was equally deplorable, blandly commended them to the young as an introduction to New Testament Greek, and at the close of his book added lines 'to the sour-faced prudes who will scorn to read it':

Lucian and Lucianism

> You strait-laced Catos, who in anger scold
> All laughter-loving scoffers, stand away.
> In youth we sport, we dote when we are old,
> And for the rest, what else is life but play?[1]

Such a whimsical defence of Lucianic *lusus* could hardly have issued from a press in Protestant Strasbourg twenty years later. One might contrast with it the tone of E.K.'s gloss on the love between Colin Clout and Hobbinol in the January eclogue of *The Shepheardes Calender* (1579): 'yet let no man thinke, that herein I stand with Lucian or hys develish disciple Unico Aretino, in defence of execrable and horrible sinnes of forbidden and unlawful fleshlinesse'. Possibly E.K. enjoyed his Lucian quite as much as Nachtgall, but it is significant that the tongue-in-cheek joking of the two academics took opposite forms when presented to the public. In Elizabethan England 'Lucianical' had become a term of abuse with devilish undertones, and if humanist writers continued to understand and even practise something similar to what we have been calling the Lucianism of Erasmus and More, they did so only covertly and certainly without using his name.

He had in fact been under attack from religious zealots ever since his work was rediscovered in the previous century. Passages in *The Passing of Peregrinus* and the pseudo-Lucianic *Philopatris* were interpreted as mockery of Christ and the early Christians. Another stumbling-block was his evident disbelief in the immortality of the soul, which not everyone could excuse, as More did, as a natural result of his paganism.[2] Especially scandalous was the denial of all certainty proclaimed in the spurious Greek epigram, 'Lucian to his Book', which took pride of place at the head of all major renaissance editions of his work. Thomas Hickes's translation of 1634 reads:

> Lucian well skill'd in old toyes this hath writ:
> For all's but folly that men thinke is witt:
> No settled judgement doth in men appeare,
> But thou admirest that which others jeere.[3]

This explains how easy it became to disapprove of Lucian and of *Folly* in the same breath. A sympathetic editor of *Hermotimus* in 1522 might defend its rejection of all ancient philosophical

systems as clearing the way for the sole Truth,[4] but for many
the sceptical spirit itself was objectionable, causing Lucian to
be conventionally labelled *atheos*. By 1529 Luther was ready
to apply the same opprobrious term to Erasmus: 'Christ will
judge him as *atheos* and as a Lucianic Epicurus.' He is 'a
light-minded man, mocking all religions as his dear Lucian does,
and serious about nothing but calumny and slander'.[5] Later
Luther calls him 'much worse than Lucian, mocking all things
under the guise of holiness'.[6]

The charge of indiscriminate mockery was levelled at Lucian
not only by the Reformers and not only on religious grounds.
Those who felt the sting of *Ciceronianus* were quick to perceive
and damn its Lucianism. Thus Etienne Dolet: 'Erasmus, whose
custom is to attack everybody, enveighs against the monks, rails,
emulates Lucian, delights in facetiousness and thinks he serves
letters and the state by this licence.'[7] J. C. Scaliger's humourless
response went even further:

You ask if for Jesus, we should say Optimus Maximus; for God, Juppiter; and
for the Virgin Mary, Diana? What a silly question. Let us say also Lucian
for Erasmus. That name would be appropriate for you; since you have
imitated him in the style of his History, have followed his despicable method
of criticism, and you like him have jeered at our religious orders. Shall I call
you Timon? Why not? You seem to hate supremely the human race and to
love yourself.[8]

Where his wit was discounted, Lucian could be made to sound
like Juvenal as a synonym for malicious abuse, and the identification with his character Timon was destined to stick.

Outside controversy, quieter voices also expressed qualms,
especially about Lucian's effect on the young. Juan Luis Vives,
an admirer of Erasmus and More in most things and probably
the most influential educationalist of his day, combined progressive humanist ideals with a passionate reverence for chastity
and simple piety, against both of which Lucian offended.
Qualifying Erasmus's enthusiasm, he warned teachers to avoid
corruptive passages, a point which Sir Thomas Elyot was to
repeat in *The Governor*: 'it were better a child should never read
any part of Lucian than all Lucian'.[9] Much more significant
was Vives's dislike of clever rhetoric. He attributed to Lucian's

Asiatic origin the fact that his language was too rhetorical for his woefully scanty subject-matter.[10] Lacking natural enjoyment of *jeux d'esprit*, Vives showed an uncompromising hostility to the rhetoric of wit which clearly threatened to embrace not only Lucian's writings but also those of his imitators:

> True and genuine rhetoric is the expression of wisdom, which cannot in any way be separated from righteousness and piety. Neither must we imitate those practices which have been in vogue among the heathen, viz. slander, tauntings, the insinuation of the basest suspicions, inversions of what is true, and the attempt to do evil from a good purpose, and to do good from an evil motive.[11]

Since Vives was to be the model for some of Jonson's most resonant and personal statements in *Discoveries*, this frank opposition to satire, innuendo, irony and all the paraphernalia of oblique teaching deserves to be noted. Erasmus, in prefacing *The Cock*, had tried to mark off Lucian from the sophists of his period, but increasingly the anti-Lucianists insisted on joining them together, seeing him as a forerunner of the clever bogeymen of their own day who devoted their skills to baffling the ignorant and to making the worse cause appear the better.

Though Vives was far from preaching a return to illiterate simplicity, his overriding concern as an educator was to foster the simple virtues which intellectual sophistication might pervert. Erasmus, by contrast – willing though he was to champion the ignorant poor against their oppressors, and native common-sense against learned folly – was always prone to assert that the philosopher's task was 'to despise those things which the common herd goggles at, and to think quite differently from the opinions of the majority'.[12] The isolation of the scholar from the mob was a self-evident fact for the humanists, but much of the immense impact of Vives on the sixteenth century was due to his having faced up squarely to its perils. He appended to his great educational treatise, *De Tradendis Disciplinis*, sections on the scholar's life which warn against arrogance, insist that the fruits of study lie in turning it to a useful purpose for the common good, and urge the scholar who goes into the world to act modestly and cautiously, lest, by behaving worse than the uneducated, he should discredit the ability of learning to promote practical wisdom.[13] Those concerns were undoubtedly shared by More, but it is an irony of history that he, a more liberal Catholic than Vives, is remembered for his opposition to the populist aims of the Reformers. His *Dialogue Concerning Heresies*, for all its humane tolerance and care to make the gospel available to the poor in their own tongue, firmly upheld the Church's authority against the right of every man to be his own theologian, and denounced such translations of the Bible into English as lacked that authority, thus bringing him directly into conflict with William Tyndale.

The relevance of this to the status of Lucianism is made clear by the line of attack which Tyndale pursued against More. Himself a learned man, he was enabled by his position in the debate to pillory his opponent as a sophistical humorist who employed the baffling rhetoric of wit and 'poetry' as a means of protecting his own corner in the Truth. More's merry tales give offence, not for their levity, but for their deceitful powers of persuasion; *Utopia*, that 'poetical fiction', is cast in his teeth; and he is repeatedly criticized for 'jesting out the truth', 'a juggler with terms' who 'mocketh a man's wits'.[14] Foxe was to repeat those objections, complaining that More in his *Dialogues* 'dallieth out the matter, thinking to jest poor simple truth out of countenance', 'filling up with fineness of wit, and scoffing terms, where true knowledge and judgement of Scripture did fail'.[15] At one point Tyndale would seem to have struck home against More, if not quite in the manner intended. He argued that More's denials of obscurantism came badly from the man to whom Erasmus, his 'darling', had dedicated *Folly*; 'which book, *if it were in English*, then should every man see, how that he then was far otherwise minded than he now writeth'.[16] In More's often-quoted reply to that gibe we can see spelled out, as simply as can be, the distinction he drew between his Latin and his English readers, and his sad conclusion that, if the barrier between them were to break, Lucianic wit and the cultural ideal it represented must necessarily be abandoned:

I say, therefore, in these days when men by their own default misconstrue and take harm of the very Scripture of God, until men better amend, if any man would now translate *Moria* into English, or some works either that I have myself written ere this, albeit there be none harm therein, folk yet being (as they be) given to take harm of that that is good, I would not only my darling's books but my own also help to burn them both with my own hands, rather than folk would (though through their own fault) take any harm of them, seeing that I see them likely in these days to do.[17]

Written in the early 1530s, these words were by no means a personal retraction of Lucianism, but they do mark the end of a stage in its history. In England there was to be small future for works of playful intelligence in the Latin tongue, and although the court would encourage its own forms of exclusive joking in the vernacular, the shift out of Latin deprived the humanists of much of their cultural assurance. Still more inhibiting was the impact on their wit of the earnest spirit of Reformation and Counter-Reformation. Use of the vernacular came to be associated with direct and unequivocal attempts to sway the religious opinions of the majority. Even writers like Elyot and Ascham, who used English to address a more select audience on secular topics, tended to do so in a straightforward manner. During the second quarter of the century, as the crucial transition from one language to another was effected by English humanists, the art of teasing was discredited and left behind.

Lucian himself was not entirely forgotten in England. He was used by Sir John Cheke in teaching Greek to King Edward, and retained his place in the Greek or Latin syllabus of grammar schools.[18] Offered in discreet selections to beginners, his linguistic usefulness seems generally to have overcome the objections of such as Thomas Becon, who declared in 1560 that this 'wicked and ungodly' author should find no place in the school curriculum.[19] On the continent scholarly interest in him remained strong. The first complete edition of the *Opera Omnia* in Latin, including the translations by Erasmus and More, was issued by Jakob Moltzer (Micyllus) at Frankfurt in 1538 and reissued at Leiden in 1549. The preface pleads for a balanced view of Lucian, admitting his impiety and that many would like to see him suppressed altogether, but urging compensatory virtues. A fair body is not to be condemned for a single wart. Recurrent terms of praise such as *suavitas*, *elegantia*, *varietas*, and *festivitas*, along with a defence of teaching through laughter, testify to the continuance of the Erasmian tradition of aesthetic as well as moral evaluation.

Erasmus and his translations reappear in a more significant edition of the *Opera Omnia*, that of Gilbert Cousin (Cognatus), published in four volumes at Basel in 1563 (reissued 1602 and 1619). This was the first to print both the Greek and Latin texts, and as such was the one most used by the next generation of humanists. Its introductory matter vividly conveys the controversial status of its subject. Cousin, who had been Erasmus's pupil in youth, contributed a eulogy of Lucian which is entirely Erasmian, even to the extent of incorporating most of the Dedication to *The Cock* without acknowledgment. Aware of how his master had made educative use of Lucian's uncommitted stance, he makes no apology for presenting him as 'one of the Pyrrhonists, who affirm nothing, but leave all doubtful issues unresolved'. Other contributors are more defensive, however, and the two later issues carry an essay by Jakob Zwinger which is positively hostile.[20] Great stress is laid in this on Lucian's intemperate bitterness, which for Zwinger invalidates his professed devotion to philosophy:

When his bitterness leads him to transgress the bounds of moderate censure, one thinks of him as actuated less by zeal for Truth than by a sort of pathological ill-will. He seems to have painted his own portrait in the misanthrope Timon who cared nothing for god or man.

This repeats Scaliger. But in respect of Lucian's atheism Zwinger had a new point to make, seeing it not simply as a matter of blasphemy or unbelief but as a mark of the pride of mind dangerously prevalent in his own day:

Such is the rankness of man's mind, which goes horribly astray by valuing itself too highly, congratulating itself on wisdom supposedly achieved by its own unaided efforts, celebrating and worshipping itself in place of God.

Side by side, then, in Cousin's edition, two contradictory images of Lucian stood ready to fascinate Jonson's contemporaries: the suave, versatile and festive wit, potentially Christian, portrayed by Erasmus, and the godless intellect, inherently Satanic, perceived by Zwinger.

Lucian and Lucianism

Because of its four volumes, Cousin's can be identified as the edition which was the subject of a playful forfeit between Gabriel Harvey and Edmund Spenser in 1578. Harvey was to surrender his four volumes if he failed to read Skelton, Skoggin, Lazarillo and Howleglas in ten days.[21] The implication of this (which we should remember before going on to take Lucian more solemnly) is that his work was enjoyed by university men at least partly as a sort of classical equivalent to the popular collections of merry tales and rogue-fiction which Spenser apparently thought that Harvey unduly despised. Puttenham, for example, would casually identify Lucian with that lively figure in Elizabethan mythology, the Merry Greek.[22] But Harvey, over a space of twenty years, has more to tell of a divided attitude to this author. In an early marginal note (?1575), when he was entertaining dreams of a courtly career, he proposes Lucian along with Democritus and Epicurus as culture-heroes for the 'rich, sweet, and delicate' life of the mind, while the active life is to be modelled on Hercules, Alexander, and Caesar.[23] At the same time he was admiring Machiavelli and Aretino for their knowledge of the world and how to use it to advantage.[24] But publicly, in one of the three letters to Spenser printed in 1580, he forsakes these gods in shaking his head over literary fashions at Cambridge:

> *Tully*, and *Demosthenes* nothing so much studyed, as they were wonte: *Livie*, and *Salust* possiblye rather more, than lesse: *Lucian* never so much: *Aristotle* muche named, but little read: *Xenophon* and *Plato*, reckned amongst Discoursers, and conceited Superficiall fellowes: much verball and sophisticall jangling: little subtile and effectuall disputing...*Matchiavell* a great man: *Castilio* of no small reputation: *Petrarch*, and *Boccace* in every mans mouth: *Galateo*, and *Guazzo* never so happy: over many acquainted with *Unico Aretino:* The *French* and *Italian* when so highlye regarded of Schollers? The *Latine* and *Greeke*, when so lightly?[25]

Of classical authors only Lucian, and to a lesser degree Livy and Sallust, are said to be holding their own in a climate that favours the Italians. Harvey's disapproval of this state of affairs does not stop him, however, from expatiating in another of the same group of letters on the exquisite pleasures afforded by Lucian and Aretino to a refined wit:

Images of Lucian

I like your *Dreames* passingly well: and the rather, bicause they savour of that singular extraordinarie veine and invention, which I ever fancied moste, and in a manner admired onelye in *Lucian, Petrarche, Aretine, Pasquill*, and all the most delicate, and fine conceited Grecians and Italians: (for the Romanes to speake of, are but very Ciphars in this kinde:) whose chiefest endevour, and drifte was, to have nothing vulgare, but in some respecte or other, and especially in *lively Hyperbolicall Amplifications*, rare, queint, and odde in every pointe, and as a man woulde saye, a degree or two at the leaste, above the reache, and compasse of a common Schollers capacitie.[26]

Poison for undergraduates could be food for dons.

In the messy controversy with Thomas Nashe (1592) it is no surprise to find that Harvey's judgements on Lucian again conflict, depending on the point at issue. The *Second Letter* attacks railers, and accordingly he is numbered along with Archilochus, Aristophanes, the Emperor Julian and Aretino in that 'venemous and viperous brood'. 'Lucianicall' is an epithet used twice to describe cruel–clever invective. But the *Third Letter* presents Lucian in a favourable light to point by contrast to the lack of 'discretion' in Nashe's *Pierce Penniles*:

Although the Grecians generallie were over-lightheaded, and vaine-spoken, yet their levitie savoured of elegant wittinesse, and the flying birde carried meate in the mouth. Even Lucians true tales are spiced with conceite: and neither his, nor Apuleius' Asse, is altogether an Asse.[27]

Nashe, for his part, was quick to find contradictions in Harvey's attitude to the satirists, but his own was equally divided. He could see them as allies in the struggle of young wits against old, 'because they have broght in a new kind of a quicke fight, which your decrepite slow-moving capacitie cannot fadge with'.[28] Yet he finally falls back on the argument of atheism (which Harvey, to the credit of his intelligence, had not employed) in order to send them packing:

Lucian, Julian, Aretine, all three admirably blest in the abundant giftes of art and nature: yet Religion, which you sought to ruinate, hath ruinated your good names, and the opposing of your eyes against the bright sunne, hath causd the worlde condemne your sight in all other things. I protest, were you ought else but abhominable Atheistes, I would obstinately defende you, onely because *Laureate Gabriell* articles against you.[29]

However much salt we take with our Harvey and Nashe, the extracts quoted give acceptable evidence on certain points.

85

Lucian and Lucianism

First, Lucian was a vogue-author at Cambridge in the 1570s and 1580s, his appeal linked to the better-known fascination of the dangerous Italians. Secondly, Nashe may be allowed to speak for his generation in appreciating and at least claiming to emulate the 'quicke fight' of the prose satirists, while remaining responsive to the horrific implications of their atheism. Lastly, though Harvey might lament that the major authors in the Cambridge curriculum were not receiving the respect they deserved, he continues to justify enjoyment of Lucian on Erasmian grounds, namely, as a challenge to discern wit 'above . . . a common Schollers capacitie' and to discern also that it had a serious function: 'the flying birde carried meate in the mouth'. Comparing that with Sidney's statement that *The Praise of Folly* and Agrippa's *On the Vanity of Knowledge* 'had another foundation than the superficial part would promise',[30] we are in no doubt that English humanist circles at the close of the sixteenth century still understood the principles of Erasmian *lusus*.

But that they approved of them can never be assumed. Since Erasmus's time they were seen to have been open to abuse. Sidney's absolution of Erasmus and Agrippa occurs as a faintly embarrassed parenthesis in the course of an attack on the scoffing mentality in general and on jesting at serious things in particular. For many, it was no great commendation of Erasmus's Silenus-theory to see that it had licensed Rabelais, or of Lucian to note that his *Dialogues of the Courtesans* had provided a model for the *Ragionamenti* of Aretino. Protestant thinkers were especially prone to the view which Tyndale and Foxe took of More, that practitioners of erudite joking were engaged in a Catholic conspiracy 'to jest poor simple truth out of countenance'. Some went even further. Zwinger's presentation of Lucian to the world as a type of the self-worshipping intellect has to be viewed in the wider context of the consternation provoked, above all, by Machiavelli. It was seriously argued that the outright attack on spiritual values which Machiavelli supposedly mounted was the logical climax of a process which had begun with the jesting on such values by irresponsible intellectuals earlier in the century and had con-

Images of Lucian

tinued with the total neglect of them by libertines – the whole process having been planned by Satan as a counter-attack to the Reformation. This theory represents a remarkable piece of historical thinking, and if we remove the idea of supernatural motivation is not altogether stupid. It can be found in the dedicatory epistle prefaced by an unidentified French Protestant to his Latin translation (1577) of Gentillet's *Contre-Machiavel*, and it deserves extended quotation (here from the later English version):

After *Solon*...had seene *Thespis* his first edition and action of a Tragoedie, and meeting with him before the playe, demaunded, If he were not ashamed to publish such feigned fables under so noble, yet a counterfeit personage: *Thespis* answered, That it was no disgrace upon a stage (merrily and in sport) to say and do any thing. Then *Solon* (striking hard upon the earth with his staffe) replied thus: Yea but shortly, we that now like and embrace this play, shall find it practised in our contracts and common affaires. This man of deepe understanding, saw that publicke discipline and reformation of manners affected and attempted once in sport and jeast, would soon quaile: and corruption, at the beginning passing in play, would fall and end in earnest ...Hereof France is unto all ages and nations a wofull view, yet a profitable instruction at this day. For when the cleare light of the Gospell began first to spring and appeare, Sathan (to occupie and busie mens minds with toyish playes and trifles, that they might give no attendance unto true wisedome) devised this policie, to raise up jeasters and fooles in Courts, which creeping in, by quipping and prettie conceits, first in words, and after by bookes, uttering their pleasant jeasts in the Courts and banquets of kings and princes, laboured to root up all the true principles of Religion and Policie. And some there were whom the resemblance of nature, or vanitie of wit had so deceived, that they derided the everlasting veritie of the true God, as if it were but a fable. *Rabelaysius* amongst the French, and *Agrippa* amongst the Germans, were the standardbearers of that traine: which with their skoffing taunts, inveighed not only against the Gospell, but all good arts whatsoever. Those mockers did not as yet openly undermine the ground work of humane societie, but only they derided it: But such Cyclopian laughters, in the end prooved to be onely signes and tokens of future evils. For by little and little, that which was taken in the beginning for jestes, turned to earnest, and words into deedes. In the necke of these came new Poets, very eloquent for their profit, which incensed unto lust and lightnesse, such mindes as were alreadie inclined to wantonnesse, by quickening their appetites with the delectable sause of unchast hearing; and pricking them forward with the sharp spurres of pleasure. Who could then bridle vices and iniquities, which are fed with much wealth, and no lesse libertie? seeing them not onely in play, mirth, and laughter entertained; but also earnestly accepted and commended, as being very excellent. Yet some troad the steps of honesty, which now lay a dying, and practised the ould manners and fashions, which were almost forgotten. For although the secret

87

faults of the Court were evill spoken of, yet shame stoode in open view; hainous and infamous crimes kept secret corners; princes were of some credit and faith; lawes were in reasonable good use; magistrates had their due authoritie and reverence; all things onely for ostentation and outward shew, but none would then have feared an utter destruction: For then Sathan being a disguised person amongst the French, in the likenesse of a merry jeaster, acted a Comoedie, but shortly ensued a wofull Tragoedie. When our countrie mens minds were sick, and corrupted with these pestilent diseases, and that discipline waxed stale; then came forth the books of *Machiavell*, a most pernitious writer, which began not in secret and stealing manner (as did those former vices) but by open meanes, and as it were a continual assault, utterly destroyed, not this or that vertue, but even all vertues at once.[31]

The author of this passage, dedicating his translation to two English noblemen, congratulates them on their good fortune in living under a Protestant monarch, and says he undertook his work for English readers as 'an Antidote and present remedie, to expell the force of so deadly poyson, if at any time it chance to infect you'. He describes the process through French eyes, but Englishmen too could see Italian diabolism as an extension of early humanist frivolity, which in turn was seen to derive from the 'conceited Grecians'. The preacher Thomas Adams was explicit in describing Lucian and Machiavelli as the beginning and end of the Satanic scriptural tradition. '*Sinnes* text is from Hels *Scriptum est*: taken out of the Devils *Spell*; either Lucian his old *Testament*, or *Machiavell* his new.'[32]

These are hardly grounds for placing Lucian in the eye of the Machiavellian storm. He and his followers were none the less caught up in it because of the attention it drew to the phenomenon of the uncommitted intellect. Lucian probably did lack moral commitment; Erasmus, More and Rabelais did not, but in their *lusus* had pretended to do so because they saw it as their function to rouse a public dormant in scholastic habits of thought. That function had been discredited in England by the bloody events of the mid-century. At a time when statesmen like Cromwell and Gardiner seemed to their enemies to have practised the worst excesses of Machiavellian craft and policy, the priority for Christian thinkers of both camps was no longer to sharpen or liberate the intelligence but to redefine its theological role and bring it back firmly within Christian bounds. As forthright commitment was increasingly called for, it became harder to justify openly authors who had obscured their true position in the interest of teaching obliquely.

Lucianism can exert a decisive influence only on writers who either adopt or pretend to adopt a relativist attitude to moral and philosophical values. Thus Donne's *Ignatius his Conclave*, written in Latin, though it marks a revival of Erasmian satiric *lusus*, cannot be called Lucianic in our sense of the term since it is quite unequivocal in its purpose of denouncing the Jesuits: it recalls the Erasmus, not of *Folly*, but of the *Julius Excluded from Heaven*. It was with the growth of relativist thinking in seventeenth-century France that the second great period of Lucian's European influence was to begin. Where tentative ventures in that direction occurred in England, his presence can occasionally be felt. Frye has noted the link between 'Menippean' satire and the form of literature known as the 'anatomy', which presupposed a measure of detached curiosity over a chosen field which was usually wide. Accordingly, there is a trace of Lucian in Ralegh's lines beginning 'What is our life?' and more than a trace of him in the *persona* of Democritus, the laughing philosopher, adopted by Burton. But Elizabethan and Jacobean 'anatomists' more commonly approached their subjects with Lear's angry motive for anatomizing Regan, to denounce sources of corruption. Their tendency to lapse from clinical objectivity is absurdly illustrated by the first published work of the young George Wither, who begins by proposing his youth and inexperience as a guarantee of disinterested observation ('So I *aloofe* may view, without suspicion') and proceeds to anatomize man:

> Mounted aloft on *Contemplations* wings,
> And noting with my selfe the state of things,
> I plainely did perceive as on a stage,
> The *confus'd actions* of this present age.[33]

Yet Wither called his volume *Abuses Stript, and Whipt*, and in the course of it resorted sufficiently to the Juvenalian scourge to be consigned to the Marshalsea Prison. Though vantage-ground of some kind is essential for all satire, Lucian's had been much too remote for the satirists of the 1590s. Spenser might cast Harvey in the role of the kataskopic don

Lucian and Lucianism

that sitting like a Looker-on
Of this worldes Stage, doest note with critique pen
The sharpe dislikes of each condition[34]

and he himself, in lost early work like the *Dreams*, may well have expressed a witty academic detachment; but when a scholar-satirist like Donne or Guilpin located himself in his 'cell', or study, it was rather to serve as a springboard for attack on the world outside. Conventionally open to attack as 'jeering Lucianists',[35] the verse-satirists were in fact too anxious to appear morally committed to be able to use the real Lucian at all. For Erasmus's Lucian they had even less time. When Marston proclaimed in 1599, 'In serious jest and jesting seriousness / I strive to scourge polluting beastliness',[36] he outlined a concept of *joco-serium* that was to have a remarkable future in melodrama but was in total violation of the witty ideal proposed by Erasmus as an alternative to the Juvenalian cess-pit.

The only satiric poem of the 1590s to reflect Lucian's shadow even faintly is Donne's *Satire III*. If we think in terms of genre, the use of verse-satire as a medium for considering alternative religions naturally places the poem in the line of Horace, whose eclecticism ('nullius addictus jurare in verba magistri') is firmly rejected at the poem's core:

but unmoved thou
Of force must one, and forc'd but one allow;
And the right.

But this also rejects scepticism, which appears in the poem as a much greater threat, as indeed it was for Donne's generation. The argument of Lucian's *Hermotimus* is attributed to 'carelesse Phrygius' who 'doth abhorre / All, because all cannot be good', and has its corollary in the easy relativism of Graccus who 'loves all as one'. Support for the view that Lucian is specifically remembered in this poem would depend on seeing Donne's parade of mistresses as a conscious variant on the slave-market of *Philosophies for Sale*. More generally, he recalls Lucian by the very pointedness with which he alters his major assumptions. Donne does not discourage a detached survey of the religious market, but only insists that the survey should be directed toward making a positive choice. 'I must not laugh, nor weepe sinnes, and be wise' means that in matters where salvation is at stake the attitude of a Democritus or a Heraclitus is incompatible with wisdom. Wisdom for Donne means the active search for God which had been folly to the doubting Greek. But within the limit of that basic contradiction the Christian poet allows full scope to the sceptical intelligence. His choice, like the poem itself, will be strenuously cerebral; his path to Truth's mountain is marked by paradox. The statement that 'truth and falsehood bee / Neare twins' belongs to the same class of paradox as Sidney's appreciation of *Folly*, 'that good lie hid in nearness of the evil'.[37] 'Doubt wisely', itself a paradox in relation to the concept of faith, has often rightly been taken as the poem's motto.

It is in drama, however, that the best-known Elizabethan comments on the morally unattached intellect are to be found, and especially in Shakespeare, whose metaphorical renderings of it are at times suggestively Lucianic. There is no need to boggle over the fact that very little Lucian was available to him in English, since one or two dialogues read at school in Erasmus's Latin – let us say, at a guess, *Timon* and *Icaromenippus* – could have provided him with all the Lucian that he needed to remember, though he may well have read more and read it later. There is a vivid study of *kataskopê* in *Love's Labour's Lost*, IV.iii. Berowne, after soliloquizing on being in love, climbs on to a commanding height of some kind (many editions retain Capell's stage-direction '*Gets up into a tree*') in order to overhear the King, who subsequently steps aside to overhear Longaville, who in turn withdraws to overhear Dumain. Hearing all three confess themselves in love, Berowne exclaims, 'Like a demigod here sit I in the sky, / And wretched fools' secrets heedfully o'er-eye.' The process then moves into reverse as each listener reveals himself, chides his victim and in turn is chidden, until Berowne descends to 'whip hypocrisy':

> O, what a scene of fool'ry have I seen,
> Of sighs, of groans, of sorrow, and of teen!
> O me, with what strict patience have I sat,
> To see a king transformed to a gnat!
> To see great Hercules whipping a gig,
> And profound Solomon to tune a jig,
> And Nestor play at push-pin with the boys,
> And critic Timon laugh at idle toys!

This is a distinctively Lucianic variant of the world-upsidedown *topos* (cf. *Icaromenippus*, 15–16). The King replies, 'Too bitter is thy jest. / Are we betrayed thus to thy over-view?' But the audience is the ultimate overviewer and knows that Berowne is as much a hypocrite as the others. His superior wit, as is usual in Shakespeare, marks him as the character with the greatest potential for maturity and wisdom, but moral approval depends on the use to which his wit is put, and has to be withheld until he accepts from his mistress (like Benedick later) a task which will tie his intelligence to a moral and selfless purpose. Similarly, in *A Midsummer Night's Dream*, where there are actual demigods, we find that the happy outcome depends on their conversion from the attitude of 'Lord, what fools these mortals be!' to one of promoting harmony and making amends. Shakespeare's reaction to satiric attitudes current in the 1590s is most clearly shown by *As You Like It*, II.vii. The tone of that scene is made subtle by the fact that Jaques, who sees the fool's motley as a licence to take up each attitude in turn, does so in an evidently playful spirit, while Duke Senior, who moralizes against him, appears somewhat heavily sententious. The result is that conventional arguments for and against satire are finally bypassed. After echoing Touchstone's 'complaint' on Fortune and Time, Jaques toys with the more fashionable aim (of Jonson's Asper, among others) to 'cleanse the foul body of th' infected world', adding the ironic afterthought: 'If they will patiently receive my medicine'. The Duke responds with the Christian objection that the satirist who finds motes in the eyes of his fellow-men is displaying the beam in his own, to which Jaques counters the Erasmian defence of general satire, that it offends only those who betray their guilt. The debate is at this point interrupted and made to look academic by Orlando's entry and account of his and Adam's distress, inducing a mood of charity in his hearers. It is then that Duke Senior ponderously introduces the world-stage metaphor to point out that other people's tragedies are worse than theirs, thus launching Jaques into the Seven Ages of Man, which is not, be it said, derived from Lucian, but is a survey of the type associated with him. This is satire wittier than the complaint, less vindictive than the Juvenalian, and persuasively comprehensive in seeming to range over the whole of human life. However, as is often pointed out, when Orlando re-enters with his 'venerable burden', the speech is seen to be far from comprehensive in its wisdom. Its moral emptiness, and indeed the uselessness of satire as a whole, are brought home to us, not by anyone's words, but by the contrasting satisfaction we derive from the relief of a weak and hungry old man.

To adopt the demigod stance and view life as a pageant is always in Shakespeare an expression of pride or weakness: a claim to be above the battle or a sign that one has given it up. His great men resort to it at their lowest ebb, like Macbeth in a moment of despair, or at the height of self-confidence, like Prospero when the triumph of his art brings him to the verge of forgetting his humanity. All simplified views of life, all renunciations of a share in its complexity, are brought under suspicion. Thus the most surprising feature of *Timon of Athens* is that Shakespeare thought it worthwhile to turn his full attention to a character capable of simplified vision only. Editors debate whether he actually consulted Lucian when he wrote, but it is at least clear that the choice of a hero so typically Lucianic – often, as we have seen, identified with Lucian – did much to determine the character of his play, making it resemble a moral fable more completely than his tragedies usually do. There could be no basis for moral conflict in the extremes of trust and distrust of human nature shown by Timon, because simplified vision, once disillusioned, does not struggle to accommodate reality but veers to an opposite simplification. Nor was it open to Shakespeare to humanize his play by involving Timon in significant personal relationships, because such relationships are impossible for those who cannot come to terms with human nature. In dramatizing such a character, all that can be done is to place him in a certain context. For the sake of his fable, Lucian had placed his Timon on a hill-top farm, a good point of vantage for hurling abuse up at the gods and stones down at mankind. Shakespeare's fable demanded the contrasting back-cloths of civilized society and elemental nature, and a context of characters with whom Timon is thematically, not personally, related. Placing and patterning by themselves, however, have a mainly intellectual impact. Lear, Antony, Coriolanus, also figures in clearly marked moral fables, become more than that by reason of their internal conflicts and involvement with people; they stir emotions in an audience that Shakespeare can steer to a kathartic conclusion. Timon's remote inhumanity, springing integrally from his author's conception of what he stands for, means that he cannot ultimately be more than an intellectual enigma. His storms of passion, breaking on the rock of an audience's emotional indifference, are only disturbing in the sense that they call for diagnosis. The clinical question 'How did he get that way?' pre-empts feelings of pity or terror. One expects to be left with that sort of question by a puzzling, open-ended fable. Lucian had himself raised it when he made his Hermes suggest about Timon

You might say that he was ruined by kind-heartedness and philanthropy and compassion on all those who were in want; but in reality it was senselessness and folly and lack of discrimination.[38]

And in a similar spirit critics of Shakespeare's play still debate whether Timon's simplified vision was a mark of madness or stupidity or greatness – much, indeed, as they respond to the final simplified vision of Gulliver.

Shakespeare is an ocean where every kind of writing can be made to find its resemblance. Instead of supposing that he abandoned *Timon* because his enigmatic hero was unsuited to tragedy, it might be argued that the play merely masquerades as tragedy and was planned as an enigma to stretch the understanding of its audience. With a little ingenuity, other puzzling plays like *Troilus and Cressida* and *Measure for Measure* might be similarly related to the Lucianic mode. It is not, however, one of the present book's aims to try to catch the ocean in its net, or to pay back old scores by trying to view Shakespeare through Jonsonian lenses. He normally mistrusted that aspect of humanism of which the art of teasing was a rhetorical expression – the author's conviction of superiority to his public. What effect this may have had on the drama before Jonson will be considered in the next chapter. Here, finally, we can remind ourselves how, at least among non-dramatic writers, the humanist poet's approach to his art did predispose him to teasing techniques.

For Sidney, Spenser, Jonson, Milton, the anti-Erasmian image of Lucian as an aloof and unprincipled scoffer was even less to be admired than it was for Shakespeare, since their more clearly articulated literary theory was built on the assumption that poetry should inculcate commitment to virtue. No concept was more basic to their thinking than that voiced by Sidney, that the aim of all intellectual endeavour was to enable man to make up as far as possible the ground he had lost by the Fall, and that the prime knowledge to be sought was that of the self, 'with the aim of well-doing and not of well-knowing only'.[39] Applied to the function of the poet, this meant that as well as encouraging his readers toward those goals he should also achieve them himself; his act of 'well-doing', as poet, is performed by embodying his self (or, as we would say, his convictions) in his work. This is a main reason why Spenser, Jonson and Milton do not, like Shakespeare, allow their intelligence to follow in the wake of their imagination but always imagine situations which embody or challenge belief; it is also why the entire *oeuvre* of each of these writers is as consistent as the growth of one man's self-knowledge will permit, why they are always (to use a term the humanists loved) *sibi aequales*, 'like themselves'. This stress on clarity and integrity of moral purpose was in large measure a response to the threat of the free-wheeling or iconoclastic intellect, which Lucian was thought to have foreshadowed, and was naturally accompanied by rejection of its two most widely anathematized vices: sophistry – the use of intellectual argument without conviction – and affective rhetoric – the attempt to persuade by emotional appeal, promoting a repetition of the Fall. But the stronger the urge toward moral engagement, the greater the problems of artistic expression; and the literary training of the humanist poets worked against, not in favour of, engagement. The root assumption in Aristotle's *Poetics* is of the work as a thing apart from its creator, conceived and fashioned objectively. The concept of decorum, in all its ramifications, presupposed an artist who would scrupulously modify his personal voice to the requirements of genre, subject, character. Even rhetoric, in teaching the art of persuasion, taught a sophisticated delight in verbal play which could never be contained within the role of pious truth-telling allotted to it by Vives. So the characteristic which most significantly unites the various achievements of Spenser and Jonson and Milton at their best is a controlled tension between their commitment to assert 'themselves' – one may almost say to preach – and an artistic theory which rendered that commitment suspect and hard to fulfil. In controlling that tension they were forced to resort in one way or another to teaching obliquely, to forms of irony and concealment of purpose through which zeal could be reconciled to art.

Thus Jonson, at a stage in his dramatic career when his art had been almost overwhelmed by self-assertion, was to be attracted by the example of the Lucianic Erasmus as a satirist who could penetrate the moral consciousness of the reader with consummate artistry and no self-assertion whatever. It would be rash to suggest that the other authors named were equally conscious of Erasmus's example, yet in all of them the instinct to challenge the reader indirectly, to make him work his own passage to the truth, was a part of their humanist inheritance. However strong their urge to proclaim a message, they wrote primarily for an audience 'fit, though few', and were prone to perpetuate the aristocracy of intelligence by setting rigorous qualifying examinations. One thinks of the deceptively negligent style with which Sidney made Gosson disappear; of how Spenser makes his readers undergo for themselves the testing experiences of his characters; above all, of the inducement Milton offers to sinners to plant their feet wrong in relation to each major issue in his epic. None of these three went as far as Jonson could go in drama toward obliterating his true point of view. They remind us, however, that even where English humanism was most deeply imbued with Protestant fervour, the art of teasing could continue to find a place.

CHAPTER 5

Teasing drama: Medwall to Marlowe

Why should a dramatist not treat his audience as More treated Dorp, or Erasmus Budé, or Swift the reader of *Gulliver's Travels*? The theatre's taboo on being nasty to customers can be said to have been lifted in the twentieth century but had a remarkably long life before. It had much to do with the mystique of a shared experience, of the play as a joint creation by playwright, actor and audience. It was also, rather obviously, a matter of economics: the dependence of the stage on large bourgeois audiences who pay to be pleased, not examined. And satirists themselves appear to have concurred in it, perhaps from a sense of fairness to their victims, letting them meditate on charges brought against them in print instead of forcing them to instant confessions of guilt through misplaced laughter or applause. Above all, the taboo was a product of artistic example. The classical drama – or at least such plays as fitted Aristotle's pattern – emphasized the integrity of the play as fiction, as an image of life, and limited the scope of the author's rhetoric to making the fiction persuasive. Most influential was the example of Shakespeare, the audience's friend – a demanding one, no doubt, but always to be trusted, always the honest sharer of visions, never the smiler with a knife.

Jonson, like Swift, found out that the masses could be pleased and examined simultaneously, especially if one chose the sources of their pleasure as the topic on which to examine them. He may have been unfair in working off on his audience his suspicion of the medium he wrote for, but he was not the first English writer for the stage to have done so. In the early Tudor period the idea of the play as self-contained fiction had been slow to take hold, and communal trust between playwright and audience had not been the norm. All forms of fiction were more likely in those days to be justified, as Erasmus justified his *Colloquies*, in terms of beneficent trickery. Thus when More sought to justify to Tyndale his own and Erasmus's *lusus*, it was to drama that he turned for an example. Answering the charge that *Folly* had ridiculed the worship of saints, he wrote: 'that book of *Moria* doth indeed but jest upon the abuses of such things, after the manner of the disour's [jester's] part in a play, and yet not so far neither by a great deal as the messenger doth in my *Dialogue*'.[1] Most forms of drama in More's time contained equivalents to the *agent provocateur* of dialogue. He could have been referring to any of them.

One possibility is that he was thinking of academic entertainments. In humanist circles little distinction appears to have been made between dialogues and plays, both being acted as part of holiday celebrations in colleges from the start of the century, if not earlier.[2] A statute of 1545, which presumably confirmed a much older practice, required the Christmas Lord at St John's College, Cambridge, to organize 'at least six dialogues or shows of a festive or literary nature'.[3] The occasion was the time of licence when the inversion of customary order and the paradox of Folly enthroned in the seat of learning were traditionally celebrated. We know that such revels were also held at the Inns of Court, and that More was named alternate Master of the Revels at Lincoln's Inn in 1528–9.[4] So he may have alluded to a Lord of Misrule in an academic Feast of Fools, or perhaps to a jesting prevaricator in a mock disputation. Though not much is known about such rituals, it seems certain that they fostered the challenge to orthodoxy characteristic of humanist *lusus*.[5]

Alternatively, he may have had Morality drama in mind, a play such as Skelton's *Magnificence*. The original meaning of 'disour' was jester in the sense of a teller of *gestes* or tales, but the phrase 'devil's disour' was a common one, used by Langland with regard to the alluring speeches of harlots and by More himself in a sense approximating to 'devil's advocate'.[6] So he could have intended a comparison between the role of Folly and that of early Vice-characters. The affinity is striking, and suggests the ease with which the humanist art of teasing could

be grafted on to native dramatic stock. Provocation or temptation of an audience was integral to the art of the medieval
dramatist, who was conscious of pitching his battle in the mind
of the spectator as much as in the action on stage. Providing
an object-lesson on the need to live by God's law, he had first
to force his public to admit that its fallen instincts pulled it in
a contrary direction. This was true not only of the allegorical
Moralities but also of the Miracle-plays. If a writer portrayed
the reluctance of Noah's wife to enter the ark or of Abraham
to sacrifice his son, his purpose was not so much mimetic – to
show how people would actually behave – as rhetorically
deceptive, to trap the audience into a 'wrong' response: an
indulgent guffaw at the wife's rebellion or a false sense of
outrage on behalf of the father. He would often reinforce such
temptations by making his characters address their misleading
appeals directly to the audience. In this way the religious drama
was able, at its best, to generate moral tensions of considerable
subtlety and power. It implicated participants in a type of
experience which, even when simple, was similar to the experience undergone by readers of *Folly* or *Utopia*.

But there were limits to the strain which could be placed on
spectators by a form of drama committed to exemplary teaching.
It could not afford to leave them in perplexity. Here the
humanist drama, generally treating secular themes for a more
select public, had much greater scope, and it will be worthwhile
to look in detail at an example of it which offers a third variant
of 'the disour's part' and indeed one of the most remarkable
displays of audience-discomfiture on the English stage before
Jonson. Henry Medwall's *Fulgens and Lucrece* (?1497) is tangen-
tially connected with More at several points. It appears to have
been written for performance at a banquet in Archbishop
Morton's household some years after More went there for his
early training; it shows characters 'stepping in among the
players' rather as More himself is reputed to have done there;
and it owes its survival to having been printed by More's
brother-in-law, John Rastell. Its central topic of debate –
whether a woman should choose a husband for nobility of birth
or nobility of character – was harmless and conventional

enough, but the marriage-choice could readily be seen as a metaphor for political preferment, thus awkwardly reflecting the struggle for influence at court which was going on at that time between feudal lords and self-made humanists, both of which groups were no doubt represented around Morton's table, the author himself belonging to the latter. David Bevington has shown how this 'potentially offensive' issue was handled by Medwall with tact and moderation, especially in his neglect of the opportunity offered by his source of arrogantly equating humanism with virtue.[7] But by laboriously explaining his moderate position he drew attention to the issue itself. Repeated clarifications of the guarded moral – that birth should yield to worth *only* when the two are not combined – seem designed to placate those unable to grasp the subtler implications of the play as a whole. Examining its rhetorical strategy, we can detect a strong element of provocative *lusus*. This would seem to be directed not only at dunderheaded barons but also at the tendency of humanists to base their social presumptions on bookish idealism.

The bafflement of the audience is practised through the two characters *A* and *B* who step from among the diners to introduce the play and later into the main action itself, continually complicating the focus in which its simple outline is to be viewed. Anonymity is essential to their function, but in giving them these labels in his script Medwall was alluding, in terms of alphabetical symbolism, to the difference between their dramatic roles. Broadly speaking, though both are ridiculous figures, one tends to function as knave and the other as fool. *A* as befits the initial letter, is an 'original' who opens the play by challenging the audience aggressively; he is self-assertive, makes his way by his wits, and acknowledges no moral code – in short, at his low-comic level, he is the worst sort of social upstart. He shows worldly scepticism about the likely effect of the play's moral on high-born members of the audience and advises that the ending should be changed, since 'truth may no be said alway' (I.161).[8] *B*, by contrast, the second or 'following' letter, shows acceptance of the feudal pattern. He likes to 'undertake' (I.28) on behalf of the host and the author. His ambition is to be 'of counsel' (I.63, 361). As a spokesman for authority he defends the moral of the play, but shows himself less intelligent than *A* in doing so, relying simplistically on the 'plain truth' he has been taught to respect in his parish, and arguing that the gentry will hardly take offence at a story about Roman characters to whom they are not related. His failure to see that they might apply the moral to themselves continues to highlight the fact that there is a moral to be applied, and inescapably suggests that those who fail to do so must be as stupid as he. He shows ignorance of the principle of self-contained fiction by deciding to enter the play, which for him has no meaning until he is part of it –

> Destroy the play, quotha! nay, nay,
> The play began never till now.
> I will be doing. (1.363–5)

A, on the other hand, takes the same decision in full knowledge of its incongruity, and jokingly confides in the audience his pragmatic reasons for doing so. Just as the main debate invites us to perceive 'some manner of difference' between two concepts of nobility, so here we are challenged to distinguish between *B*'s confusion of play and reality which springs from ignorant delusion and *A*'s which suggests his cynical perception that life is in any case just a matter of playing roles for one's own advantage. Only in one section of the play, the weakest (II.166–355), do these two characters become virtually indistinguishable as foolish servants. For the most part Medwall uses them in different ways to stimulate the play of mind around his central theme and so to bamboozle the goats in his audience. It seems reasonable to guess that academic purists would deplore altogether the intrusion of farce into a dignified debate on a dignified occasion, while yawning gentry would be relieved to laugh thoughtlessly at *A*'s knavery or complacently at *B*'s stupidity. Only those in touch with the author's drift would be able to balance the farcical and solemn elements against each other, appreciating the irony in relation to the play's theme of seeing the feudal order upheld by a dunce and questioned by a rascal. They would also perceive that the author plants a doubt about his safe moral by entrusting its defence to *B* and exposing it to provocative criticism from *A*.

Those who laughed idly were apt to have the laugh turned against them. A simple foretaste of Medwall's technique occurs near the start when *B* is indignant at being mistaken for an actor by *A*. Condescending mirth at the absurdity is punctured by *A*'s ironic explanation of his mistake:

> There is so much nice array
> Amongst these gallants nowaday,
> That a man shall not lightly
> Know a player from another man. (I.54–7)

The satiric point is not that actors dress as garishly as the banqueters but *vice versa*. More seriously, Medwall makes telling criticism of upper-class values through his clever pairing of masters and servants. Each servant shares his master's attitude to the feudal principle but totally misjudges his moral worth. Thus *B* is naïvely impressed by Publius Cornelius, the decadent patrician, and makes an enthusiastic speech in praise of his 'liberality', equating with reckless expenditure a term which humanists would recognize as having lofty moral connotations. Correspondingly, *A* is flabbergasted rather than pleased when his master, the virtuous but plebeian Gaius Flaminius, is finally chosen by Lucrece. Here he makes the most significant of his thrusts at the assembled company:

> How say ye, good women, is it your guise
> To choose all your husbands that wise? (II.848–9)

His last speech in the play wistfully complains that the ending is not true to life:

> And I would have thought in very deed
> That this matter should have proceed
> To some other conclusion. (II.878–90)

At one level, these words mark the moral insensitivity of the worldly man, but they also alert high-minded members of the audience to the satisfaction they have derived from seeing life as it ought to be, not as it is. *B*'s scornful and smug rejoinder on behalf of the author, that the purpose was to provide a moral *exemplum*, does not deny that a different conclusion would have been reached if the play had been offering an *imago vitae*. Medwall's talent for analysing his medium can be seen in the way he plays these two rival theories of drama off against each other.

We recognize in *A* and *B* versions of 'the disour's part' well suited to the art of teasing whether in dialogue or comedy. The wise-guy is used to force a response which is sharp but uncomfortable, while the dimwit tempts a response that is comfortable but slack. But it is in the concealed relationship of *jocus* and *serium* that Medwall's teasing should most interest us. After the interval, *A* reopens the play with a conventional defence of its farcical ingredients. All tastes must be catered for, and he divides these abruptly into two:

> For some there be that looks and gapes
> Only for such trifles and japes,
> And some there be among
> That forceth little of such madness
> But delighteth them in matter of sadness
> Be it never so long. (II.30–6)

If these groups correspond to mindless barons on the one hand and scholars with an insatiable appetite for doctrine on the other, it is clear that Medwall has ironically omitted reference to his ideal spectator. This conclusion is strengthened by *A*'s assertion that the 'trifles' in the play are 'impertinent / To the matter principal'. The subplot's relevance is obvious. The main action is elaborately burlesqued in the wooing by *A* and *B* of Lucrece's maid Joan, the 'flower of the frying-pan'. *A*'s motives are worse than those of Publius (he already has several 'wives' and lives off their earnings); *B*'s intentions are as honourable as those of Gaius but stupider (he offers no means of support); Joan's handling of proposals is as prudent as her mistress's but less sincere (she is promised elsewhere); and the obscene joust of 'fart prick in cule' debases the disputation of the noble wooers to its lowest possible equivalent. It is generally agreed that the effect of the parodic parallel is not only to let us giggle at foolish servants but also to comment on the unreality of the main action. Though farce has its own exaggerative tendencies, *jocus* for Medwall (as later for More) clearly inclines to the representation of human frailty as it is, while *serium* involves the exemplary triumph of ideal wisdom. Thus the burlesque, while not utterly undermining its object, keeps open an alternative and more realistic channel of vision. Since *A* and *B* are in any case, by their deeds and comments, inextricably bound up with the serious action, it is clear that the 'understander' of the play was expected to bring *jocus* and *serium* into a single paradoxical focus. What is required of him is the balanced intellectual response that is proper to dialogue. Though Medwall himself enters into his fiction whole-heartedly enough to be tedious for great stretches of time, his distinction lies finally in his detachment from the game and his ability to turn it against us. We should learn, through *A* and *B*, that to enter the play-world by no means destroys it – rather helps it along – but poses a dangerous threat to our moral and intellectual bearings.

The early date of *Fulgens and Lucrece* corrects the impression, which the design of this book might very well give, that humanist *joco-serium* was exclusively bred out of Lucian by Erasmus and More. It is none the less natural that we should hope to find further dramatic examples of it in More's circle, especially since this included the dramatists John Rastell and John Heywood; natural, too, that we should be disappointed to find nothing in their work that equals Medwall's in force and subtlety. A simple explanation is that neither of those writers was temperamentally able to unite these two qualities. Rastell had intellectual power and the desire to challenge, but was deficient in dramatic skill, and lacked – a crucially important factor – the patience to play wittily with an audience. His *Interlude of the Four Elements* (?1519) repeats Medwall's specious division of his public into those disposed to 'sadness' and those disposed to mirth, and in fact carries further his contrast between strenuous philosophic material and knockabout farce. When he defends *jocus* as a mere palliative and box-office draw ('To give men comfort, / And occasion to cause them to resort / To hear this matter'), we suspect that he meant something more. But whatever his intentions the two levels are not brought together effectively. They are much better integrated in *Of Gentleness and Nobility* (?1527), where the Ploughman who provides the farce is also the most seriously challenging figure. As Bevington notes, this character is 'always on the offensive, raising questions that cannot always be answered. He becomes the gadfly, like Hythloday in *Utopia*.'[9] The problem of how to react to his radical attack on the prerogatives of the upper classes is firmly and awkwardly dumped in the upper-class audience's lap. Rastell wrote, it would seem, for his own private theatre, the audiences of which presumably enjoyed hard-hitting engagement, and it is chiefly he who gives a tantalizing sense of the potential for teasing drama which existed in the first quarter of the sixteenth century.

Heywood was a better dramatist than Rastell but a less fervent humanist, a professional entertainer who seems never, if we may judge from his work, to have wished to offend anyone. His social criticism was expressed through a basically genial irony that has usually been described as Chaucerian. He has the distinction, however, of being the first English dramatist to have drawn inspiration directly from Lucian. His *The Play of the Weather* (published 1533) has its origin in *Icaromenippus*, 25, where Zeus is shown listening to prayers:

The prayers came from all parts of the world and were of all sorts and kinds...Among seafaring men, one was praying for the north wind to blow, another for the south wind; and the farmers were praying for rain while the washerman was praying for sunshine.

He copes with conflicting prayers by suspending judgement, which would mean letting the climate take its course. This is essentially what Heywood's Juppiter does too ('Now shall ye have the weather even as it was'),[10] with the important difference that he professes to keep the matter in his own hands, carefully allotting to each section of the community as much of what it wants as is consistent with the good of the whole. Accepting that the play is an allegory on factional rivalries under Henry VIII,[11] we can credit Heywood with some boldness in presenting it, especially if it was played before the king. But the approach is disarming and pacific rather than provocative. What he has imitated from Lucian, apart from the delicately humorous handling of fable, is the use of the kataskopic viewpoint as a means of cooling emotional temperatures and providing perspective. This perspective is transmitted to the audience not only by Juppiter but also by his servant, Merry Report, who organizes the proceedings with amused detachment and impartiality. It is a moment of some piquancy in the development of drama when a character described as 'the Vice' explains his name by translating the Horatian tag which Erasmus and More had applied to Lucian: 'Reporting alway truly, / What hurt to report a sad matter merrily?' ('ridentem dicere verum / quid vetat?').[12]

Among early Tudor plays Heywood's alone breathe something of the original spirit of Lucian, yet by reason of their frankness barely belong to the teasing mode we have labelled Lucianic. On the other hand, *Fulgens and Lucrece*, which exemplifies that mode very fully, was almost certainly written without reference to Lucian at all. Again we are reminded that Lucian's impact on the humanists merely strengthened an instinct for teasing play which was prevalent before, and indeed had been a feature of medieval court cultures (notably reflected in Chaucer's treatment of his audience in *The Parliament of Fowls* and the *Troilus*). What the art always required, however, was a political climate stable enough to tolerate stimulus. Thus it found expression more easily in Morton's household in 1497 than in the tense atmosphere at court in the early 1530s. That was not a time or place for making mischief. Rastell survived only by turning his pen to the service of Thomas Cromwell. More, who may never in any case have recommended the vernacular drama as a medium for disturbing stimulants, certainly would not have done so at a time when he was offering to burn *Utopia* and *Folly* rather than see them translated into English, fearing that misconstruction could imperil the souls of the ignorant. As is well known, his fear that ambiguities of speech could be misrepresented to the peril of his life led him finally to cultivate public silence. The stage shared in the paralysis of wit which that silence symbolized.

Though there was ample provocation in the drama of the next fifty years, the political climate gave little more inducement to wit. From Bale to Preston, most writers favoured the Morality form in preaching on public issues, but even with the

weapon of the Vice in their hands they showed little sophistication in playing with their public. When he did write as
humanist more than as preacher, the mid-century playwright
was notably reluctant to tease. Partly he was influenced by the
growing prestige of the self-contained drama based on Roman
models; still more he seems governed by respect for his audience.
Farcical plays like *Ralph Roister Doister*, *Jack Juggler* and *Gammer
Gurton's Needle*, written for performance in schools and colleges,
are excellent instances of humanist *lusus* in the sense of being
erudite jokes, incongruously applying to English conditions the
conventions and paraphernalia of Plautus and Terence familiar
from the classroom. But the joke is mainly at the expense of the
curriculum, and is genially shared with the students. These
plays provide interesting background to Jonson in several
respects. Roister Doister and Merrygreek are recalled in the
interplay of impostor and ironist in *Volpone*, and there is the same
conscious emphasis on 'lowness' in Gammer Gurton's village
that we find in *Bartholomew Fair*. All of them keep alive the
provocative practice of indulging amiable rogues, and in the
fate of the cleric, Doctor Rat, in *Gammer Gurton* we sense how
that play, with the beggar as hero, has been slyly directed at
academic pride. But recalling the Erasmian defence of *lusus* as
'laxandi vel exercendi ingenii gratia' one is bound to note that
these delectable plays rest the mind rather more than they
stretch it. At the other main centre of humanist drama, the
court, still less encouragement was given to the art of teasing.
Neither Mary nor Elizabeth could afford to encourage the free
play of wit. The latter, in the same way as she told preachers
to keep to their texts, probably did more than Aristotle to
promote the self-contained drama. Richard Edwards in his
prologue to *Damon and Pythias* (?1564) implied that it was in
response to a royal injunction that he had departed from 'toying
plays' and 'sports'. In describing the matter of his 'tragical
comedy' as 'mix'd with mirth and care' he was not reviving
the challenging mixture of *jocus* and *serium* as Medwall knew it
but was launching the Elizabethan mixed drama on its relatively
inoffensive course, in which all that was demanded of low
comedy was a thematic link with the main action, broadening

but not seriously complicating the spectator's perspective. Perhaps significantly, Edwards's most interesting character, the joking philosopher Aristippus, is shown as a moral failure who refuses to jeopardize his favour with the tyrant by intervening on behalf of Damon's innocence. His reputation for *jocus* renders him incapable of *serium*, and he is dismissed from the play because no room can be found for him in the simple moral pattern of the conclusion.

When the wits of the late 1580s turned to writing for the new public theatres, they respected their audiences only as a source of income, and their disregard of Aristotle was a symbol of freedom from academic shackles. The situation was one where the temptation to play ironically with the public very obviously arose. Kyd, on the limited evidence available, seems to have resisted it best. The pervasive irony of *The Spanish Tragedy* is entirely at the expense of the characters, and spectators are invited to share with the author his enjoyment of the ultimate overview. In what spirit Greene approached his public is more doubtful. He appears to have taken a pragmatic satisfaction in putting together gallimaufries of attractive material in better shape and language than was usual, but as Bevington observes 'the suggestion of mockery through caricature is never entirely absent' from his plays, especially in romantic passages,[13] while in the Oxford scenes of *Friar Bacon and Friar Bungay* he parades pseudo-science with evident relish. Yet he conspicuously refrains in that comedy from the needling of his public's ignorance which Jonson was to practise in *The Alchemist*, and in general his mockery seems directed at himself in the hack writer's role. Clearly it is Marlowe who concerns us most here. Much evidence suggests that he was a born mischief-maker, a precocious intellectual quite likely to make game of his popular audience. To see Marlowe in this way is in no sense to cheapen him, but is rather to explain what sometimes seems cheap in his work. It is not to deny the seriousness of his vision, but is a way of relating his vision to his curious rhetoric.

Marlowe would have questioned, without necessarily denying, the Sidneyan absolute that man's 'erected wit' had been given him for the sole purpose of repairing the ravages of his 'infected will' and bringing him closer to salvation. To explore the conflict between theological views of that kind and the human aspirations which they checked was for him more exciting than to take sides on the question and so to sweep the greatest issue of his age under a carpet of certainty. Thus the Tamburlaine plays, *Doctor Faustus*, and *The Jew of Malta* are expressions of the 'self' more in the Montaignean sense of attempting intellectual honesty through scepticism than in Sidney's or Jonson's sense of being statements of moral conviction. But is a writer's inclination to be honest with himself any guarantee of plain dealing with his public? Marlowe is praised for his honest way of challenging spectators to applaud Tamburlaine's fortunes as they please, to make up their own minds about Faustus's fortunes 'good or bad', to balance the evil of the Jew's Machiavellism against the evil of religious hypocrisy. A system of counterpointing is uncovered in the texts which shows him weighing man's need to free himself from theology against the pride, crime and folly involved in doing so. Seen in this light by modern readers, for whom relativism tends to be a habit of mind, the plays appear as marvellously fair dramatizations of conflict. And so ultimately they are. Plainly, however, to achieve that balance, Marlowe had to puff the devil's case rather hard. To stretch an audience accustomed to orthodoxy, he knowingly perverted the arts of discourse as taught in his time.

He gave the stage its head (against Aristotle's advice) in catering to instincts for violence, farce and spectacle. He bypassed the intellect with emotive appeals, and subjected piety to hammer-blows and pin-pricks. Into Tamburlaine's speeches he poured much of himself, but in doing so was surely aware that their 'astounding terms' – i.e. stupefying logic as well as language (*OED*) – threatened the world with an extreme example of what teachers and preachers deplored as affective rhetoric. The Tamburlaine plays test how far the auditor can be swept from his accustomed moorings by word-power. Similarly, in writing *Faustus*, Marlowe must have known that to debate theology on the commercial stage without total commitment to the Christian scheme was by academic standards flagrant sophistry ('the art of making money by pretending to be wise' was how Aristotle defined sophistry in the *Sophistical Elenchi*). He sought to implicate spectators in his own uncertainty by exploiting their contradictory reactions to Morality drama. On the one hand, he built on its appeal as popular entertainment, making devils and deadly sins seem like old-fashioned bugbears which deserved to be laughed at; on the other, he revived the capacity of the form to rouse powerful feelings of religious awe, so that the play could also become solemnly and intimidatingly orthodox. Concealing his sophistry in the latter respect, he actually compounded it. As for *The Jew of Malta*, its harsh, sardonic vision is projected rhetorically through the scandalous practice of suppressing the truth. Abigail is killed in Act III and dismissed from the stage with a salacious gibe as her epitaph. In a play of which the main target is hypocrisy, the spectator is forced into the hypocrite's role – to forget the saint in his enjoyment of the sinners and finally to applaud Ferneze's *Te Deum*.

This is to say that the source of Marlowe's 'danger' as a playwright lay less in his thought than in his method, his use of logic and rhetoric in the fallacious ways he had been trained at university to detect. Consciousness of method had been heightened in his time at Cambridge by the popularity of Ramus, whose *Dialectique* distinguished between the 'natural method' of arguing, which moves from what is conspicuous to what is less conspicuous according to the perceptions of a well-trained mind, and the 'prudential method' used by poets, orators and historians, which is adapted to the capacity of less educated hearers and readers. This secondary method had been played down and almost suppressed in English versions of Ramist logic.[14] It is touched on only briefly and distorted in Roland MacIlmaine's version of 1574, where it is called 'the craftie and secrete methode', to be used 'when with delectation or some other motion thy chief purpose is to deceave the auditor'.[15] (Among its techniques which MacIlmaine notes with disapproval are irrelevance, digression and inversion of antecedents and consequences). Though Ramus had meant his prudential method to 'deceive' only in the limited sense of relaxing logical rigour for the sake of clarity, his Scottish disciple shows why it was mistrusted, warning earnestly in his preface against deceit of all kinds. The method, all too clearly, could be used as a cloak for the dissemination of error by writers of 'poysonable sophistrie'. Fear of false logic was as much a product of defensive Protestantism as was the fear of irresponsible jesting described in the previous chapter. Both these bogeys would seem to be tilted at in the mischievous logic and rhetoric of Marlowe's plays, which reflect the *succès de scandale* at Cambridge of 'diabolical' authors such as Lucian, Julian, Machiavelli and Aretino who had supposedly devoted their verbal skills to perversion of truth.

Just how much serious purpose lay behind Marlowe's mischief is the most slippery problem posed by a notoriously elusive writer, a problem impossible to handle persuasively in a few pages. But an appropriate approach to a summary judgement can be made by glancing at his use of a central Lucianic image. As well as being the source of his most famous single line,[16] Lucian appears to have had meaning for Marlowe in relation to his intellectual detachment – the stance from which he launched his offensives – and thus also to the question of the value to be attached to moral commitment.

Lucian's influence is clear in the opening of *Dido, Queen of Carthage*, where the dalliance of Jupiter and Ganymede is closer in tone to the *Dialogues of the Gods* than to Virgil and sets the mood for the comic deflation and distancing of heroic figures which is a feature of the play.[17] This lets us see that Marlowe's other play which juxtaposes men and gods also used Lucianic tricks to set human aspirations in a limiting perspective. Among the best moments of *Faustus* in performance are the appearance of Lucifer and attendant devils as silent witnesses of the hero's first encounter with Mephostophilis and their later reappearance to watch his final torments. Almost certainly they entered 'above', symbolically taking the place of God allowed to them by Faustus. The use of an upper stage-level to signify hierarchical station is combined by Marlowe with its use for dramatizing the ironic viewpoint of the *kataskopos*, thus stressing Lucifer's power over the 'fond worldling' whom he watches. The *kataskopos* image is of major importance in *Faustus*. It has three manifestations, the two most central being the figures of the universal scholar and the controlling deity, used to illustrate the distinction between uncommitted knowledge and the power which can be achieved by turning knowledge into action. Each half of the play opens with a scholarly survey followed by a decision to act: Faustus's survey of his library at the start is matched by his later voyages. The latter are strictly speaking divided into an 'anaskopic' or upward-looking inspection of the heavens from below (starting, like Lucian's Menippus, from Olympus) and a kataskopic inspection of the earth from the sky. Astronomy and geography satisfy the heavenward and earthward impulses to be recalled pathetically in his final speech. The downward vision owes little to Marlowe's main source and appears as an interesting blend of *Icaromenippus* and the Devil's temptation of Christ from the high mountain:

> So high our dragons soar'd into the air
> That looking down the earth appear'd to me
> No bigger than my hand in quantity.
> There did we view the kingdoms of the world,
> And what might please mine eye I there beheld.[18]

Up to that point, Faustus's scientific curiosity has been satisfied by 'beholding', but Mephostophilis, the provider of shows and tours, has derived a deeper satisfaction of power from guiding his victim. In the scene between them where these words are spoken, the oddly-repeated exchanges of 'come, then' / 'nay, stay' begin to emphasize the distinction between viewing and doing. Faustus ('Then in this show let me an actor be') has now observed enough, and longs to come to grips with the Pope, but is restrained by Mephostophilis:

> first stay
> And view their triumphs as they pass this way;
> And then devise what best contents thy mind.
> (VIII.78–80)

Remaining for a while as observers, presumably 'above', their subsequent *exeunt* and re-entry on the main stage as cardinals mark the beginning of Faustus's attempts to use his knowledge to achieve power in the public sphere. Foolish as these attempts are, we may guess that his eagerness to commit himself to action was something which the playwright could admire. Marlowe's own compulsive scepticism and relativism can fairly be inferred from his habit of treating the world's religions on equal terms, but conversely his absorption with dynamic characters who act on their beliefs suggests that he was dissatisfied with his paralysing cast of mind. It was probably to illustrate the degradation of such a mind that he introduced into *Faustus* a third version of the *kataskopos*. Benvolio at his window has the character, not in the source, of a cynical scoffer, very much the conventional hostile image of a Lucianist. And the contrast between the two major versions – the detached don and the controlling god – would seem to imply Marlowe's consciousness that knowledge by itself is *not* power, that to control others ideological commitment is essential.

But even if he did feel a need for such commitment, one must assert that it was his lack of it which ultimately differentiates his art of teasing from Erasmus's or Jonson's and aligns it rather with that of more sceptical wits, like Lucian himself, for whom disruption of orthodoxy and stimulus to thought were sufficient ends in themselves. This is not, of course, to deny him a place among practitioners of humanist *lusus*.[19] For far too long his witty offensives have been explained exclusively in terms of the survival of medieval dramatic conventions. Morality humour has normally been used to shed light on his farce, especially in *Faustus* and *The Jew*. Of his principal characters, Tamburlaine in his man-drawn chariot has been compared to a Herod or a Cambyses as a simultaneously laughable and frightening symbol of pride; Faustus's frivolity is said to reflect the heedlessness of an Everyman figure getting worse instead of better; Barabas, sinister and funny, is to be seen as an extension of the Vice. Those, without doubt, as Marlowe well knew, were the ways in which spectators were conditioned to accept and enjoy his humour. But since it is clear that he wrote from a standpoint well outside the medieval religious tradition, one must also acknowledge the learned art with which he applied those techniques of the popular stage to his own teasing purposes. His bids for easy and thoughtless laughter were a tactic of the same mocking mind which enjoyed more erudite joking of the kind typified by Barabas's allusions to Agamemnon and Iphigeneia and Faustus's last-minute quotation from Ovid. It was an academic wit which devised his parodies of Morality patterns (as when the traditional opposition between wise doctor and foolish devil is inverted between Faustus and Mephostophilis) and which conceived and controlled the games of counterpoint already referred to (the playing-off of Tamburlaine's infectious grandeur against lower-key reminders of his sinfulness and folly). And Marlowe's disconcerting habit of embroiling his great men in farce, so that actors cannot play them *au grand sérieux*, shows a touch of the 'Menippean' method of character-portrayal which compels the understander to adjust his levels of response intellectually from moment to moment and denies him the satisfaction of total emotional involvement. It is in areas such as these that we recognize the best and most thoughtful achievements of Marlowe's teasing rhetoric, where his innovative genius cuts sharply through terrain on which Jonson was to build with more weight.

One of Marlowe's major contributions to the English stage was to bring back *jocus* and *serium* into a challenging relationship which had been lost since the days of Medwall and Rastell. Even at its least aggressive, his humour is used to complicate our view of his heroes. For example, as one critic has noted, the effect of Wagner's ridiculous logic-chopping in the second scene of *Faustus* could be either to increase admiration for his master's learned reasoning in the previous scene or to show up its sophistry.[20] (One suspects that the author himself meant the latter while actively encouraging the former, since the blinding of the audience with science is an important part of Faustus's initial function, creating a potent first impression which later events are to render untenable). And in *Tamburlaine* the comic coward figures can similarly work in either of two ways: to reinforce or to undermine the hero's martial values. More commonly, however, Marlowe's humour forms part of a contemptuous frontal attack on the spectator's moral sense, as with 'Holla, ye pamper'd jades of Asia!' or when Tamburlaine ends his insidiously persuasive speech on *virtù* with 'Hath Bajazeth been fed to-day?' The constant encouragement to morally dismissive laughter is what makes Marlowe's humour so peculiarly sardonic. As with the rhetoric and pageantry of *Tamburlaine* or the glamour of Helen of Troy, so it is with the comedy of Faustus's antics or Barabas's poisonings – 'if you can enjoy all this and still not *think*...' seems to be the dramatist's underlying attitude. We remember that one of the statements attributed to Marlowe was 'that it was an easy matter for Moses being brought up in all the arts of the Egyptians to abuse the Jews being a rude and gross people'.[21] Scorn of his audience enabled him to revitalize the drama of confrontation which Jonson was to continue. But it was also a mark of his relative immaturity. Whether we look forward to Jonson or back to Erasmus, we find in the more deeply-rooted humanists an educative concern which it is hard to feel that Marlowe shared. They rarely, as he frequently does, aim merely to shock; nor do they attack complacency and narrowness to relieve their own private uncertainties. Moral assurance helped them to a more relaxed and varied sense of comedy, to an enjoyment of the ridiculous which can make us forget their moralizing purpose. More significantly, it helped them to the cool control of moral implication essential to teasing as an art, the control which makes *Volpone*, while no less ferocious, a finer work of art than *The Jew of Malta*.

PART TWO

Ben Jonson

Quid laedit, si totus populus in te sibilet, modo tute tibi plaudas?
Erasmus, *Stultitiae Laus* (*LB*, IV, 433B)

CHAPTER 6

Before *Volpone*

In most of his work and what is known of his life Ben Jonson
seems sharply at odds with the tradition we have just explored.
Were it not for a handful of well-known plays, charges of
deviousness would be hard to bring against a writer so forthright,
so given to the poetry and prose of unequivocal statement – a
man, moreover, who told William Drummond that 'of all stiles
he loved most to be named honest'.[1] Posterity's image of plain,
honest Ben may reflect too readily the face Jonson showed to
his public; too often, certainly, the force of his mind has been
stressed at the expense of its subtlety. Yet the image is ultimately
a just one in the sense discussed earlier, that everything he
published was a considered expression of his poetic self. Paradoxically, it was his care to protect the integrity of that self
which led him to the oblique mode of statement in comedy.

How a humanist writer distinguished the poetic from the
actual self is most memorably illustrated by Machiavelli in the
well-known letter to Vettori where he describes his life in exile
on his farm near Florence. He tells how he would pass the day
gossiping, gambling, drinking with the peasants, and in the
evening would retire to his study, take off his dirt-covered
daytime clothes and put on curial robes, enter the courts of the
ancients, partake of the food he was born for, and write his
Prince and his *Discourses*.[2] There Machiavelli propounded a
central and recurring renaissance myth, both emphasizing and
bridging the gap between the humanist and common humanity.
Jonson, too, was apt to contrast his forays into the world with
his return 'home' to the candle-lit cell where as poet he strove
for self-realization, 'to come forth worth the ivy, or the bayes'.
Each of his non-dramatic poems is a response of the poetic self
to a particular occasion, a response determined by the poet's

Ben Jonson

sense of what is ethically proper in the circumstances and formally warranted by poetic tradition. The poems which modern readers tend to like best are those where the poetic and the actual self have been brought into conflict, as when the Christian Stoic and the loving father struggle in reaction to the death of a child, or when the middle-aged lover pits the poet's right to celebrate beauty against a bemused awareness of his 'mountaine belly'. Being poems, however, they resolve the conflict as the poet determines.

This approach limits what we now call self-expression but gave Jonson ample freedom to express his ideals through censure or praise. Taking in hand his lyre, he could strike his 'proper straine'; the poet had no standards to satisfy but his own. The limitations he did acknowledge were in dramatic poems, where an audience had to be satisfied on the spot, and an instant verdict was apt to be given by majority vote. His theoretical preference for non-dramatic poetry had nothing in common with the romantic exaltation of personal lyric over impersonal drama. For Jonson the idea that the poet should express the man in his naked human essence had no meaning at all, since in his view the mere act of writing a poem, however slight, was a claim to the superhuman status of being a 'maker' and an assertion of the moral authority which that status conferred. Human nakedness was something he would be forced to expose if he pandered to the mob in the theatre. Leaving his study, discarding his robe, he would then enter the arena as a mere man.

None of the plays by which Jonson wished to be judged shows the least abandonment of his poetic self, though he was constantly on guard against self-prostitution to the strumpet stage, and was perpetually vexed by the problem of coming to terms with his audiences. *Sejanus* and *Catiline* make clear that his concept of 'high' tragedy meant a stern exposition of his views on political morality through exemplary warnings from Roman history. Standing on the height of his argument, he challenged his public to rise to his level and see the truth as he saw it himself; hence the didacticism, the refusal to probe into mysteries of human behaviour or destiny, which disqualify these plays by usual tragic criteria. For comedy he drew his materials from lower strata of the world around him, but his didactic approach was normally similar, demonstrating truth through the twin pointers of satirized characters and moral spokesmen, only in a few plays denying his audience the helping hand of the latter. And in the masque, at least for a while, the poet found his highest earthly fulfilment in sitting metaphorically at the king's right hand, guiding the court and with it the kingdom in the way it should go.

Jonson in his poet's robes, garlanded with laurel, is not a figure easy to accept on his own terms. There are times when his unwavering ideals seem blind fixations, remote from reality, not a little ludicrous. Even those who are undisturbed by his personal arrogance may charge him with monotony, an artistic fault to which his forty-year cult of constancy to the self was naturally prone. None the less, if there is any poem or play of his that we particularly admire and enjoy, it is risky to say that there he has succeeded in spite of himself, having stepped from his high horse, spoken from the heart, relaxed his moral judgement, or allowed his garland to slip. We can talk in such terms of his Conversations with Drummond but less easily of his *Works*. *The Alchemist* and *Bartholomew Fair* are realizations of the same self as *Cynthia's Revels* or *The Magnetic Lady* – more complex and subtle, and as different as can be in rhetorical method, but not different in their underlying beliefs and aims. Here we shall be mainly concerned with the comedies from *Volpone* onward where he expressed himself obliquely, but first we must see how his use of the Lucianic tradition was foreshadowed and in part made necessary by his earlier writings.

An important period in his life was the one about which we know least, the years before 1598, when the first play he thought worth preserving, *Every Man in his Humour*, formally inaugurated his public career as poet. Jonson was then twenty-six, and the few facts we know of his earlier history hint at the conditions under which his ideals were formed. He was brought up in a working-class home; received, by good luck, about five years of excellent grounding in Latin and Greek at Westminster School under its Second Master, William Camden; thereafter did not go to the university but was apprenticed as a bricklayer to his stepfather; served as a soldier in the Netherlands; and finally turned to the stage, first as a strolling player and then as an author working for Henslowe; meantime marrying and having children. If we assume that he left Westminster at the age of seventeen, it is clear that for the next ten years he lived poor and lived rough, at the same time steadily compiling a remarkable stock of erudition. By the standard of a Bacon or a Milton, Jonson's mind may never have become a storehouse of universal knowledge; perhaps also his pretensions to learning need to be viewed with some scepticism as reflecting the pride of a self-educated man. But efforts to discredit his scholarship by showing that his classical references were not always derived from original sources merely emphasize that he was learned in the manner of his time. To take some of his material, as he did, from mythological manuals or collections like Erasmus's *Adagia* was to use such books for their intended purpose, as a basis for new constructions. The measure of Jonson's learning, like Shakespeare's, is that it was adequate to his creative needs. This meant in his case, first, a high degree of linguistic competence, so that he could read Greek authors in Greek where Latin translations were not available, and Latin almost as easily as his own language, thus having free access not only to classical authors but to the vast resources of medieval and renaissance learned writings. Secondly, it meant that he had a firm understanding of the principles on which ancient literature was based, and a sense of intellectual parity with the authors he read, enabling him (as he later put it) 'to convert the substance, or Riches of another *Poet*, to his owne use'.[3] If Jonson in his late twenties had been merely an ostentatious smatterer in the learned tongues, he would not have become the friend of Donne or a protégé of 'true-bred' scholars such as Camden and Selden. A sufficient guarantee of his ability to digest what he had read is *Every Man in his Humour* itself, a play notable for the mature and unobtrusive assurance with which it blends classical and native comic traditions.

Where self-education did have a decisive effect upon him was in leading him to discover for himself, and so to adopt as his own, ideals which in the 1590s were going out of vogue. For example, his enthusiasm for the Sidneyan ideals of the poet and the courtier, and of the two in relation to each other, probably sprang from an excited reading of the *Defence* on its publication in 1595, but could hardly have been shared in the same generous spirit by those of his contemporaries who were then emerging from the universities to find the court in decline, openings blocked, and cynicism heavily in the air. Even his most basic tenet, the Stoic concept of the fixed and well-grounded self, was one which for Donne's generation of wits had been put in perspective, if not actually displaced, by flirtations with Machiavelli. All Jonson's literary and ethical commitments give the impression of having been formed and nurtured in isolation. He joined with his contemporaries in taking the conflict between old and new standards as the subject of his satire, and was as quick as any to understand the new, but he was unique among them in never doubting that the ground he himself stood on was firm. This is a characteristic of the man who has built his own structure of belief as opposed to the man whose beliefs have been imbibed from others and then challenged by experience. It explains why the figure of the battered idealist, so common in the period's literature, is not to be found in Jonson's plays. It also explains why, in *Cynthia's Revels* and *Poetaster*, naïve visions float so readily and conspicuously to the surface of 'comicall satyre'.

Every Man in his Humour was written and later rewritten as an example of 'correct' comedy, 'one such...as other playes should be'.[4] It is a brilliant exercise in genre-imitation, adapting structure, plot-patterns and traditional type-characters from Roman comedy to a milieu and spirit which even in the early 'Italian' version were distinctively English and contemporary, acceptable even to those who cared nothing for the value of imitation as such. That it succeeds primarily as a well-managed farce and differs from the three more strenuous plays which followed it is indisputable; none the less, Jonson's description of it as 'comoedie' and not as 'comicall satyre' should not blind us to its nature as the work of a satirist who focussed on shortcomings in order to point to ideals. For example, in his

minimal and apologetic treatment of love Jonson made a
radical departure from precedent – 'the most truly original
thing he ever did', in J. B. Bamborough's view⁵ – in order to
avert a collision between his critical purpose and the indulgence
toward lovers which Plautus and Terence had established as a
part of comic decorum. His critical purpose is underestimated
by commentators who use the play to distinguish between
comedy and satire. 'Unlike satire', J. W. Lever wrote of it,
'comedy functions through a system of checks and balances.
Instead of upholding a norm of good sense against foolish
aberrations, it offsets one extreme by another, leaving the norm
to build itself in the minds of the spectators.'⁶ But Jonson's light
comic touch in this play covers an absorption with particular
positives which renders his total vision satiric. His 'norm' is
more precise than a *via media* between extremes of temperament
– is indeed not a norm at all so much as an ideal – and it is forced
on our attention by the terms in which the characters discuss
one another, the ethical currency exchanged.

The clearest evidence of idealism underlying the play's
original design is Lorenzo Junior's speech on poetry near the
end of the earlier version (V.iii.312–43), combining a lofty
affirmation of the 'true Poet' with contempt for poetasters in
a manner which recalls Sidney and looks forward to a long
succession of Jonsonian utterances. Cut in the revision, and
usually described as an enthusiastic excrescence, the speech
violated the tone of the play by allowing the author's fervent
voice to intrude, but was not irrelevant to its theme, and there
is no cause to doubt that its culminating position was planned
from the start. Even if we allow that Lorenzo-as-poet is not too
convincing, his status as a poetic idealist is stressed at the
beginning and end of the play, while Matheo's pretensions to
poetry keep the issue alive in between. The burden of his final
speech is that judgement as opposed to 'opinion' is needed to
appreciate poetry in its true essence, 'such as it is', when she
is 'like her selfe'. When Clement retorts, 'but election
[judgement] is now governd altogether by the influence of
humor', we see that the discussion of poetry has been aligned
with the unifying message of the play, that selfhood can only

be realized by a firm exercise of judgement, exalted above humour and will.

Jonson's thinking on this subject is best explained by the passage from Sidney we have already referred to, where knowledge is justified as an attempt to repair the ruins of the Fall, and the 'mistress-knowledge' is said to be 'the knowledge of a man's self, in the ethic and politic consideration, with the end of well-doing and not of well-knowing only'.[7] Sidney had theorized that the poet could promote that knowledge most effectively, and in *Every Man In* Jonson aims to turn theory into practice, in line with Sidney's view of the purpose of comedy, by parading examples of failure in self-knowledge 'so as it is impossible that any beholder can be content to be such a one'.[8] He matches Sidney's distinction between 'the ethic and politic consideration' by showing that ignorance of the self makes a man not only a fool but also a public menace, unaware or neglectful of the obligations attached to his place in society. Even Bobadilla, Stephano and Matheo, the most simply foolish characters who cultivate a false self to conceal the void within, pose some threat to the noble professions of soldier, gentleman and poet which they ape, while the social consequences of a maladjusted self or indulged eccentricity are apparent in the way Thorello treats his wife, Giuliano his brother, Lorenzo Senior his son, and Clement his magistrate's functions.

By means of a ground-swell of ethical comment, the play constructs a paradigm for the cult of the 'mistress-knowledge'. A familiar peg on which to hang it is offered to the audience by Lorenzo Senior's sententious speech in couplets on the rule of king-reason over subject-affections, recommending a state of mind where emotions 'rang'd / By reasons rules, stand constant and unchang'd' (II.ii.29–30). But it is always in such traditional terms that the old man's fears for his son are expressed. Relying on his trite maxims, he shows little interest in the concept of the individual self, and accordingly is seen to 'betray himselfe' to Musco (line 104) through complacent faith in his own reason-ableness. Selfhood is a subject more talked about by the young, as when Lorenzo Junior gives Stephano the ironic injunction, 'let the *Idea* of what you are, be portraied in your aspect'

(I.ii.109–10). To understand oneself, however, requires what Stephano lacks: intelligence (*ingenium*) and the capacity for self-examination. Without these qualities a character will remain trapped in the limited self imposed by his humour, unconsciously the slave of a ruling passion. Thus Prospero says of the angry man Giuliano: 'a tall man is never his owne man til he be angry: to keep his valure in obscuritie, is to keepe himselfe as it were in a cloke-bag: whats a musition unlesse he play? whats a tall man unlesse he fight?' (IV.iii.9–12). In Jonson's paradigm the progression is first from self-examination to self-knowledge; then judgement (*judicium*) submits the self to a process of moral ordering so that it can finally be realized in virtuous action. The completed ideal is hinted at in Thorello's recollection of Prospero as he had first known him:

> Me thought he bare himselfe with such observance,
> So true election and so faire a forme:
> And (what was chiefe) it shewd not borrow'd in him,
> But all he did became him as his owne,
> And seemd as perfect, proper, and innate,
> Unto the mind, as collor to the blood. (I.iv.38–43)

Thorello himself, the most complex character in the play, has stuck halfway up the ladder. Knowing himself all too well, both as he is and as he ought to be, he finds it difficult to achieve the next stage of 'well-doing' which would constitute self-realization:

> Ah, but what error is it to know this,
> And want the free election of the soule
> In such extreames? Well, I will once more strive,
> (Even in despight of hell) my selfe to be. (I.iv.218–21)

These lines are the cue for Musco to enter 'disguised like a soldier', observing: 'S'blood, I cannot chuse but laugh to see my selfe translated thus, from a poore creature to a creator.' It is the kind of remark, rather common in Jonson, which is not exactly natural to the speaker but makes a clear point for the author. Thorello's anguished struggle to realize the self is contrasted with the light-hearted evasion of the self by the rogue-disguiser. Both are intelligent enough to know themselves, but the latter declines the task of self-improvement imposed on all human 'creatures', preferring to manipulate the delusions of others and so become the 'creator' of Jonson's plot. Musco points again to the symbolism of disguise when he enters (V.ii.1) dressed as a varlet: 'Of all my disguises yet now am I most like my selfe.' As has often been noted, he anticipates Jonson's later and greater dissemblers by wilfully suppressing the moral self and becoming a type of the merely ingenious creator or artist. In the Folio revision he is described as an 'artificer' and 'architect' (III.v.25–6). It is chiefly he who manoeuvres the action of the play toward its conclusion at the judgement-seat of the magistrate Clement.

As the champion of Musco, Clement becomes the main vehicle for the play's irony, and the conclusion over which he presides, with its clear resemblance to that of *The Alchemist*, makes nonsense of the notion that Jonsonian comedy becomes ironic in *Volpone* for the first time. Several characteristics of humanist irony are to be found in *Every Man In*. One, the presence of which in the first version is shown up by being more sharply pointed in the revision, is the hidden exploitation of ambivalent concepts – the game Medwall played with regard to 'liberality'. A simple instance can be found in the Folio text's expansion of a passage near the start, where Kno'well (Lorenzo Senior) reflects on his youthful (and Sidneyan) enthusiasm for poetry:

> That fruitlesse, and unprofitable art,
> Good unto none, but least to the professors,
> Which, then, I thought the mistresse of all knowledge:
> But since, time, and the truth have wak'd my judgement,
> And reason taught me better to distinguish,
> The vaine, from th'usefull learnings. (I.i.18–23)

'Usefulness' was a criterion Jonson was eager to apply to poetry, but not of course in Kno'well's narrowly utilitarian sense. As the end of the play affirms, the poet cannot be valued by the same standard as an alderman or a sheriff. Similarly, and more pervasively, we find Jonson playing on the implications of 'judgement' (*judicium*), especially in relation to 'wit' (*ingenium*). Judgement means the critical faculty of the mind (discrimination or 'election'), and was for Jonson a moral concept,

Ben Jonson

differing from wit in being necessarily an exercise of the moral sense. *Every Man In* encourages confusion between moral and non-moral connotations of the term. Most of the characters criticize each other, but lack the moral equilibrium of achieved self-hood, and so have no right to pass judgements at all, their critical faculty having failed in its primary task. This is most piquantly illustrated by the 'humorous' Clement, in whom society has vested judicial authority. His alliance with the rogue is a symbolic abdication of *judicium* in favour of *ingenium*. In the early version he hails Musco as *ingenium magnum* (V.iii. 210–11), a point reinforced in the revision by his sentence on Brainworm, which is worthy of Erasmus in its loaded simplicity: 'Thou hast done, or assisted to nothing, in my judgement, but deserves to bee pardon'd for the wit o' the offence' (V.iii.112–14). Since Jonson refrained from clarifying the anomaly, he left his play to that extent open-ended.

If this has an Erasmian ring, other aspects of the conclusion also strike familiar chords. Thematically, Clement functions in two ways. As an exponent of judgement he is satirized, yet in defending poetry he has the full weight of Jonson's authority behind him. One could explain this by saying that his final verdicts, though erratically based, were meant to appear as accidentally sound. It seems more likely, however, that here we have an example of Jonson's tendency to slip into the 'Menippean' mode of fiction which we noted in Erasmus's *Colloquies*, whereby ideas are more important to the author than the character who voices them, and the reader is not asked to form a 'whole' view of the character by reconciling his admirable and defective traits or opinions. It would of course be crass to complain of inconsistency in Clement, since his dramatic impact is single and overwhelming, as Jonson well knew that it would be:

an excellent rare civilian, and a great scholler, but the onely mad merry olde fellow in Europe.
...and he hath a very strange presence me thinkes, it shewes as if he stoode out of the ranke from other men. I have heard many of his jests in Padua: they say he will commit a man for taking the wall of his horse.
...or wearing his cloake of one shoulder, or any thing indeede, if it come in the way of his humor. (III.ii.48–57)

The portrait recalls the popular image of More. What Jonson

is getting at is the public delight in humanizing the magistrate and scholar by making him a jest-book figure of comic disorder. The assumption is that Clement will be enjoyed as a Lord of Misjudgement. His 'strange presence...as if he stoode out of the ranke from other men' does, strictly considered, raise the moral spectre of an 'exorbitant' judge who is a law unto himself, but it caters more immediately to the Elizabethan love of an outsize eccentric who can turn order upsidedown at a whim and get away with it by sheer force of personality. When he reaches for his armour to overawe the would-be soldier and makes verses *extempore* to subdue the would-be poet, it is open to us to criticize the pride he takes in playing other people's roles while neglecting his own; and when he flourishes his sword over Musco we can, if we choose, recognize a visual perversion of the emblem of Justice. But in all this his *bravura* is theatrically irresistible, sweeping us along on an exhilarating tide. He and Musco are the characters who make the strongest impact upon us precisely because they are actors who abandon the self in favour of more dramatically exciting roles. Thus their alliance symbolizes a further anomaly, the triumph of the theatre over morality. In as much as Jonson presumably hoped that this would be perceived, *Every Man In* represents his first and clearest attempt to square his distrust of the stage with his own and his audience's delight in it by building the former implicitly into the fabric of his play.[9]

Quintessential Jonson this comedy certainly is, not only in its underlying themes but also in its concealed challenge to the understander. Witty rogues and comic justices were far from being his inventions, but Jonson's deliberateness in exploiting their appeal and opposing it directly to the moral current of his argument produces a kind of irony that is very much his own. Compared to later comedies, however, *Every Man In* is distinguished by the mildness of its challenge. Although critics have tended to underestimate its idealistic base and its satiric thrust, in the last resort it remains what it has always been supposed to be, a light comedy, where the poet's own 'self' has been realized mainly in artistic terms by scrupulously observing the decorum of the genre.

In his following experiments with 'comicall satyre' Jonson's

Ben Jonson

eye was trained much more on his audience, but didactic fervour led him to abandon the structure of Roman self-contained comedy and with it the stance of the concealed ironist. Dramatizing instead the standpoints of explicit satirists and moralists, he turned the stage into a battleground where moral issues could be openly debated and resolved. These plays were certainly influenced by the vogue of verse-satire, reflecting many of its concerns and some of its techniques, but in spite of their satiric label are chiefly of interest by proclaiming Jonson's positive ideals with uninhibited freedom. Though for that reason they are remote from the tradition we are examining, they concern us in a number of ways.

In the first place they offer the earliest proofs of Jonson's familiarity with the writings of Erasmus and Lucian. Carlo Buffone in *Every Man out of his Humour* (1599), when he advises the rich bumpkin Sogliardo on how to appear to be a gentleman, extensively adapts Erasmus's colloquy *The Ignoble Knight, or Faked Nobility* and more briefly his *Inns*.[10] *Cynthia's Revels* (1600) alludes lightly but centrally to *The Praise of Folly* through the names of Madam Moria and one of her nymphs, Philautia (Self-Love). In that play, too, we find Jonson's first use of Lucian. Four of his *Dialogues of the Gods* provide matter for the opening scene between Cupid and Mercury, and he has the honour of being quoted and defended in passing by that paragon of judgement, Crites.[11] In *Poetaster* (1601) the climactic plot-motif of the pill which makes Crispinus vomit his outlandish vocabulary is taken from Lucian's *Lexiphanes*, and an earlier scene, the mock banquet of the gods staged by Ovid and his friends, has rightly been described by Herford and Simpson as Lucianic in tone and treatment.[12]

Grounds for inferring how Jonson thought of Lucian can also be found in these plays. Since Cupid and Mercury are introduced with Lucian in their mouths, they should not be seen as mere Lylyan derivatives but rather as vehicles for what Harvey had admired as the 'elegant wittinesse' of Grecian 'levitie'. In a satire which makes its points through deliberate distinctions of style, Lucian appears to have been the classical model for the spritely but morally inoffensive wit which Jonson (following Castiglione) thought appropriate to courtiers. Mercury recommends to Cupid that they should 'act freely, carelessly, and capriciously, as if our veines ranne with quick-silver, and not utter a phrase, but what shall come forth steept in the verie brine of conceipt, and sparkle like salt in fire' (II.i.7–10). Their 'sparkle' contrasts with the dreary language of courtly affectation. During the central section of the play their functions fall within Lucian's province: distanced by their divinity, they comment, ridicule, and provoke. In the last act, however, as Jonson moves toward judgement and correction, they cease to be adequate for his purpose. Cupid must be banished from Cynthia's presence, and even Mercury, though as the 'sacred god of wit' (V.iv.612) he is allowed to remain, opens the act by preparing to hand over the role of reformer to the sober Crites. Mercury's capacity to rise from scintillating prose to lofty verse in his last scenes marks the meeting-point in Jonson's scheme between the highest level attainable by wit and the higher standards of judgement and virtue, represented by Crites and Arete respectively. A similar association of Lucian with the disputed boundaries of allowable wit helps to explain Jonson's attitude to the two Lucianic scenes in *Poetaster*. Many readers have found inconsistency in the fact that the banquet of the gods is condemned on high moral grounds by Caesar and then excused by Horace in terms of 'innocent mirth, / And harmlesse pleasures, bred, of noble wit' (IV.vii.41–2). But it has to be remembered in *Poetaster* that Jonson's Roman figures are carefully placed according to the standpoints they represent, those of emperor, patron, epic-poet, satiric-poet, love-poet, and so forth. Horace is constantly presented as a 'middle-brow' writer who mediates between forms of poetry higher and lower than his own. He is the main champion of poets in respect of their social status and involvement, but he never appropriates to himself the stance of the poetic idealist which Virgil exemplifies and which Caesar uses as a basis for courtly judgement. Thus, while the Lucianic charade was bound to strike Caesar as a perversion of the poet's identity and sacred function, Horace could reasonably defend it as a harmless example of *lusus ingenii*, especially in a context where he was asserting that poets should be free of interference from political spies. Lucianism is always ultimately allowed or disallowed by Jonson according to the motives behind it, so that the later participation of Caesar and Virgil in the pill-episode, which troubled Herford as a 'moral descent', could be justified by the reformative and exemplary purpose of the joke. On the other hand, Horace will not be the last of Jonson's 'authoritative' characters who is allowed to complicate a moral issue by making a case for Lucianic wit on non-moral grounds.

Apart from such references, the 'comicall satyres' show links of a broader kind with the tradition of humanist satire. One of these is their preoccupation with games. This need not refer to *lusus* as a game in which the author engages his public, but rather to games played by the characters themselves, dramatized on the principle that men are to be judged by the quality of their amusements. Ovid's banquet of the gods is an instance of this where the value of the game can be assessed by different criteria. *Cynthia's Revels*, concerned as it is with the way a court should amuse itself, makes more extensive and less ambiguous use of the device, contrasting the supposedly enlightened pranks of Mercury and the profitable entertainment of the masque with the idiotic word-games played by the satirized courtiers. The diversions of single characters seeking to escape from the self are a prominent object of satire in *Every Man Out*, notably Puntarvolo's charade in Act II and Buffone's 'drunken dialogue' in Act V. Jonson remained willing, throughout his career in comedy, to risk boring his audience to distraction with prolonged displays of his characters' mindless amusements. In later plays certainly, and perhaps from the start, his tactic was to tempt the ignorant spectator to enjoy such scenes at face value while encouraging the understander to share in his own satiric contempt. But the root of his interest in games was the humanist concern with standards of *festivitas*, a concern which Erasmus in particular had never tired of emphasizing in the long series of his 'convivial' colloquies, aiming to show that 'the very amusements of a Christian ought to have a philosophical flavour'.[13] The commonest way of implying the festive ideal was by dramatizing lapses from it, and Lucian had provided the *locus classicus* of this method in *The Carousal, or the Lapiths*, which describes how a wedding-feast attended by learned guests degenerates into a chaos of drunken brawling and squalid animality.

Although Jonson's urge to be explicit in the 'comicall satyres' led to a negation of Lucianic irony by committing him transparently to the point of view of certain characters, he tried to counter this involvement by encouraging a detached view of the action as a whole. All these plays were designed as 'anatomies', examining a broad cross-section of society instead of focussing on a particular intrigue. The main movement of *Every Man Out*, matching the ambition of its characters, is socially upward from the country to the city to the court, ending with an appropriate drop into the debtors' prison. Though *Cynthia's Revels* deals solely with the court, it attempts to cover the whole range of vice and virtue on the understanding that the court is a mirror for the entire realm.[14] And *Poetaster*, too, spreads its net widely over society in hunting down ignorant attitudes to poetry. Jonson often used visual effects to heighten the impression of his victims as engaged in a pageant or ritual dance: most obviously in the masque for Cynthia, where the Vices dance in the dress of their corresponding Virtues, but also in the more realistic setting of the Middle Aisle of St Paul's (*Every Man Out*, III), where we find the revealing stage-direction '*Here they shift. Fastidius mixes with Puntarvolo, Carlo and Sogliardo, Deliro and Macilente, Clove and Orange, four couple.*' The principle of the full stage, 'to behold the *Scene* full, and reliev'd with varietie of speakers' (*Every Man Out*, II.iii. 297–8), would seem to have been linked in Jonson's mind with the spectacle of a 'great stage of fools'. Whether visually realized or not, his panoramic surveys of human folly bear comparison with the kataskopic metaphors we associate with Lucian and Erasmus. Crites, indeed, elaborates one such metaphor, 'the strangest pageant, fashion'd like a court' (*Cynthia's Revels*, III.iv.3ff.), demonstrating that the man of true judgement is entitled, in Jonson's opinion, to the kind of demigod viewpoint which Shakespeare invariably distrusted.

It has always been recognized in respect of these plays that devices such as prologue, induction, and chorus, and the use of authorial spokesmen, were meant to train the audience's critical sense as well as to tell it what to think. *Every Man Out*, one of the most astonishing experiments in all renaissance drama, shows Jonson practising 'alienation' more insistently than Brecht ever does, while transferring to the stage the 'Menippean' principle of subordinating fiction to moral analysis. Its episodic structure bears some resemblance to a sequence of Erasmian colloquies, with choric interludes explaining issues which Erasmus would have left implicit. But clearly Jonson's stimulus to criticism here stopped a long way short of letting his public form its own conclusions; the play of mind we associate with 'Menippean' writing was never more rigidly controlled. Even in *Cynthia's Revels*, written for the Blackfriars Theatre – where, if anywhere, Jonson hoped that 'the lights of judgements throne' would shine[15] – he provided an induction to explain his allegory and anticipate the lapses of his 'gentle' audience. Yet his preoccupation with audience-response in the 'comicall satyres' is a mark of the 'Menippean' writer, a sign that every line is being weighed for its rhetorical impact more than for its place in a fictional design. It is likely that Jonson carried over this concern even into plays where he ceased to draw attention to it and where he chose to cultivate the appearance of fictional integrity.

The same will be argued with regard to the preaching of his personal convictions, the 'egotistical sublime' so blatant in those early comedies. Assertions of what Jonson called 'allow-able selfe-love' (*Cynthia's Revels*, V.vii.29) or 'the faire title of erection' (*Poetaster*, V.iii.364) were common among humanist writers, but we may note a final parallel with Lucian and Erasmus in the occasional passages of self-mockery with which Jonson tried to balance and so in a sense validate his arrogant postures. Toward the end of the high-pitched and strenuous induction to *Every Man Out* we are given a glimpse of the poet off duty: 'when hee comes abroad (now and then) once in a fortnight, and makes a good meale among Players, where he has *Caninum appetitum*...and then (when his belly is well ballac't, and his braine rigg'd a little) he sailes away withall, as though he would worke wonders when he comes home'. Demetrius in *Poetaster* alludes to the author in the guise of Horace, 'a meere spunge; nothing but humours, and observation; he goes up and downe sucking from every societie, and when hee comes home, squeazes himselfe drie againe'. Comparable passages of ironic self-portraiture are common in Lucian where he gives scope to the unflattering views of him held by his detractors. Erasmus twice makes Folly refer to him by name as her disciple; in his colloquy *Cyclops* he describes his persistence in writing colloquies as his contribution to the calamities of mankind; and he makes Nosoponus deny him the title of author except in the sense of 'one who smears a great quantity of paper with ink'. Other writers such as Horace, More and Montaigne offer more intimate laughs against themselves, and are felt to be more human as a result. Jonson's self-mockery resembles that of Lucian and Erasmus, first, because he dwells on his professional image – the two passages quoted describe the poet's sorties into society and his resumption of his proper self 'when he comes home' – and secondly, because in doing so he seems to be practising a literary gambit rather than revealing his natural temperament. The *eironeia* of these authors, if we wish to moralize, appears as a devious form of self-advertisement, a reflex of vanity. More pertinently, it can be seen as another expression of 'Menippean' wit, which can as easily be turned against the author as in any other direction, and at such times has the function of strengthening his credibility by suggesting that he is human after all.

Those, then, are ways by which even the 'comicall satyres' show some affinity to the Lucianic tradition. For our purpose, however, they are chiefly important for the evidence they give of Jonson's practice of appropriating classical authors, blending their voices with his own and applying them to contemporary issues. This practice is somewhat obscured in his 'ideal' figures, such as Crites and Cynthia or Virgil and Caesar, for the obvious reason that his ideals were formed by a variety of influences, modern as well as ancient. Crites, for instance, is a curious confection of severe Stoicism with elements of courtliness borrowed from Castiglione and Sidney, fused also with Jonson's own aspirations to be accepted as a court poet. But in the more objectively conceived satirist-figures his imitations are easier to detect. Asper and Macilente in *Every Man Out*, played by the same actor, constitute a diptych-study of the Juvenalian character as it was understood in the 1590s, the satirist as indignant outsider. In fact there are three panels in that portrait: Carlo Buffone's mindless and habitual carping represents the lowest form of Juvenalian *petulantia*, opposed at the other extreme by the vindicated fervour of Asper which is based on judgement and self-possession, while Macilente (like Thorello in *Every Man In*) occupies the intermediate position of one who struggles but fails to realize the self he envisages, his valid satiric insights being vitiated by envy and self-pity. In *Poetaster*, Horace is used by Jonson, as by Boileau and Pope in later years, to defend the position of the satirist under attack. Here again, though the strain of equating Jonson with Horace has always been great, there is evidence of critical objectivity in the way the Horatian defence has been adapted to modern circumstances. By allowing Horace and his problem to be overshadowed first by Ovid and then by Virgil, representing types of poet who are of lesser and greater value to the court respectively, Jonson not only placed his personal apologia in a broad perspective but also emphasized his interest in assessing the contemporary usefulness of various kinds of writing through reference to their classical exponents. Even in later comedies, where his eye is fixed firmly on his own world, he retains this awareness of the ancient authors whose guidance he follows, and places them critically in his own moral scheme.

Poetaster was written in a hurry to anticipate *Satiro-mastix* and is an openly pugilistic play. Championing himself and his cause, Jonson plunged into the public *fracas* known as the War of the Theatres to deal body-blows against Dekker and Marston as well as side-swipes at lawyers, soldiers and actors. In view of these circumstances the play's merits are remarkable. It illustrates, like *Ciceronianus*, *The Battle of the Books*, and *The Dunciad*, that the humanist writer could combine personal polemics with idealistic fervour and a high degree of artistic skill. Like the authors of all these works, however, Jonson paid a price

in peace of mind for the pleasure of playing God in public.
Moreover, unlike the others, having fought his battle in the
market-place and lost it, he felt a sense of having vulgarized and
brought into public derision the very poetry he had aimed to
defend. This feeling may explain why the close of the 'Apologeticall Dialogue', appended to *Poetaster*, has a power beyond his
usual expressions of pique and pride:

> But, that these base, and beggerly conceipts
> Should carry it, by the multitude of voices,
> Against the most abstracted worke, oppos'd
> To the stuff'd nostrills of the drunken rout!
> O, this would make a learn'd, and liberall soule,
> To rive his stayned quill, up to the back,
> And damne his long-watch'd labours to the fire;
> Things, that were borne, when none but the still night,
> And his dumbe candle saw his pinching throes:
> Were not his owne free merit a more crowne
> Unto his travailes, then their reeling claps.
> This 'tis, that strikes me silent, seales my lips,
> And apts me, rather to sleepe out my time,
> Then I would waste it in contemned strifes,
> With these vile *Ibides*, these uncleane birds,
> That make their mouthes their clysters, and still purge
> From their hot entrailes. But, I leave the monsters
> To their owne fate. And, since the *Comick* MUSE
> Hath prov'd so ominous to me, I will trie
> If *Tragoedie* have a more kind aspect.
> Her favours in my next I will pursue,
> Where, if I prove the pleasure but of one,
> So he judicious be; He shall b' alone
> A Theatre unto me: Once, I'le 'say,
> To strike the eare of time, in those fresh straines,
> As shall, beside the cunning of their ground,
> Give cause to some of wonder, some despight,
> And unto more, despaire, to imitate their sound.
> I, that spend halfe my nights, and all my dayes,
> Here in a cell, to get a darke, pale face,
> To come forth worth the ivy, or the bayes,
> And in this age can hope no other grace –
> Leave me. There's something come into my thought,
> That must, and shall be sung, high, and aloofe,
> Safe from the wolves black jaw, and the dull asses hoofe.

To assert the value of poetry and his own merit as a poet was
for Jonson a single objective. He pursues it here in the most

telling way possible, by writing well. Underlying the passage is a recognition of the need to rescue both poetry and the poet from the messy situation they had been placed in by his tactic of open confrontation with the audience, not only in *Poetaster* but in all three 'comicall satyres'. Later, when he returned to comedy, he would know that the unclean birds, the wolves and the asses were still there, but instead of trying to convert them he would mock them indirectly, keeping 'safe' the integrity of his art.

In the meantime, however, he felt drawn to tragedy, to sing 'high, and aloofe'. The epithets are revealing. This was the period in Jonson's career when he climbed conspicuously on to the pedestal he had erected for the poet; when he cultivated the friendship of noblemen and scholars; when he left his family to lodge with Sir Robert Townshend and later Lord D'Aubigny; when he began his career as a writer of courtly entertainments. The pose of 'odi profanum vulgus et arceo', the epigraph attached to Sidney's *Defence*, is at this time consciously adopted as professional strategy. In the rhetoric of *Sejanus* (1603) the concepts of height and aloofness are partly separable. If the former refers to the dignity of the genre and the high plane of seriousness to which the audience will be required to rise, the latter forecasts the artistic detachment in the handling of moral issues which Jonson was to cultivate with unremitting care in this play and all those that he wrote during the next decade. This detachment, and its peculiar relationship to strong moral commitment, is the chief factor which marks *Sejanus* off from the preceding comedies and links it to those that follow.

The story of *Sejanus his Fall* is nominally tragic in the usual Elizabethan sense of reporting a fall from power and a revolution of Fortune's wheel.[16] Jonson did his best to adapt this pattern to neo-classic requirements, notably in his fifth act which opens with Sejanus's hybristic boast ('Swell, swell, my joyes') and ends with an account of his dismemberment. But he made little attempt to raise the stature of his central figure above that of the 'small-town adulterer' portrayed by Tacitus. His interest was not in the personal tragedy of one of Fortune's favourites but in the concept of Fortune herself and the problem of how to treat her, subjects extensively discussed not only by the

Roman Stoics and Boethius but also by renaissance writers as different as Machiavelli and Lipsius. He sought to show that opportunists who stop at nothing to court and manipulate Fortune succeed only in binding themselves more firmly to her wheel, whereas those who decline to acknowledge her deity and instead practise constancy to the moral self develop an inner strength to withstand her blows. Politically, the response of rulers to this issue determines their country's welfare. *Sejanus* imparts its moral with laborious clarity, but also with a remarkable degree of emotional restraint, and this, though often identified as a cause of its coldness and failure in the theatre, is equally the source of its curious intellectual distinction. Rigorous concentration on art marks Jonson's handling of his sources, his plot-construction, and his language, and appears most clearly in his controlled treatment of the moral issue. While not showing the least sympathy for his Machiavels or in any way undermining the essential rightness of their opponents, he analyses the Machiavellian position with an objectivity and intelligence almost worthy of the master himself, and certainly unequalled in contemporary drama. He studies it from various angles. The close of Act III, where soliloquies by Sejanus, Tiberius and Macro follow each other in quick succession, reveals once again his talent for composite portraiture. These miniature discourses on statecraft describe, in turn, how an upstart may gain power by encouraging the ruler's weaknesses, how the ruler may retain power by playing off the ambitious against each other, and how a political agent may thrive by ruthless suppression of personal feelings. In terms of their position on the wheel, we see that the most secure figures are the emperor, who can exploit his position at the top, and the agent, who has just climbed on and therefore has least to lose, while the climber at the mid-point of his rapid ascent is easily blinded by over-confidence. Less than 200 lines, centrally placed in the play, convey this *résumé* of 'politique' attitudes. The pattern is evident; and the pattern, one feels, is what matters.

Jonson's refusal to play on the emotions is especially clear in his portrayal of Tiberius. By laying more emphasis on the craft than on the vice and debauchery, he refrains from exploiting sensational materials lavishly provided by history. He offers none of the easy attractions of the stage Machiavel. Tiberius's grim humour, imitated from Tacitus, is not developed broadly like that of Shakespeare's Richard III or his own Volpone but is of a kind which must be enjoyed intellectually, depending on the recognition of fine ironies, subtle hypocrisies and ambiguities of speech. Throughout the play, appeal to the judgement is constant. Even near the end, where the speeches of Terentius and the Nuntius have the conventional purpose of arousing fear and pity, affective rhetoric is kept well under control. It is charactersitic of Jonson that he attributes the order to rape Sejanus's little daughter not simply to the 'cruel' Macro but to the 'wittily, and strangely-cruell' Macro (V.851). Every Machiavellian horror is seen as the product of a type of mind, and our minds, too, must be brought to bear on its implications.

Virtue is submitted to the same test. However evident his moral approval, Jonson does not reinforce it with emotional appeals. He does not throw his weight behind Arruntius, as behind Asper. Agrippina's scorn for expediency ('Vertues forces / Shew ever noblest in conspicuous courses' (II.456–7)) is criticized as improvident by Silius. The disablement of virtue in Tiberius's Rome is continuously presented as a topic for rational analysis. Jonson's men of principle are as various as his Machiavels, ranging from Drusus, who slaps Sejanus on the face and gets poisoned, to Lepidus, who owes his survival to a 'passive fortitude' amounting almost to a policy of non-involvement (to 'live at home, / With my owne thoughts, and innocence about me, / Not tempting the wolves jaws' (IV.296–7)). Again we have the impression of an author more interested in patterning political attitudes than in 'moving' his audience to virtue by direct means, as a naïve disciple of Sidney might have tried to do. Stifling of emotional response is nowhere more remarkable than in the scene of Silius's suicide. Trapped in the Senate, with no longer anything to gain from discretion, Silius speaks out boldly, opposing his virtue to the threats of Fortune in the ringing tones of Jonson's most committed non-dramatic poetry. Yet for an audience the emotive power of the speech is sapped by the stronger dramatic interest which attaches to the silent presence of the watching Tiberius. The emperor's reaction to the suicide as 'this sad accident, / That thus hath stalled, and abus'd our mercy' (III.344–5) immediately diverts admiration to a master-stroke of conscious hypocrisy, which Jonson has transferred from another context in Tacitus to achieve this intellectually distancing effect.

So the aloof stance produces a play of which the vision, at least, is essentially ironic. We are shown a self-contained world in which Machiavels pursue a seemingly interminable pattern of subordinating the public interest in their attempts to dislodge each other from Fortune's wheel, while the practitioners of virtue, though constant in man's primary duty of living and dying well, are incapable of altering the course of events. To call such a vision pessimistic would be scarcely accurate, since what we are given is not so much a statement about life as an object-lesson on which conduct, especially in the political sphere, is meant to be based. It is in the objectivity that irony resides. With respect to rhetorical method, irony operates in *Sejanus* only at the remote level where it operates in most works of self-contained fiction, namely in leaving the audience to determine for itself its involvement in the story. Increasingly in the last scenes of the play Jonson focusses attention on the inconstant and unthinking 'multitude'. That this term is not to be applied merely to the *plebs* is made clear when Terentius pointedly links the behaviour of the shifty senators to that of the murderous rabble (V.777ff). And by the motto from Martial which Jonson placed on his title-page –

> Non hic *Centauros*, non *Gorgonas, Harpyasque*
> Invenies: Hominem pagina nostra sapit

– he reminds us, as so often, that his work is concerned with men not monsters, typical human behaviour rather than grotesque aberrations from the norm. The savagery of both senate and populace in destroying its fallen idol ('Deeds done by men, beyond the acts of *furies*' (V.758)) is an expression of the same human weakness that set up the idol in the first place. To the extent that 'all are the multitude' (*Discoveries*, 644), the audience is to recognize its putative responsibility for a state of affairs in which virtue is hamstrung and vice licensed. But further than that in the direction of implicating his audience Jonson does not go. In the following comedies the pose of aloofness would enable him to strike obliquely at his public while appearing to cater to its tastes. The tragic writer in his opinion – and here he would seem to have differed from Marlowe – cannot stoop to such tricks. His duty is rather to help his hearers to rise to his level of perception, to offer them a vision which allows for complexity but eliminates distractions, and to place moral issues squarely before their minds in a way that gives them every opportunity to form a true judgement and profit accordingly.

Yet it is perhaps not fanciful to see in the figure of Tiberius, 'acting his *tragedies* with a *comick* face' (IV.379), a preview of the deceptive approach that Jonson was soon to adopt. The common observation has already been made that his clever rogues, from Musco onward, were conceived as types of the false artist, their wilful neglect of the moral self freeing them to manipulate characters and create plots to suit their advantage as the fictional writer can do. Even in tragedy, Jonson could make Macro enthuse on the creative, moral-free delights of politic art in a soliloquy which, in its excited rhythms, plainly anticipates Mosca's on the art of the parasite. But Macro and Mosca advance their interests by pretending to be instruments of a higher power. Tiberius is a study (Jonson's most complete) of the master-artist in irony, the Sphinx-like dissembler of his purposes, whose 'heart / Lyes a thought farder, then another mans' (III.97–8). He achieves his greatest successes by remote control, advertising the efficacy of aloofness especially in two major scenes. If, as is tempting to suppose, he moved to the upper stage at III.154 to watch the proceedings of the Senate against Silius, he there visually embodied the ironic *kataskopos*, observing with a pretence of detachment the acting-out of a charade that he himself had planned, a stage-spectacle which Jonson may have copied from Marlowe's presentation of Lucifer. As Silius strenuously prepares for suicide, Tiberius might well be shown paring his finger-nails. But the controlling artist refines himself still further in Act V when Tiberius's letter is read to the Senate. There, most acutely, we are reminded of the dramatist who directs the action of his play without being present on the stage. He is merely a style, recognizable even through another man's voice. In that superbly-written scene, the ambiguous twists and turns of the absent writer, arts which are clear to the constant characters but which throw the inconstant time-servers into comic confusion, vividly prefigure the arts by which Jonson was to test the responses of his audience in his subsequent comedies.

CHAPTER 7

Volpone

In *Volpone* (1606) Jonson achieved the kind of breakthrough to brilliance which humanist poets quite consciously hoped for, when the rewards of apprenticeship would at last come to hand, and moreover come easily, or at least appear to. The play still conveys its author's excitement in deploying a new comic formula, one which released and combined his best powers and was to win him the favour of audiences as different as those of the Globe and the 'sister universities'. Whether Jonson was accurate in saying that he wrote it in five weeks we can no more tell than we can test Erasmus's claim to have written *Folly* in one, but essentially what both authors claimed in these statements was a hard-won access of *furor poeticus*, a mastery of art which could be flourished with zest and a touch of *sprezzatura*.

Gauging the Lucianic contribution to *Volpone* will soon lead us to the springs of the play's vitality, but the proper way to start is by listing drily some factual evidence from its early pages:

1. The action opens with a mock-encomium, a Praise of Riches.

2. Lucian's dialogue *The Dream, or The Cock*, as well as being the source of incidental passages on the power of gold (I.i.8; I.ii.98–105), formed the basis of Mosca's interlude on the transmigration of the soul of Pythagoras (I.ii.5–53).

3. At the conclusion of this, Androgyno's 'Song' (66–81) summarizes in the same order a series of arguments in praise of fools advanced by Erasmus's heroine.[1]

4. Since Folly had introduced that passage by referring inaccurately to Lucian's cock – 'this cock ranked simpletons, on many counts, above the learned and great' – it was clearly she who gave Jonson the notion of making his fool the final recipient of the philosopher's soul.

5. When Voltore's arrival heralds the comedy of delusion, Mosca draws first on *The Cock* and then on *Folly* in explaining why he finds the situation so funny.[2]

This is enough to establish that Jonson had Lucian and Erasmus on his desk as he wrote the first pages of his play.[3] Since it is virtually certain that he read *The Cock* in Erasmus's version, he would also have before him the critical preface in which Erasmus urged the superiority of Lucian not only to other satirists but also to writers of comedy, praising his mixture of *jocus* and *serium*, his teasing allusiveness, and his revival of the sharpness ('dicacitas') of Old Comedy without its abusiveness ('petulantia').[4] All these points have a bearing on *Volpone*, but the last is the most significant, since Erasmus returned to it in defending *Folly* in his *Apologetic Epistle to Dorp*, which in turn was Jonson's main prop in defending *Volpone*. His dedicatory epistle repeatedly scorns the 'petulancy' of vulgar rivals, and its central section, admitting to 'sharpnesse' but disavowing personal satire, follows Erasmus's apology very closely indeed.

Though literary allusions are legion in *Volpone*, this network of reference at the start to the theory and practice of Lucianism is quite without parallel. Critics have been quick to take account of it in exploring the play's themes. Asserting that 'Lucianic influence has penetrated to the core of the drama', Harry Levin took up the topic of metempsychosis and showed how the link made by Jonson between gold-worship and the degenerating soul had been easily extrapolated from Lucian's dialogue.[5] Others have variously interpreted the play as a Praise of Folly. It is ultimately more helpful, however, to perceive that Jonson's early references to Lucian and Erasmus were acknowledgment of guides who had helped him to formulate a new satiric method. Indeed, to distinguish between themes and methods – between art as mimesis and art as rhetoric – is peculiarly urgent in the case of *Volpone*, the impact of which in the theatre is apt to be at odds with the meanings it reveals in the study. Put most simply, a grim conspectus of human depravity is expressed through exhilarating farce. Though none of the play's critics would deny this, most have stressed either its sombre vision or its farcical energies, and

Ben Jonson

found difficulty in writing about one without neglecting the other. What needs to be studied is the rhetorical method by which both were combined.

Volpone classically illustrates the ways by which farce can be moral. One of these is its capacity to express moral vision in an exaggerated and symbolic manner. Like Molière's Orgon hiding under the table, Volpone shamming sickness on his couch provides a ludicrous but vivid symbol of his spiritual state.[6] All Jonson's *farceurs* reveal by their antics the absurdity to which greed drives them. As farcical situations accumulate and cohere in an elaborate plot, the play's moral vision is correspondingly clarified and enforced. But farce is also a weapon which can be moral in the sense that it tests the audience's powers of discrimination. Instead of clarifying, it can actively obscure what is seriously at issue. In *Volpone* the temptation to 'laugh off' a predominantly evil world, and indeed to take part in it joyfully, is at least as strong as the encouragement to see it clearly for what it is and to reject it with the scornful laughter prescribed by Sidney.

Since both these moral uses of farce were widespread in sixteenth-century drama, we shall not claim too much for the influence of any one tradition. *Volpone* is a triumph of synthesis, its extraordinary dynamism resulting from many influences, modern as well as ancient, popular as well as learned. For example, it was Horace who had associated *captatio* (legacy-hunting) with the fable of the fox who flattered the crow into dropping its cheese; but it was Jonson who saw how the other fable of the fox who lured the carrion-birds within range by shamming death could fit the situation of the *captator captus*, the legacy-hunter deceived by his prey. Linking a well-known fable to a classical theme, he showed fine intuition in seeing how both could be used for a new kind of comedy. In both, broad humour was combined with an indictment of competitive greed. In the *captatio* stories of Petronius and Lucian the skill of the successful party was offered for amusement against an assumed background of moral contempt, just as the fox in the popular tradition that survived into Jonson's own day was enjoyed as a paragon of comic resourcefulness while also being recognized as a symbol

146

of diabolic cunning. For a dramatist who was trying to escape from the device of using moral spokesmen to pillory satirized characters, such situations had the advantage of containing their moral point within themselves, requiring no added comment unless perhaps the fox or the rich man might be made to moralize archly at the expense of his victims. Rather similarly, as we saw in Chapter 1, Lucian in his ninth *Dialogue of the Dead* involves his reader in a world of apparently determinate evil when his two old men in Hades chortle over the success of Polystratus in cheating his suitors without giving the least hint that any other code of behaviour might exist. *Volpone*, like Lucian's dialogue and like the fable, presents outrageous standards as morally normative throughout most of its length, inviting us to share in the laughter they validate, subjecting us to trial by farce. Clearly Jonson's synthesis also embraced the dramatic tradition of the Vice, with whom Reynard the Fox had much in common. If Barabas was to be recognized as a Vice, so certainly were Volpone and Mosca. One of the main contributions to *Volpone* of Erasmian *lusus* (in the sense of a deceptively playful testing of moral intelligence) was that it provided Jonson with a learned equivalent for techniques made familiar by Morality drama, thus giving them an authority which the humanist poet required.

But Erasmus's example also helps to explain why Jonson could practise the art of teasing more effectively than earlier dramatists. In the first place, he shared with Erasmus a consciousness of rhetoric more highly developed than Marlowe's. In *Discoveries* he stakes his reputation as an 'artificer' on his persuasive skills. Posterity, he says, will acknowledge

with what strength hee doth inspire his Readers; with what sweetnesse hee strokes them: in inveighing, what sharpenesse; in Jest, what urbanity he uses. *How he doth raigne in mens affections; how invade, and breake in upon them; and makes their minds like the thing he writes.*[7]

It is plain that the more deliberately such skills are practised, the more devastating they will be when turned against the audience. He also, like Erasmus and unlike Marlowe, worked from a foundation of firm moral certainty which enabled him to test the standards of his audience with vigour and consistency.

Ben Jonson

He shows awareness of his roles as rhetorician and inquisitor by mirroring both within the action of *Volpone*, creating characters who are expert in devious rhetoric and a story which centres on temptation and trial. Volpone is made to mimic the 'astounding terms' of Marlowe in a context of attempted seduction. The salesman in the piazza and the lawyer in court 'try' the judgement of their hearers with what Jonson contemptuously calls 'language',[8] mere word-power divorced from conviction. Mosca's flatteries furbish the central temptation of the inheritance and lure his master, too, toward the fox-trap, until 'each tempts th'other againe, and all are sold'.[9] After the first court-scene, where folly and greed have overwhelmed judgement, the rogues note with amusement how the plainest arguments of truth have been shunned as Satanic rhetoric:

MOSCA.   Too much light blinds 'hem, I thinke. Each of 'hem
        Is so possest, and stuft with his owne hopes,
        That any thing, unto the contrary,
        Never so true, or never so apparent,
        Never so palpable, they will resist it –
VOLPONE. Like a temptation of the divell. (V.ii.23–9)

It is to a comparable state of moral confusion that Jonson takes pleasure in luring his spectators, while at the same time dazzling them with the evidence they need to form a true judgement. The way his cleverer characters vex and torment the less clever similarly parallels his rhetorical purpose. In Volpone's description of how he plays with his victims –

        still bearing them in hand,
    Letting the cherry knock against their lips,
    And, draw it, by their mouths, and back againe (I.i.88–90)

– we recognize an extension of the cat-and-mouse tactics employed by Tiberius, tactics which Jonson himself could practise for worthier ends.

Volpone's first speech has been thoroughly studied as an index of his inverted theology, but it should also be seen as a complex piece of audience-provocation. Visually, the ritual of gold-worship – the priest before the shrine, elevating a coin with an acolyte in attendance – offers a spectacle as theatrically compelling as it is morally outrageous. Jonson's lifelong belief

that the sensationalism of the theatre militated against moral
discrimination ceases to inhibit him, and becomes a source of
strength, as soon as he starts to write obliquely. The insidious
appeal of this opening becomes clear when we pick up its
allusions to others. One is to the opening of *The Jew of Malta*.
We have not been forewarned to regard Volpone with the
suspicion which Marlowe's Machevill-prologue had directed to
Barabas. The hint of churlish impatience in Barabas's first
soliloquy ('Fie, what a trouble 'tis to count this trash!') has
been replaced by the exultant, life-welcoming note of 'Good
morning to the day'. The first words of Jonson's previous
comedy, *Poetaster*, had been 'Light, I salute thee', but the
speaker there had been Envy, wreathed in snakes, complaining
of 'wounded nerves' from which Volpone is blessedly free. It
is the positive tone of Volpone's hymn, achieved by the placing
of stress ('*Open* the shrine...', '*Haile* the worlds soule...', '*More
glad*...am I...', '*Well* did wise Poets...'), which builds up a
persuasive mood of buoyant optimism. There is no need to
speculate too precisely on how the content of the speech affected
its Jacobean auditors; whether, for example, they were more
shocked by Volpone as a saint-worshipper or as a worshipper
of gold.[10] What matters is the blatant use of rhetoric to disturb
and confuse the 'affections'. As with Folly's speech, the proper
response to Volpone's cannot be a simple matter of turning his
white into black:

> Deare *saint*,
> Riches, the dumbe god, that giv'st all men tongues:
> That canst doe nought, and yet mak'st men doe all things;
> The price of soules; even hell, with thee to boot,
> Is made worth heaven! Thou art vertue, fame,
> Honour, and all things else! Who can get thee,
> He shall be noble, valiant, honest, wise –

By dismissing the speaker too readily one would overlook the
measure of worldly truth he expresses. Money is indeed the main
motivating force in society, does speak louder than words, does
buy souls, and can even buy a good moral reputation. Merely
to retort that this should not be the case would be to substitute
naïve idealism for the kind of prudential morality, based on

understanding of the ways of the world, which Erasmus had aimed to promote in his *Colloquies*. Response to these lines is in any case conditioned by a more outrageous statement made just before. Gold has been praised as

> far transcending
> All stile of joy, in children, parents, friends,
> Or any other waking dreame on earth.

Even that passage contains bleak truth in the sense that people can be more disillusioning than cash, but it was mainly meant as a stab at the human heart. The Oxford editors show that Jonson adapted it from a fragment of Euripides' *Danaë* preserved by Seneca, who records that when the lines were spoken in the Athenian theatre

the whole audience rose with one accord to hiss the actor and the play off the stage. But Euripides jumped to his feet, claimed a hearing, and asked them to wait for the conclusion and see the destiny that was in store for this man who gaped after gold.[11]

There one glimpses the drama of confrontation which excited Jonson. Blandly violating natural affections, Volpone for a moment points forward to Swift's Modest Proposer, as he also does a little later when he reveals 'I have no wife, no parent, childe, allye.'

The first scene closes with Volpone's ironic survey of the clients whom he coins into profit. As he speaks, however, we realize that he is being secretly viewed in the same light by Mosca, while at a third and more recondite level of irony we ourselves are being 'borne in hand' by the author. Recognizing that what the characters in *Volpone* do to each other often represents a subtle perversion of what the author is doing to us, we have the clue to understanding how Jonson was using Lucianism. Its controversial status in his time was explained in Chapter 4. In particular, we saw that Cousin's edition of Lucian, which he probably used, epitomized the controversy by printing an Erasmian appreciation of Lucian's moral worth side by side with Zwinger's blunt criticisms of the blasphemer and mocker, the champion of the intellect liberated from the service of God. We saw also how *Folly* had embroiled Erasmus in the same controversy, and how Jonson, in his glances at Lucianic wit in *Cynthia's Revels* and *Poetaster*, appeared to treat it as a disputed boundary-mark between the provinces of *ingenium* (wit) and *judicium* (judgement). If the Comicall Satyres rated Lucianism no higher than 'harmlesse pleasures, bred, of noble wit', requiring to be supplemented by the sterner purpose of a Crites or a Caesar, *Volpone* reflects a revised estimate of its potential as a moral weapon, in keeping with Jonson's interest in seeing how traditional satiric approaches could be usefully applied in the theatre. As before, however, his study was nothing if not critical. In his scrutiny of the Juvenalian temper in *Every Man Out* most of his characters had been used to illustrate its defects, while its valid function, though embodied by Asper in the induction, had been illustrated in the play proper only by the dramatist's own procedures. So we find in *Volpone* a concealed distinction between the morally responsible or Erasmian use of Lucianic techniques by the author and the morally reckless use of them in the action by Volpone and Mosca.

Seen in this way the packed allusions to Lucian and Erasmus in Act I take on fresh meaning. Mosca's interlude is in the main a debased parody of Lucian's *Cock* culminating in a debased parody of Erasmus's *Folly*. Its mimetic purpose is to portray the sick humour of Volpone's household (as far as possible removed from Erasmus's notion of Lucian's *festivitas*), but also, rhetorically, it seeks to infect the audience with the same sickness. Like the puppet-show in *Bartholomew Fair* and many other examples of debased 'play' within Jonson's plays, it tempts the spectator in the theatre to share the amusement of the spectators on stage instead of recoiling in proper disgust. And the second pair of references which we noted to Lucian and Erasmus has a similar function. When Mosca draws on them in response to Volpone's 'Why dost thou laugh so, man?' he sets the tone for our reaction to the scenes that are to follow. Perverted Lucianism is again being used to induce mirth of a morally dismissive kind. Jonson no doubt remembered Sidney's disapproval of 'scornful matters' in comedy:

the great fault...is that they stir laughter in sinful things, which are rather execrable than ridiculous; or in miserable, which are rather to be pitied than scorned.[12]

Yet we find, as the play progresses, that we increasingly do share in the malicious merriment of the rogues at the expense of their despicable victims. Mosca's task is to feed our appetite as well as his master's for this kind of laughter. How well he succeeds becomes clearest in the scene after Volpone's supposed death when he sends away the disappointed clients, delivering a moral lecture to each in turn. Volpone refers to this scene as 'a rare meale of laughter', a 'feast' – another perversion of the *convivium* – but we share it so gladly that we find ourselves trapped into accepting Mosca as a distributor of justice. That is the culmination of a process which the early allusions to Lucian and Erasmus had set in train. It is thus possible to detect that the humanist debate about the morality of Lucianic laughter provided Jonson with a fresh set of terms in which to ask the uncomfortable question 'Why dost thou laugh so, man?' – the basic question of all moral comedy traditionally posed by the Vice.

At the risk of categorizing more neatly than Jonson himself would have done, we can identify three aspects of the Lucianist's role which correspond not only with Jonson's own role as the author of *Volpone* but also with roles played by Mosca and his master. They are, first, the artist as detached observer or *kataskopos*, watching the stage of fools; secondly, the Protean artist whose personality is disguised by, and expressed through, the creation of characters; and third, the artist as a teasing manipulator of his public's responses. Abstractly considered, these represent constant factors in the artistic process – vision, creation, and intent – each subordinated to irony. Within the play, though there is some overlapping, it is roughly true to say that the teasing role is played by the Fly, while those of spying observer and disguised actor belong to the Fox. Of Mosca as gadfly one need only emphasize that his chase always has a beast in view: not even his soliloquy on the parasite's art (which 'spiritualizes' Lucian's *The Parasite* and so parodies the humanist habit of 'overgoing' classical models) is meant to suggest that his delight in pure skill makes the object irrelevant. Volpone, on the other hand, in spite of his opening speeches, pursues pleasure and especially mirth more obsessively than

profit. As a Protean, he delights primarily in creating roles for
himself to act; but also, like the actor on the raised stages of
Jonson's time, he enjoys watching the effect of his performance
on others. A hint of the *kataskopos* has been noted in his attitude
at the end of the first scene, where he surveys the working and
counter-working of his clients. He goes on to assume the posture
physically when, as Scoto of Mantua, he 'mounts' his 'banke'
and looks down on the ignorant throng, and again when he
watches the discomfiture of his clients:

> I'le get up,
> Behind the cortine, on a stoole, and harken;
> Sometime, peepe over; see, how they doe looke;
> With what degrees, their bloud doth leave their faces!
>   (V.ii.83–6)

Jonson's stage-pictures often result from his practice of thinking
in emblems. In the mountebank salesman he seems to hint at
an emblem of fraud and hypocrisy which had a common
religious application in medieval painting and wood-carving:
the fox, robed as a friar, looks down from his pulpit on a
congregation of trusting geese; from his cowl the head of a dead
duck can be seen to dangle, and he preaches on the text 'God
is my witness how I desire you all in my bowels.'[13] Later, on
his 'stoole', Volpone's overviewing has a different significance.
He appears as a broadly comic variant of Tiberius watching the
downfall of Silius, or of Tiberius as one might imagine him if
he could have watched the blood draining from the faces of the
senators on hearing his letter. But he is unlike Tiberius, and
relatively foolish, because in indulging his appetite for ironic
laughter he forfeits control of the situation. He 'kills' himself
for the sake of a jest and installs Mosca at his desk as his heir.
'I'le to my place', he says, 'Thou to thy posture...Play the
artificer now, torture 'hem, rarely' (V.ii.109–11). In this
contrast of postures it is the vulnerability of the overviewer that
is pictured. His grip on the artifice lost, his intelligence faulted,
the ironist's distance from the action becomes a liability. His
stool, so to speak, can be knocked from under his feet.

The corresponding roles played by Jonson himself have
already been made clear in outline. His vision is kataskopic and

his creative method Protean in the sense that he offers a self-contained world on which none of the characters he creates expresses his view with complete authority, his intent being in that way fundamentally teasing. But does he at any point acknowledge a parallel between his own techniques and those of his characters? Arguably, he does so in the mountebank-scene, a strange feature of which is that Volpone–Scoto speaks in distinctively Jonsonian tones when voicing high claims for his art and contempt for his vulgar rivals.[14] We now understand the paradoxical way in which the 'Menippean' writer's detached manipulation of the fictional medium was felt to license occasional subjectivism of this sort, so that a degree of personal allegory can legitimately be looked for in the performance Volpone puts up on this occasion. It does not constitute a straightforward sales-pitch, as even the sceptical Peregrine supposes. Scoto, appreciated by the aristocracy, condescends to appear in '*an obscure nooke of the* Piazza', steadily lowers his price, and in the end sells nothing. Volpone seems to fail, but in fact achieves his secret purpose, which was to glimpse Celia. A plausible guess at Jonson's private meaning is that he was not trying to do what even the more intelligent members of his public expected of him. After years devoted mainly to cultivating an exalted image of the moral poet at court and at the Blackfriars Theatre, his object in coming to the Bankside was not to sell a stern moral message, or indeed to sell anything:

Gentlemen, know, that for this time, our banke, being thus remov'd from the clamours of the canaglia, *shall be the scene of pleasure, and delight: For, I have nothing to sell, little, or nothing to sell* (II.ii.69–73).

Rather, while flattering his audience into a sense of security, his aim was to subject it to his private purpose, the test of a searching inquisition.

It is clear that the teasing deceptions of Lucianism could only be countenanced by Jonson on very strict terms. 'So fertile and flexible is Lucian's genius', writes an early seventeenth-century editor, 'that he assumes all the shapes of rhetoric like a Proteus, and takes on all its colours like a Chameleon.'[15] Such baffling versatility, admirable in the artist, had its deplorable corollary in the moralist's lack of settled convictions. A condition of using his techniques responsibly was therefore that the ironic artist must maintain the integrity of the self, constant and positive behind his endlessly-shifting visors. This, most crucially, is where Volpone and Mosca fail. Total identification with their roles is a mark of their shallow cynicism, and also a cause of their downfalls in that it robs them of self-possession and self-control. Their two most important soliloquies are designed to make this plain. Mosca's, at the start of Act III, shows an equation of his self with his art; 'I feare, I shall begin to grow in love / With my deare selfe, and my most prosp'rous parts.' He acknowledges a 'whimsey' in his blood, symptomatic of the overconfidence in manipulation which causes his initial error of involving Bonario and his final mistake of misjudging his master. Volpone's parallel soliloquy at the start of Act V reveals that, during the trial, role-playing has for the first time failed to bring him self-fulfilment ('I nère was in dislike with my disguise, / Till this fled moment'), and has instead resulted in a terror of self-doubt which he must banish with wine. 'This heate is life; 'tis blood, by this time' – a grosser variant of Mosca's 'whimsey' – similarly forecasts a failure of judgement and the disastrous exchange of roles between master and servant, fox and fly. His final 'uncasing' appears on the surface, and was meant to appear, as a rejection of play-acting and a heroic assertion of his identity, but it ought rather to be understood as a climax to the most pretentious and false of all his roles. Like his last remark in Act I, 'I must / Maintaine mine owne shape, still, the same', and his boast to Mosca that in the first court-scene he was 'never, but still my selfe', his 'I must be resolute...I am Volpone' lays claim to the Stoic virtue of constancy to the self which is precisely the standard by which he is measured by Jonson and found wanting. Volpone does, of course, have an identity of a sort: he is an actor, an impersonator of others, just as Mosca is an artificer, a manipulator of others. But to the extent that they are these things only, or even mainly, neither can be said by Jonson's reckoning to have cultivated the self at all. Having 'liv'd, like *Grecians*', they cannot do more than talk (III.viii.14–15) of dying 'like *Romanes*'.

It should go without saying that the proper response to

Volpone and Mosca is not to condemn them coldly but rather to engage with them as we do in Erasmian *lusus*, with intelligent enjoyment of the game being played and excitement heightened by awareness of its threats. We are meant to feel the strain between morality and theatrical appeal, not as a pretext for rejecting the theatre but as an experience which makes playgoing a morally significant activity. All Jonson's ironic comedies employ the same strategy of challenging spectators to keep their moral bearings, requiring them to maintain the integrity of their 'selves' against the onset of theatrical rhetoric and the author's insidious attempts to 'make their minds like the thing he writes'. The challenges of most potentially damaging, just as Mosca is the most seriously incriminating of his agents. We should take note that Mosca's repeated technique is to plant the seed of a vicious notion and then wait until his victim brings it to fruition and claims credit for having thought of it himself. To read the passage (II.vi.59–95) which begins

> Thinke, thinke, thinke, thinke, thinke, thinke, thinke, sir.
> One o' the Doctors offer'd, there, his daughter

and ends with Corvino's

> sweare it was,
> On the first hearing (as thou maist doe, truely)
> Mine owne free motion

is to recognize a process by which the audience also is continually induced to proclaim its worst instincts through its responses to the action.

The area where Jonson's probing is most profoundly uncomfortable has its centre in Celia, who is a more exciting figure than critics allow who dwell solely on her place in the play's thematic pattern or vision. Arguing that her simple integrity and constant virtue are intended to contrast with her husband's duplicity and the Protean vice of Volpone, they show how much point can be missed by hurrying to a right conclusion. What they miss *en route* is Celia's sex-appeal, and how they miss it is hard to conceive in view of the notably sensuous language with which Mosca presents her to the play:

> The blazing starre of *Italie*! a wench
> O' the first yeere! a beautie, ripe, as harvest!
> Whose skin is whiter then a swan, all over!
> Then silver, snow, or lillies! a soft lip,
> Would tempt you to eternitie of kissing!
> And flesh, that melteth, in the touch, to bloud! (I.v.108–13)

Certainly, he is tempting Volpone, but Volpone is not disappointed by what he later sees for himself; and the spectator, whose appetite has been whetted at the same time, is not disappointed either by the lady's first action of tossing a handkerchief from her window. Why Jonson should have introduced his paragon in this compromising posture ought to be worth a thought. Examining the text, we find that the handkerchief was a means of transmitting money to the salesman who would then presumably return it to the donor with his product wrapped inside. Thus Celia's action is in fact innocent, at worst an impulsive indiscretion. But that is not, of course, how it appears. We do not need *Othello* to remind us that a handkerchief was a woman's conventional token of sexual favour, or Corvino to tell us that the dropping of a handkerchief was a conventional ploy for seeking 'parlee' with a stranger. Celia's first appearance is a stage-picture which falsely confirms the impression already given by Mosca of Corvino's 'gallant wife'. Even after her purity of character has been established, her allure remains a potent factor in the play's rhetoric, inviting a complex of wrong reactions. She is proffered as the voluptuously beautiful woman whose sexuality appears to be channelled into religion – a phenomenon, often Catholic and southern, of which Pope's Belinda is a more delicate English example ('On her white breast a sparkling cross she wore'). By tradition it arouses lewd incredulity in the Anglo-Saxon Protestant male, for whose attention the treatment of sex in *Volpone* angles. Mosca's cynicism in assuming that the real Celia is only waiting her opportunity to 'do' ('What woman can, before her husband?'), and her detractors' delight in repeatedly picturing her as a lustful animal, titillate the audience at a psychological level where rational awareness of the speakers' unreliability may count for little. Connected with this is the appeal to darker, more sadistic instincts. Corvino's impulse to bully and degrade

Ben Jonson

his wife ('no pleasure, / That thou shalt know, but backe-wards' and so forth) can also strike answering chords. If we feel pain at the sight of an innocent, dutiful and intelligent lady being dragged about by an unworthy husband, manoeuvred as a sacrificial victim toward Volpone's bed, and praying to '*God, and his good angells*' at his idolatrous altar, we need to remember, as Jonson surely did, that this sort of material is a recognized source of pleasure in the sadistic and pornographic fiction of all ages. The long and slow build-up to the attempted rape caters openly to prurient interests. Celia is not tempted by Volpone's 'sensuall baits'; rather it is she who is the sensual bait, and we who are tempted to see her as Volpone does. When he argues that an attractive woman with a psychotic husband deserves to be wooed by a capable lover, only an audience of vision-critics will be totally insensitive to his argument. Sympathetic concern over Celia's predicament must surely have been mixed at the Globe with a vicarious delight in Volpone's virile posturing and lustful designs. Jonson's anticipation of this effect would seem to be indicated by his making her appeal, with disastrous results, to her seducer's 'manlinesse'. To snigger at the line 'If you have...any part, that yet sounds *man*, about you' would be to stand self-condemned of a lewdness equal to Volpone's. It is necessary to postulate such responses if only to insist that, in portraying the corruptive influences of sex as well as gold, Jonson's searching eye looked beyond the characters on stage to take in his audience also. Both influences, like the appeals of farce and heroism, are notoriously apt to send the compass of judgement spinning.

Ironically enough, it is Volpone who points out that the connotation of Celia's 'heavenly' name is that she cannot be appreciated by 'earth-fed mindes'. Jonson as moral idealist has conceived her according to the Platonic equation of beauty and virtue, the heavenly aspect reflecting the heavenly soul. As pragmatic satirist, however, he is concerned to show that a rarefied ideal of that type, appropriate enough to a masque, wins acceptance with as much difficulty on the Bankside as in Volpone's Venice. Convinced that he is dealing in both spheres with degenerate humanity, he must expose his ideal to be trampled on by the wolves and the asses, just as Celia herself, because of the world she inhabits, must reject her beauty in a harshly ascetic spirit as a 'crime of nature'.

He plays with a virtuous ideal somewhat differently in the case of Bonario, who also, however, deserves to be seen as an effective tool of the author's strategy rather than as an ineptly realized paragon. The temptation here is not to cheapen the ideal but to accept it too readily, since the standard of 'goodness' Bonario invokes, again appropriate to an ideal world, is plainly inadequate to combat the evil generated and enjoyed in the play. By drawing the good man in simple outline Jonson may well have intended to point a contrast with the complexity of evil, but his use of simple characterization is also a bid for an over-simple response. The context in which Bonario's honesty is placed requires us to see it as ambivalent. His first scenes show him 'maz'd' by Mosca's allegations about his father: 'I know not how to lend it any thought' – 'Yet, / Cannot my thought imagine this a truth.' To the extent that this disbelief marks resistance to Mosca's wiles it is to be favourably construed as a mark of healthy judgement; but at the same time the speaker is made to seem naïve because he knows less than we do about the corruption of the society he lives in. Similar ambivalence is the key to his much-mocked rescue-speech, where the sentiments are not ridiculous or out of place but the style and the tone are. Parodic recollections of Spenser pervade it, establishing Bonario as an Arthurian knight saving the lady from an ogre's den. Old-fashioned chivalry is a tempting standard for the spectator to fall back on but of doubtful validity among Machiavels.

Erasmian interpreters of the play's moral pattern have argued that Bonario and Celia stand for the 'Christian folly' of ineffectual unworldliness. To this one must only add that Jonson throws their unworldliness into the arena: hers to be mauled by the wolves, his to be applauded by the asses. Like all great satirists, he has a knack of anticipating the comforters that his public will turn to when its *amour propre* is threatened. It was to twist his knife in that self-protective habit that he developed the role of Corvino further than was otherwise necessary. Execrable in all his actions, Corvino none the less displays from start to finish a compulsion to protect his image of himself as 'a good catholique', a man of 'conscience' and 'scruple'. He even classes himself among the Christian fools ('My conscience fooles my wit'), requires moral reassurance from Mosca after slandering his wife in court ('There is no shame in this, now, is there?'), and in his final words ('I shall not see my shame, yet') sums up without knowing it the essence of his spiritual state. His unconscious hypocrisy makes him by far the most complex figure in the play. But complex figures in Jonson never compete for a Shakespearean 'roundness'. Like unusually simple ones, their nature is ultimately determined by their rhetorical function: what they will force the spectator to acknowledge or betray in himself. Accordingly, when Corvino overcomes his reluctance to shout filth in Volpone's ear as soon as he knows that it is safe to do so, or when his scruples about smothering the invalid vanish on the understanding that the responsibility will be Mosca's, we should conclude that Jonson is not simply 'imitating' horrid behavioural patterns but is also confronting the audience with a correlative of what may be its own experience as it witnesses the play. It should recognize in Corvino its own reluctance to admit to disreputable instincts, and its own delight in indulging them when encouraged by the artificer to do so. If Mosca and Volpone parallel the roles of the satiric artist, Corvino mirrors the unshakeable complacency of the satirist's victims, determined to think well of themselves in the teeth of the most damning evidence.

That the Would-Bes implicate the audience will be readily granted, since all agree that the English travellers were meant to bring the lessons of *Volpone* 'home'. 'England', wrote Barish, 'is warned to heed the lesson of the Italian state lest its own follies turn to vices and destroy it.'[16] But in this area of the play we may again suspect that Jonson's critical purpose was less monitory than teasing. More than in the main plot we sense a learned wit at play; the humour, though broad in its effects, has its springs in the erudite joking of humanist *lusus*. Literary parody is at the root of the Would-Bes' roles, Sir Pol an inversion of Ulysses and his wife of the Castiglionean courtly lady. On their emptiness Jonson takes delight in lavishing a preposterous display of technical virtuosity. His use of verse to track the wandering of their imbecile minds, to detail Pol's project for the water-works or his diary-entries about cheapening sprats and urinating at St Mark's, is 'mock' writing in the humanist tradition, literary humour with an esoteric base. So, too, with the parrot's part in the beast-fable, a joke not fully detected until Barish wrote in 1953. And it is no surprise to find that the tortoise's passport to relevance, unearthed even later,[17] was derived by Jonson from a learnedly funny entry in Erasmus's *Adagia*.[18]

It was as an extension of this kind of private humour that the Would-Bes were made available to the audience as scapegoats baited with the popular appeal of zanies. Since comedy's aim is to

> sport with humane follies, not with crimes.
> Except, we make 'hem such by loving still
> Our popular errors, when we know th'are ill[19]

the Would-Bes probe the popular habit of converting eccentricity to vice by loving it. Native drama lent support to the view that the English were too nice or too stupid to make good Machiavels. In giving his English characters that 'stagey' quality of which critics are apt to complain, there are signs that Jonson was specifically eliciting stock responses to a theatrical convention. Pol's harping on the death of Stone, the fool, for example ('Is *Mass' Stone* dead?'...'*Stone* dead?'), echoes Justice Shallow on the death of Double ('Dead!...Dead!...And is old Double dead?'). Peregrine retorts,

> why? I hope
> You thought him not immortall? O this Knight
> (Were he well knowne) would be a precious thing
> To fit our *English* Stage. (II.i.55–8)

Through the Would-Bes Jonson first offers and then snatches away the comfort Shakespeare's audiences were accustomed to derive from bumbling, lovable native types in contexts of state-intrigue or Italianate romance-plots. Detecting that the popular delight in shuddering at Machiavellism sprang from a

Ben Jonson

complacent sense of its foreignness, he subjects his would-be English Machiavels to the devastating treatment he reserved in later comedies for would-be moralists: harsh derision meted out within the action by cleverer characters with whom the audience prefers to identify. In *The Alchemist*, Surly loses credit by being hooted off the stage when on the point of exposing the conspiracy, and similarly the Would-Bes, instead of providing a reassuring norm of innocent English folly in *Volpone*, become the most humiliated figures in the play: the lady trying to achieve her ends through the offer of favours which no one wants, and her husband 'creeping' in a politic disguise transparent to all.

To see that the 'relief' provided by the Would-Bes is itself comprehended in Jonson's satire takes us some way to reconciling the main kinds of humour which the two plots purvey. But it is not in the last resort possible to label the humour of one plot as 'savage' and of the other as 'playful', since in each plot both tones are combined; nor should we suppose that in mixing them together Jonson aimed to promote a wholeness of dramatic experience through fusion of disparate moods. On the contrary, it is the clash of moods, deliberately induced and unresolved, which finally points us to the satiric tradition he worked in. We sense this perhaps most acutely in Act III, where the 'rape' of Volpone by Lady Would-Be is made to precede the attempt on Celia. Ludicrous subjection to the Englishwoman's tongue destroys Volpone's sinister aspect at the moment when it should be most threatening. With whatever emotions we anticipate Celia's arrival, we are thrown off balance by Volpone's comic groans of passive despair, and can hardly recreate our previous tension when the episode is over. It is chiefly through Volpone that Jonson practises his 'Menippean' method, making him by turns impostor and buffoon, seriously threatening and broadly laughable. The character's immense dramatic force depends on no inner complexity reconciling its opposite facets, but rather on the skill by which its various roles are combined, alternated and projected against the audience, each separately and all together exerting a dangerous fascination from moment to moment. Thus, in terms of rhetorical impact, the spectacle of

Volpone cowering beneath the bedclothes under the torrent of Lady Would-Be's verbiage affects us like the 'delusive sleights' of the fox before he seizes his prey; it forces from us a kind of comic sympathy just as we prepare for the alienating spectacle of Volpone leaping lustfully at Celia. A mark of 'Menippean' non-dramatic satire is that it demands from the reader an agility of mind, an emotional aloofness, equal to that of the writer. In *Folly* or *Utopia*, in Rabelais or Swift, for a reader to try to develop a consistent emotional response to the characters or the story is to risk losing contact with the author's drift. In drama, very plainly, the possibilities of such a method are curtailed by the nature of the medium. Actors, present in the flesh, simply cannot convey Folly's multiple *personae* or the changing perspectives of Gulliver. And when a playwright opts for a logically coherent plot, with the degree of consistency it imposes on his characters, the scope of the method is reduced still further. Yet it operates sufficiently in *Volpone* to make it perilous for a spectator to 'settle' in the world of the play; and one suspects that a reason why the play fell from favour between the mid-eighteenth century and our own was resentment at Jonson's cynical juggling with emotional responses. It is not only that he violates our trust. He also appears to have accepted and exploited the equation of theatrical appeal with moral delusiveness, so that to appreciate him properly our enjoyment of the former has to be constantly checked by recognition of the latter – a feat which, in the theatre, calls for a high degree of intellectual detachment.[20]

This is most needed, naturally enough, in assessing his conclusion, where the conflict between our instincts for justice and for comic indulgence is brought to a head and by no means resolved. Few feel that goodness and justice triumph in exemplary fashion. The ineffectuality of the good characters, the vacillation and venality of the court, the refusal to link Celia and Bonario romantically – these have often been noted, and are signs of Jonson's persistence in robbing the public of its anticipated moral satisfactions, just as the harshness of the sentences on Volpone and Mosca sternly blocks comedy's traditional dispensation of favour toward rogues. The resonant emphasis on judgement in the last scene does indeed, as Jonson claimed, provide an answer to Puritan critics of permissiveness in comedy, but that is not to say that the values of the leading Avocatore are Jonson's or were meant to transcend the Venice of the play. 'Mischiefes feed / Like beasts, till they bee fat, and then they bleed.' The metaphor is apt to a society which fattens its beasts well and a court whose ideals scarcely rise above licensed blood-letting. Celia's plea for mercy has been quickly suppressed, and the play has offered no support for Bonario's piety in crediting Heaven with the tendency of evil to destroy itself. Even as the farce turns acrid in the last fifty lines, the challenge to our judgement is sustained. In escaping the trap of responding complacently, we need not fall into the opposite one of calling *Volpone* pessimistic. It is not a vision of the world as Jonson saw it so much as a fable, the objectivity of which masks an inquisitorial purpose. In that connexion the twist Jonson gives to Volpone's *plaudite* hardly needs comment:

> The seasoning of a *Play* is the applause.
> Now, though the *Foxe* be punish'd by the lawes,
> He, yet, doth hope there is no suffring due,
> For any fact, which he hath done 'gainst you;
> If there be, censure him: here he, doubtfull, stands.
> If not, fare *Jovially*, and clap your hands.

It is a device, borrowed and expanded from the last line of *Folly*, to which Jonson was to return more than once. Wryly he forces the spectators to acknowledge that their approval of his play, the seal of its theatrical success, depends on their refusing to see that it has been directed against them.

CHAPTER 8

Epicoene

━━━

'To make a snare, for mine owne necke! and run / My head into it, wilfully! with laughter!' So Volpone acknowledged that his appetite for sport had trapped him into an error of judgement. 'Out of mere wantonnesse! O, the dull devill / Was in this braine of mine, when I devis'd it.'[1] Casual as it is, this talk of the devil was doubly appropriate. Like the archetypal setter of snares, Volpone had planned to laugh at his victims, but at last, like the archetypal ass, has fallen into the pit that he dug for others, and had the laugh turned against him for having wantonly set up his wit in defiance of higher wisdom. Volpone's downfall through his compulsion to 'be merry', his pursuit of what he calls '*Crotchets*' and '*Conundrums*', fittingly punishes his perversion of the art of teasing, which was sanctioned for Jonson by his higher purpose and justified by his demonstration that improper laughter rebounds on the head of the joker. Many years later, in *Discoveries*, he used the same diabolic metaphor in arguing that 'moving of laughter' was not always comedy's aim, but was rather 'a fowling for the peoples delight, or their fooling'[2] – a statement which critics have tended to discount as a theorist's denial of the secret of his practical success. But what Jonson attacked there was the type of comic humour which 'depraves' an audience by playing down to base instincts with no testing purpose whatever. His own sense of humour, on the contrary, was validated – was released to fly high and giddily and wide – precisely by his knowledge that he held it under moral control. The ironic comedies are none the less hilarious because they force us, along with Volpone, to admit that living for laughs ensnares and entangles judgement. The ways in which they do this become a source of their more recondite humour and wisdom, alerting

Ben Jonson

the understander to pitfalls which the ignorant spectator will rush into 'wilfully', 'with laughter'.

But Jonson took pride in varying his modes of operation, with the result that the differences between *Volpone* and *Epicoene, or The Silent Woman* are more obvious than their points of contact. The later play shows a sophisticated lightness of touch unique in the Jonson canon. In place of *Volpone*'s religious undertones its music is consistently secular; its challenges hardly jeopardize our souls. Yet it is scarcely less abrasive than its precursor in the sense of surreptitiously devastating the values of the audience it set out to delight. Even critics most wary of moralistic readings of Jonson no longer claim to enjoy the play as so much light-hearted froth. Ian Donaldson does not find it as 'gay' or as 'genial' as Castelain, Palmer and Herford had said it was, and he described its main action as 'viciously' high-spirited.[3] Its moral tone, according to J. B. Bamborough, is 'looser and more ambiguous' than that of any other of Jonson's comedies.[4] To be disturbed by the play – to find it 'equivocal' with one editor, or be impressed by its 'unrelenting irony' like another[5] – is nowadays a normal response.

Because its last moments constitute the most flagrant example of audience-bafflement in English drama, a case could be made for repeating the approach of the previous chapter. But Dauphine's trick differs in effect from the examples we have just been considering. The result of mistaking Epicoene's sex is not to find oneself morally compromised, as one would be by responding wrongly to Celia. We are not made to share the humiliation of Daw and LaFoole who claim to have been to bed with Morose's bride, nor does our mistake lay us open to anything like the sexual blackmail which awaits the Collegiate Ladies. We share the discomfiture of these characters on a different level. It is our wit, not our moral composure, that is put out of joint by the final revelation. At the moment when our ingenuity is fully taxed in the search for a comic *dénouement*, we and most of the characters are suddenly deprived of our bearings, and the buzz of discussion as we leave the theatre is in admiration of the author's wit more than Dauphine's. Jonson's last-minute *coup de théatre* is primarily an epideictic assertion that 'the better half of the garland' is due to him. Yet the play is morally disturbing in its own unique manner, and a part of that uniqueness can be explained in terms of the Lucianic tradition. Even a few points of literary reference will clarify what Jonson was doing.

First, however, something can be learned about the nature of the play from the circumstances in which it was first acted 'in the year 1609 by the Children of her Majesty's Revels' who were at that time operating at the Whitefriars Theatre. We hardly need background studies of London's private or 'coterie' theatres to form a clear idea of the audience for which Jonson was writing. Harbage's description, 'the fashionable set and its hangers-on', is warranted by the prologue to *Epicoene* which he quotes.[6] This offers matter

> fit for ladies: some for lords, knights, squires,
> Some for your waiting wench, and citie-wires,
> Some for your men, and daughters of *white-Friars*.

The last line slyly alludes to the disreputable elements which Jonson associated with the Whitefriars district. If we are to believe Lady Would-Be (*Volpone*, IV.ii.51), these included transvestite prostitutes whose inclusion here gives point to the theme of epicenity in the play and especially to the treatment of Clerimont's boy at the hands of Lady Haughty (I.i.16–17). Other sectors of the audience anticipated by the prologue are well represented in 'The Persons of the Play'. Of the fifteen named characters nine are described as either 'ladies', 'knights' or 'gentlemen'. (This number does not include Truewit, a point of which the significance will be touched on later.) Mistress Trusty is a 'waiting wench' and Mistress Otter is a 'citie-wire': both are listed as 'pretenders', socially inferior women who enjoy associating with their betters. Jonson's text depicts a milieu obsessively conscious of the court, though connected with it somewhat precariously. Clerimont has just come from it (I.i.72), and Dauphine could go to it (IV.i.58), but the latter is prevented from going by his diffidence, and the former prefers the company of the Collegiates, 'an order betweene courtiers, and country-madames' (I.i.75–6). Mistress

Ben Jonson

Otter has been 'the servant of the court, and courtiers' since they patronized her china-shop, but her social orientation is summed up in Truewit's complex gibe, 'the onely authenticall courtier, that is not naturally bred one, in the citie' (III.ii.34; 28–9). For her cousin Sir Amorous it has been sufficient to have shown himself at court once (I.iv.64) in order to take lodgings in the Strand and give himself courtly airs, while Sir John Daw takes refuge from the failure of his courtly lyrics by complaining that he has not been called to the Privy Council (I.iii.20). Morose's interest in the court is alleged repeatedly. According to Truewit he has friends there (II.ii.6); Lady Haughty assumes that he has sucked its milk (III.vi.78); and he himself demands that his bride must be able to match his own courtly breeding (II.v.31ff.). The subject of courtly pretence is kept prominently in view. There is a pervasive stress in *Epicoene* on a *demi-monde* of characters who fail to be themselves through aping their superiors. It therefore seems likely that the prologue's promise of catering to all tastes was not just the tame repetition of a platitude but was also a warning that the author had identified his audience in advance and determined to show it its face in a mirror. His play 'fit' for ladies, lords, knights, squires and so on, has been planned in the spirit of a Hamlet or a Hieronimo: 'Why then I'll fit you.'

The theatre and actors for which the play was written offer further clues to its intended character. By reason of its rapid dialogue, the absence of choric or idealized figures, and the portrayal of a world familiar in every detail to its public, *Epicoene* can be seen as a work in which Jonson moved further than he had previously gone toward *vraisemblance*, 'things (like truths) well fain'd'.[7] But the enclosed theatres, while smaller and more intimate than their open-air counterparts, by no means encouraged 'naturalism'. Artificial lighting and music between the acts must have emphasized a theatre of artifice. Jonson would seem to have relied on this factor to distance his action and establish a convention in which improbabilities like Morose's obsession with noise, and the mastery of legal Latin shown by Cutbeard and Otter, could be happily accepted. The use of child actors further enforced a patently artificial convention. The induction to *Cynthia's Revels* shows how Jonson could exploit their curious blend of animal spirits and precocious sophistication, and unless we accept the theory that by 1609 the children had grown up,[8] we can see that in *Epicoene* he assigned to them a crucial role in his rhetorical strategy. The mirror-image he showed to his public was not made more flattering by being reduced in scale. To a society of pretenders Lilliputian treatment is lethal. Jonson also exploited the fact that the popularity of the children's companies at this time had come to depend on their being given erotic and sexually suggestive material to act.[9] Seeing this tendency as a debasement of an acting medium associated with humanist court-drama, he typically built it in to the structure of his rhetoric, encouraging his public to indulge its spurious taste. When he made his actors discourse in their childish voices on cosmetics and contraception and other matters which he associated with the 'adulteries of art', he implicitly invoked standards of innocence and nature by which his audience would be apt to stand condemned.

Some of these inferences concerning *Epicoene* are strengthened by its prefatory material. Jonson's dedications of individual plays in the 1616 Folio provide interesting evidence of how he categorized each in his mind. *Every Man In* to Camden, *Every Man Out* to the Inns of Court, *Cynthia's Revels* to the Court, *Poetaster* to a lawyer who had got him out of trouble, *Sejanus* to D'Aubigny, *Volpone* to the Sister Universities: each dedication can be developed into a central comment on the play concerned. The inscription of *Epicoene* 'To the truly noble, by all titles, Sir Francis Stuart' is almost enough by itself to suggest that the play investigates 'titles' to nobility. Stuart's descent from the royal house of Scotland gave him a title not shared by LaFoole (I.iv.60), and for further information about him editors cite Aubrey: 'He was a sea-captain...a learned gentleman and one of the club at the Mermayd...with Sir Walter Ralegh, also, of that sodalitie: heroes and wits of that time.' An all-round man, it would seem, no doubt a better captain than Otter and more learned than Daw, he was probably selected by Jonson to typify the gentlemanly virtues which the play's 'wits and braveries' fail to embody. His reputation as a good club-man leads us on

Ben Jonson

to consider the supposedly sociable nature of the first prologue, which has been much misunderstood. Its devious argument is best revealed by paraphrase:

> There is truth in the old saying that the playwright's skill and his ultimate reward lie in pleasing the people (1–3), but nowadays there is a sect of dramatists who eschew popularity and cater to an élite (4–6). From such an élite we actors dissociate ourselves (7–9), yet, if they were to come to our play, they would not be disappointed (10–11). They might not find everything to their liking, but they would at least acknowledge that the author was a clever man who could have written entirely for them if he had not preferred to popularize knowingly (12–15). A good play should, after all, be substantial and sharp as well as merely amusing (16–18). Therefore the author offers something for everyone...(19ff.).

The frequent assumption that this prologue is genial and placatory seems to rise from a careless reading of lines 8–9:

> Our wishes, like to those (make publique feasts)
> Are not to please the cookes tastes, but the guests.

The speaker is thought to be Jonson. Instead, what we have here is the fiction common to prologues in which an actor mediates between the author and his public. Actors must indeed please the audience rather than the author; they stand to lose from élitist dramas that are played once only. Accordingly, their representative begins by making an easy bid for popular support against highbrow cranks, stating the extreme populist view (anathema to Jonson) that the dramatist's true function and reward is 'to content the people'. Having made this point, he can afford to suggest that room will be made at the feast for the connoisseurs ('those cunning palates') if they care to come along. But at the same time he is gradually shifting his ground until, at line 19, he begins to speak openly on behalf of the author ('The *Poet* prayes you...'). In the course of that transition it becomes clear, though not obtrusively so, that the author of this prologue is himself one of the highbrows, and that his offer of a popular entertainment is slyly motivated. The claim that he could have written an élitist comedy 'but that, he knew, this was the better way' is naïvely interpretable as a concession to popular taste, but it conceals the subtler suggestion that a popular mode has been chosen as a more effective means of achieving the author's objective. That this was a matter of nourishing his public on a salutary diet of satire is clarified by the following triplet with its emphasis on 'bread' and 'salt' at the expense of 'custard' and 'tart'.

If it is agreed that the prologue's offer to 'fit' all tastes covertly meant that each sector of the audience had been marked out as a target, we can fairly conclude that Jonson's use of the feast-metaphor here is somewhat disingenuous. So, we must ask, in exactly what sense of the term is *Epicoene* a 'festive comedy'? Donaldson gives it that name on the score of its debt to the native tradition of revels and times of licence: 'the decorum of the play seems to be governed by the nature of a festive occasion [a marriage] which the play depicts'.[10] His point is supported by a wealth of reference in the text to conventionally festive events. Morose's rejection of society is in large part expressed through his hatred of the rituals surrounding Shrove Tuesdays, Maydays, coronations and especially weddings; and allusions to almost every Jacobean holiday pastime, from courtly tiltings to popular bear-baitings, combine to back up the 'festive' invasion of Morose's seclusion by the revellers. It becomes clear that Donaldson associates this term with the behaviour sanctioned by holiday occasions, so that he can call the play 'festive in mood'[11] in spite of not finding it altogether 'gay' or 'genial'. He admits that the mood established by Morose's persecutors is open to criticism, and sees evidence of a wry attitude to festivity on Jonson's part in the fact that the comedy ends, not in marriage, but in divorce. Indeed the effect of *Epicoene*, according to Donaldson, is to expose a radical disharmony between public and private ways of enjoying oneself. 'What the revelry of the play "celebrates"...is a complex and pervasive notion of isolation and disunity, the opposite qualities to those which wedding revelry should celebrate.'[12]

There, once again, the disturbing effect of a Jonson play is traced to its vision, where it might equally well be traced to its challenging method. We may suspect that the packed allusions to ritual merry-making in *Epicoene* were intended not only to invoke a familiar standard of festivity but also to imply a higher and more exacting one by which the audience is asked to measure its own amusements, including its enjoyment of the play. We often glimpse the intent behind Jonson's ironic comedies by noting inversion or parody of ideals which he states explicitly elsewhere. Thus Donaldson himself observes how the tumult and disorder surrounding Morose's marriage invert the ideals of peace and harmony solemnly proclaimed in the masque *Hymenaei* (1606). One could similarly conjecture that the three Graces who attended the *Haddington* wedding-masque of 1608 are parodically recalled in the three Collegiates, dedicated as these are to adultery and avoiding pregnancy. More generally, much of the festive ideal which underlies *Epicoene* can be gauged from cross-reference to the poem 'Inviting a Friend to Supper':

> To night, grave sir, both my poore house, and I
>   Do equally desire your companie:
> Not that we thinke us worthy such a ghest,
>   But that your worth will dignifie our feast,
> With those that come.

The poem provides a good illustration of the point made in an earlier chapter that all Jonson's poems are expressions of himself as 'poet'. Since the invitation is to a poet's supper, it is itself a poem, and it carefully communicates a style of festivity appropriate to such an occasion. By echoing poems of Horace, Juvenal and Martial it recalls their preference for the simple pleasures of a party among friends over the vulgar delights of ostentatious banquets, where informers lie in wait for indiscretions, and at the same time it emphasizes a literary taste which the host and his guest will share. In tone, too, it skilfully evokes the different moods that will contribute to a successful evening. Basically relaxed and colloquial, with touches of playful wit ('Ile professe no verses to repeate'), it begins on a formal note signifying the courtesy due to a 'grave sir', and insists that good company is better than good fare. Yet the 'cates' are not unimportant; so the menu is rehearsed with just enough relish to stir the appetite, while the wine is praised in a tone of hyperbole that suggests the bolder mood it can legitimately induce. 'Of this we will sup free, but moderately.' In the versification of the last six lines –

> Nor shall our cups make any guiltie men:
>> But, at our parting, we will be, as when
> We innocently met. No simple word,
>> That shall be utter'd at our mirthful boord,
> Shall make us sad next morning: or affright
>> The libertie, that wee'll enjoy to night

– Jonson achieves a flexibility within the discipline of couplets which matches his guarantee of true festivity, that freedom of behaviour and liberty of wit will be kept within the bounds of moderation and innocence.

In his commentary on that poem Wesley J. Trimpi observes that it can best be glossed by the *Leges Convivales* which Jonson wrote for his room in the Apollo Tavern. Some of these Laws, here in Trimpi's translation, are helpful in turn as a gloss on *Epicoene:*

Let no one...who will pay for nothing come, unless he be a guest of someone who has been officially invited. Let the insipid, melancholy, and frowzy fool stay away; let the learned, the urbane, the gay, and the honest be admitted; nor should well-chosen ladies be kept out...There must be no wrangling about the seating arrangement...It should be permitted that the toasters challenge one another in moderate cups, but let the competition be more in anecdotes than in wine. Let no guest talk too much or be silent, and let no one who is full of food and drink discourse on serious or sacred matters. Let no musician in who has not been summoned. It is allowed that our private mysteries be celebrated with laughter, dances, choruses, songs, jokes, and all the festivity of the Graces. All jokes must be without gall, and no flat poems may be recited...There must be no clamour of argument...No one shall be permitted to fight with great goblets in the manner of the Lapithians, to break glassware, to knock out windows, or rip apart the furniture. Let him be let out who lets out to the world what we do or say, for the liquor must make no one a culprit.[13]

Taking the poem and the Laws together, one can hardly doubt that the revels of *Epicoene* are described with similar standards in mind. LaFoole's invitation to supper contrasts with the poet's by being a blatant piece of self-advertisement. Instead of the 'poore house' and modest company which Jonson proffers, LaFoole seeks to show off his 'delicate lodging' and his 'great ladies'. His attempt at *sprezzatura* borders on insult

Ben Jonson

when he negligently boasts of his brace of does, his pheasants and his godwits, which should be eaten 'while they are good' (as though the delicacy of his lodging were at risk), whereas the poet converts frugality into compliment by suggesting that his 'short-leg'd hen' or his 'coney' will not even be bought until he knows that his guest has agreed to come. Other points of contrast are obvious. Daw repeats his own verses, and contemns the very authors (Virgil, Tacitus, Livy) who are to be read at the poet's supper. Mavis and Mistress Otter jostle for precedence. Otter and the knights challenge each other in immoderate cups. None of the guests is invited; all talk too much; all show a singular lack of charity. And most of the participants at Morose's 'mirthful boord' will have reason to feel sad next morning.

Jonson's scrutiny of festive behaviour and festive wit was based on a Roman ideal. Four lines of Martial, alluded to in both the poem and the Laws, appear to have served him as a special touchstone:

To crown these [delights] shall be jests without gall, and a freedom not to be dreaded the next morning, and no word you would wish unsaid; let my guest converse of the Green and the Blue [chariot-teams in the circus]; my cups do not make any man a defendant.[14]

Mirth without bitterness, discussion without heat, a liberation of the spirit that will not be regretted later: those are the yardsticks by which the action of *Epicoene* should be measured. They are not, however, openly championed in the text, not even by the three young gentlemen whose familiarity with Roman authors would have enabled them to do so, had Jonson not wished to suggest their shortcomings. 'What should a man doe?' asks Clerimont, and Truewit replies, 'Why, nothing: or that, which when 'tis done, is as idle. Harken after the next horse-race, or hunting-match; lay wagers, praise *Puppy*, or *Pepper-corne*...'(I.i.32–5). This recalls Martial's talk of the Green and the Blue, but the emphasis has shifted from harmlessness to idleness. If *Epicoene* teaches a standard of festivity, it does so in a highly oblique manner, and it is again to the Erasmian tradition that we should look for help to explain its methods and identify its comic genre.

174

In a manner quite different from *Volpone*, *Epicoene* is a *lusus festivus*, or *lusus ingenii*, according to an interpretation of these words that the Lucianists had encouraged. There are three counts on which the label is apt, corresponding to the tripartite concern of rhetoric with author, work and audience. On the first, the play's sustained lightness of touch, its seemingly total commitment to the idiom of a frivolous society, suggests that the author regarded it at least on one level as a *jeu d'esprit*, a relaxation from work involving strenuous moral commitment; it is what Erasmus would have called a camel's attempt to prove that it could dance. With regard to content, the action described is clearly a festive game of wit, or rather an overlapping series of such games, played at the expense of most of the characters in turn. Finally, the play is a *lusus* in the sense now familiar to us of a game which the audience also must understand and play by examining its own standards of festive behaviour proclaimed by its responses. Author, characters and audience alike are engaged in an enjoyable holiday relaxation, and *Epicoene* is mainly 'disturbing' because it forces awareness of the moral conditions which surround such pleasant activity. It is primarily in that way that it brings *jocus* and *serium* together.

There are also other aspects of the play which link it to the broad field of attitudes and styles which we call Lucianic. The two main sources on which Jonson drew belong to the edge of that field. The outline and many of the details of Morose's story are taken from a declamation by Libanius, an Asiatic rhetorician of the fourth century A.D. who was patronized by the Emperor Julian at Constantinople and thus belonged to an even later stage of the Greek decadence than Lucian. The title-page of the Latin translation which Jonson used describes this speech as 'a witty declamation by Libanius the Sophist'.[15] With this Jonson blended the device of the boy bride, taken, it is now generally agreed, from Aretino's *Il Marescalco*,[16] a comedy the light-hearted cynicism of which can be inferred from the fact that the hero, though willing to plead impotence rather than marry a woman, is finally delighted with his boy. We cannot go so far as to argue that the nature of *Epicoene* was predetermined by what Jonson thought of his sources. It is none the less true that,

except where he deliberately parodied or distorted a source,
Jonson did take care to observe a decorum in his choice of
source-authors, matching them in his mind with the mood he
intended to create, thus linking the attitudes of another time and
place with those of contemporary London. We saw how Gabriel
Harvey had responded to 'the fine conceited Grecians and
Italians' as to a single cultural phenomenon. An affinity was
felt between Lucian and Machiavelli, or Julian and Aretino, in
spite of the thousand-odd years that divided them, because
Grecians and Italians alike had overlaid an appalling godless-
ness with an attractive veneer of wit. One can therefore
recognize some appropriateness in Jonson's choice of a decadently witty Greek and a decadently witty Italian as basic
ingredients in the dish he served up to his Whitefriars audience.
And the play itself takes us into a world which, to a far greater
extent than the world of *Volpone*, is dominated by equivocal
standards of 'elegant wittinesse'.

Lucian's own work is recalled by Jonson only once, in a
passing remark of Truewit to Daw when the plot against the
two foolish knights is opened in Act IV:

If you love me, JACK, you shall make use of your philosophy now, for this once,
and deliver me your sword. This is not the wedding the CENTAURES were at,
though there be a shee-one here. The bride has entreated me I will see no
bloud shed at her bridall (IV.v.44–8).

An allusion to the battle fought at a marriage-feast between the
Centaurs and the Lapithians was entirely to be expected at this
point in the play, but the injunction to Daw to make use of his
philosophy shows that Jonson was thinking of the myth as
parodied by Lucian in his account of how a dispute between
philosophers broke up a marriage-feast and brought it to a
bloody conclusion. Lucian's dialogue, *Convivium, sive Lapithae*, as
translated by Erasmus, served the Renaissance as an *exemplum*
of how educated people ought not to behave at parties. It opens
with Lycinus virtuously refusing to gossip about what has been
said and done by men in their cups; but his bluff is soon called,
and he launches into a full and joyful description of events,
having (like a good Lucianist) 'stood by the wall and watched

the whole performance without taking part in it'.[17] His hilarious account has its moral core:

> I could not help wondering whether what everyone says might not after all be true, that education leads men away from right thinking, since they persist in having no regard for anything but books and the thoughts in them...The unlettered folk [*idiotai*] were manifestly dining in great decorum, without either getting maudlin or behaving disreputably...The learned men, on the contrary, were playing the rake and abusing each other and gorging themselves and bawling and coming to blows; and 'marvellous' Alcidamas even made water right there in the room.[18]

This contrast between simple good manners and learned boorishness is not at the heart of *Epicoene*, where there are no simple heroes, and not all the satirized characters are boors. But Lucian's dialogue was part of the background of Jonson's comedy as an early and brilliant example of the mock-*convivium*, implying a festive ideal by dramatizing departures from it.

Where Lucianism is crucial is in helping to explain the central and controversial character of Truewit. As master of revels he controls the play's mood, and as the principal instrument of Jonson's purposes he deserves to be taken as their gauge. He is taken as such by both Dryden and Jonas Barish, his two most persuasive interpreters. Dryden saw *The Silent Woman* as an approach to the Restoration ideal of comedy as expressing 'the conversation of gentlemen',[19] and accordingly he admired Truewit as 'the best character of a gentleman which Ben Johnson ever made'.[20] He regretted that Truewit's wit was excessively bookish ('he would be a fine gentleman in an university'[21]) but saw that fault as reflecting the same tendency in Jonson himself. Barish is similarly inclined to equate Truewit's character with that of the play and of its author as well. Taking at face value the prologue's promise 'to content the people', he finds this confirmed by Truewit's accommodating attitudes and also by Jonson's corresponding willingness 'to relax his moral stringency and accept the limitations of the society in which he finds himself'.[22]

Barish's brilliant chapter has become inseparable from the modern reader's enjoyment of *Epicoene*, and his discussion of Truewit, in particular, will be useful to us here. But the notion that Jonson projected his own attitudes through any character in his middle comedies must be viewed with suspicion. It is better to assume that Truewit has been created with critical objectivity and to try to place him accordingly. For a start, we should look at 'The Persons of the Play':

MOROSE. *A Gent. that loves no noise.*
DAUP. EUGENIE. *A Knight his nephew.*
CLERIMONT. *A Gent. his friend.*
TRUE-WIT. *Another friend.*
EPICOENE. *A yong Gent. suppos'd the silent Woman.*
JOH. DAW. *A Knight, her servant.*
AMOROUS LA FOOLE. *A Knight also.*

Truewit alone is given no badge of social status. Perhaps Jonson meant to mark him off from his mirror-images of the knights and gentry of the Whitefriars audience, and was obliquely suggesting that Truewit alone is a real gentleman. But a simpler inference is that the character for Jonson had an intellectual rather than a social orientation: he was conceived to represent a type of mind rather than a class of gentleman. It is in fact true that he exists on a slightly different plane of reality from the other characters in the play. Though intimately familiar with their world, he himself has no defined place in it; he alone has no 'off-stage' life referred to. For example, one cannot imagine him interested in a woman, as opposed to women. This view of his 'otherness' is supported by the contrast between his name and those of his more socially-integrated friends. 'Dauphine' is a plot-name, suggesting the heir, and 'Eugenie' hints at the concept of noble birth which may or may not be matched by nobility of character. 'Clerimont' is a courtly-romance name, apt for a servant of the Ladies' College.[23] 'Truewit' is distinguished from these by claiming, in plain Saxon, to represent the perfection of a quality of mind. Jonson had peopled *Cynthia's Revels* with characters called Hedon, Asotus, Crites, Arete, Philautia, and so forth, names which bring to mind the tradition of humanist dialogues and dramas. 'Truewit' is an anglicization of a name of that type, and it is worth asking what this character might have been called if Jonson had named him in the idiom of his earlier festive comedy.

He would probably have called him Eutrapelus. That may

familiar in the sixteenth century and is of major importance in
this play.[24] Erasmus, as we shall later see, gave the name
Eutrapelus to speakers in his *Colloquies*; More, as we saw, applied
the noun to 'proper pleasant talking' in *A Dialogue of Comfort*;
and Stephen Gosson, much later, glossed it as 'the *Grecians* glee'
with reference, once again, to 'pleasant talk'.[25] It was derived
chiefly from two famous passages of Aristotle, whose influence
can often be detected in renaissance discussions of pleasantry,
even where the Greek word itself is not used. The first of these
passages occurs in the *Ethics* as an illustration of the virtue that
consists of a mean between extremes. Since it reads like a
comment on *Epicoene*, it may be quoted at length:

One form of relaxation is playful conversation. Here too, we feel that there
is a certain standard of good taste in social behaviour, and a certain propriety
in the sort of things we say and in our manner of saying them, and also in
the sort of things we allow to be said to us; and it will also concern us whether
those in whose company we speak or to whom we listen conform to the same
rules of propriety. And it is clear that in these matters it is possible either to
exceed or to fall short of the mean.

   Those then who go to excess in ridicule are thought to be buffoons
[*bomolochoi*] and vulgar fellows, who itch to have their joke at all costs, and
are more concerned to raise a laugh than to keep within the bounds of
decorum and avoid giving pain to the object of their raillery. Those on the
other hand who never by any chance say anything funny themselves and take
offence at those who do, are considered boorish [*agroikoi*] and morose. Those
who jest with good taste are called witty [*eutrapeloi*] or versatile [*eutropoi*] –
that is to say, full of good turns; for such sallies seem to spring from the
character, and we judge men's characters, like their bodies, by their move-
ments. But as matter for ridicule is always ready to hand, and as most men
are only too fond of fun and raillery, even buffoons are called witty and pass
for clever fellows; though it is clear from what has been said that Wit is
different, and widely different, from Buffoonery. The middle disposition is
further characterized by the quality of tact, the possessor of which will say,
and allow to be said to him, only the sort of things that are suitable to a
virtuous man and a gentleman: since there is a certain propriety in what such
a man will say and hear in jest, and the jesting of a gentleman differs from
that of a person of servile nature, as does that of an educated from that of an
uneducated man. The difference may be seen by comparing the old and the
modern comedies; the earlier dramatists found their fun in obscenity, the
moderns prefer innuendo, which marks a great advance in decorum. Can we
then define proper raillery by saying that its jests are never unbecoming to
gentlemen, or that it avoids giving pain or indeed actually gives pleasure to
its object? Or is it impossible to define anything so elusive? for tastes differ
as to what is offensive and what amusing.[26]

There, quite explicitly, *eutrapelia* means 'true wit' in the sense not only of a virtuous mean but also of a gentlemanly ideal. The term also occurs in Aristotle's *Rhetoric*, in another much-studied passage, where he insists that the orator must understand the characteristics of different age-groups in his audience. The wrongdoing of the young, he observes, is due not to wickedness but to insolence (*hybris*): 'they are fond of laughter, and therefore witty [*eutrapeloi*]; for wit [*eutrapelia*] is cultured insolence'.[27] The old, on the other hand, do wrong not out of insolence but out of vice: they are 'querulous, and neither witty nor fond of laughter'.[28] Here *eutrapelia* carries a suggestion of youthful excess and over-boldness but is preferred to the negative peevishness of old age which is its opposite. Whether by accident or otherwise, those two Aristotelean passages point to two of the main thematic contrasts underlying *Epicoene* between different capacities for wit (Truewit flanked by *bomolochoi* on the one hand and by the *agroikia*, or 'meere rusticitie' of Morose on the other) and between youth and age (since Truewit and Morose show many of the characteristics of their age-groups which Aristotle's catalogue had made conventional).

The semantic history of *eutrapelos* has an immediate bearing on our study. Its root-meaning of 'easily turning or changing' was sometimes interpreted favourably, as by Thucydides, in Pericles's funeral oration, to express the versatility which he admired in the Athenians, and by Aristotle, in the passages cited, to cover dexterity and nimbleness of wit. But it was also applied pejoratively. Earlier than Thucydides, Pindar had used it in the sense of 'tricky', 'dishonest', 'time-serving', and a passage in Isocrates shows that even in Aristotle's time old-fashioned moralists used it to denote wit of an abusive and morally objectionable kind, a sense which it retains in St Paul's *Letter to the Ephesians*.[29] This spread of meaning in the word was to provide Matthew Arnold with lecture-material for a contrast between the 'moral steadiness' prized by the old Dorians and the early Christians and the 'graceful flexibility' of the Ionian Athenians.[30] The Renaissance also recognized *eutrapelia* as an ambiguous concept. Robert Estienne in his *Thesaurus Lingua*

Latinae classed it as a Greek word 'perhaps signifying what we call *urbanitas, lepor, festivitas & facetia*'; but he also acknowledged its sharper side by translating Aristotle's 'cultured insolence' as 'learned insult' ('eruditum convicium'), and by glossing Paul's use of it as 'the scurrilous wit of a light-minded man' ('scurrilis urbanitas, viro gravi indigna'). For Jonson, we may be sure, the *eutrapelos* was a fascinating figure: one who, by his name, claimed to make a virtue out of turning his coat and changing his shape. We also notice how closely the various connotations of the word correspond to sixteenth-century images of the Lucianist. The debonair gentleman, the versatile artist, the time-serving moralist and the erudite mocker are all included in its semantic pedigree.

If this is indeed the background on which to view Truewit, it will be apparent that he was introduced to the Whitefriars stage as an equivocal culture-hero for a wit-oriented audience and not as the emissary of a suddenly indulgent author. The irony of *Epicoene* is a refinement on that of *Volpone* in that our admiration is directed toward a character who is wholly admirable in the terms propounded by the play, but in those terms only. As has often been remarked, we are required to look outside the play for the norms by which its action should be judged. That does not mean, however, that critics should focus morosely on Truewit's defects. Dryden defended his moral blemishes – that he was 'not ashamed to pimp' for Dauphine, for example – on the ground that comedy has no need to instruct by offering perfect characters but ought rather to delight 'the ill-nature of the audience' by examples of deformity which cannot be enjoyed without a sense of shame.[31] That is an over-simple account of how Jonson deploys Truewit, but it at least has the virtue of focussing on the character as he operates in his context instead of finding his significance exclusively in relation to an unstated moral paradigm. To assert bluntly that 'Truewit' is an ironic appellation for a character whom the author secretly condemned as 'Merewit' would exaggerate the severity of Jonson's intention as Barish exaggerates its leniency. The right way to respond to Truewit is not by denying our admiration for him but by recognizing the moral dilemma we are put in by accepting and enjoying him. Just as the ultimate subject of *The Praise of Folly* is the difficulty of being a wise man, and of *Utopia* the difficulty of political science, so *Epicoene* explores the difficulty raised by Aristotle of how to define 'proper raillery', or in other words how to reconcile wit with morality, discussing the problem in relation to that sector of society which always has to face it in its most acute form.

Barish's account of Truewit is authoritative because it stems from a close study of his linguistic and mental habits, especially as these are contrasted with those of the other principal characters. Accordingly, even if we have quarrelled with his ultimate view of what the character meant to Jonson, we can use his intermediate findings to reveal its kinship with the figure of the Lucianist. After commenting that Truewit exercises his linguistic talent 'disinterestedly, unmotivated by the itch for gain or by moral fervour', he proceeds:

His imagination discloses so many planes of possibility to him at once that he can scarcely choose between them. He embraces all with an Olympian impartiality. He can welcome the shortcomings of ordinary existence without blinking the fact that they are shortcomings. He can philosophise on time at one moment and deprecate his own philosophy in the next. He can praise feminine artifice and undermine it in one breath. He can describe the Ovidian life of seduction as an ideal, and then expose the embodiments of that ideal – the collegiates – as shams. And as he shifts his attitudes, so he shifts his style of speech... Truewit speaks through so many masks that one is not sure when, if ever, he is speaking *in propria persona*. He resembles a disembodied intelligence flickering over the action and lighting up its dark corners.[32]

'Disembodied intelligence' is exactly right. Truewit is a knowing and fascinated but profoundly uncommitted observer of society; a relativist who takes up and drops literary and philosophical poses not so much out of a quarrelsome spirit of contradiction as out of a mischievous delight in the play of mind as an end in itself; a sophisticated reasoner who argues for the sheer joy of doing so; a master of paradox who shows not the slightest concern to use his art in the service of truth. Evidence for all these assertions can be found neatly assembled in embryonic form in Truewit's first conversation with Clerimont, where his blatant shifts of position and cool way of changing the subject would seem to give a clear indication of how Jonson interpreted

Epicoene

eutrapelia. And at the same time as we identify Truewit's heritage we should also notice how it descended past him to his successors. Dryden's view of him as an almost completely polite gentleman was precisely matched by the way the seventeenth century came to regard Lucian. The old reservations about his scoffing and his moral evasiveness are less and less frequently heard, and he is hailed instead as a *bel esprit.* D'Ablancourt, whose free translation into French of 1654 was the medium through which he was most widely known in Restoration England, admitted that Lucian's knowledge of philosophy was only just sufficient to enable him to take sides on any sort of subject,

mais on ne peut nier, que ce ne soit un des plus beaux Esprits de son siècle, qui a par tout de la mignardise et de l'agrément, avec une humeur gaye et enjouée, et cette *urbanité Attique,* que nous appelerions en nostre Langue une raillerie fine et délicate, sans parler de la netteté et de la pureté de son stile, jointes à son élégance et à sa politesse. Je le trouve seulement un peu grossier, dans les choses de l'Amour.[33]

That is as good an expression as any of the ideal of polite wit which the English Restoration dramatists cherished but were never quite able to embody on stage, being always uncomfortably conditioned by their habit of thinking morally, especially when reacting against it. It is an illuminating tribute to the artistic control which Jonson derived from the oblique methods of Erasmian *lusus* that he, though a much more committed moralist than Dryden, Etherege or Congreve, was none the less able to dramatize the appeal of the uncommitted Lucianist more effectively than they.

But there is more to be said about Truewit's engagement with his audience. He is used, not to shock or subvert moral judgement, but to induce a frame of mind which dismisses the whole business of judging moral issues as a boring irrelevance, while delighting in the issues themselves as an object of witty contemplation. Jonson masks his distrust of that attitude by letting Truewit's authority appear to rest on a firmer foundation than mere wit and virtuosity. He is not always made to seem to be the rootless and inhuman Lucianic cipher which he basically is. Exposing the rootlessness of others he can moralize like Jonson himself, and because he is totally wrapped in the ironist's cloak he can even ask to be credited with a latent humanity, especially when he allows (or pretends not to allow) a laugh against himself. His genial treatment of his friends invites us to share Clerimont's view of him as 'a very honest fellow', and the generous opening of his last speech, so far from transferring our admiration to the others as it professes to do, serves finally to confirm our sense of his cultural superiority.

It is as the champion of youth and high spirits against crabbed old age that he is most obviously persuasive. His knowing effrontery, or 'cultured insolence', is not only forgivable but almost lovable by contrast with the querulous Morose. In what has long been recognized as the play's central thematic contrast, the exponent of living as a sophisticated art achieves a natural freedom and spontaneity of manner, while his naturally boorish opponent talks of 'discipline', 'doctrine', and 'impulsion' as means of restricting life and keeping it at bay. It is of some interest here to glance back at two Erasmian dialogues which Jonson may have recalled in his treatment of the art–nature opposition.

Morose's 'ridiculous disease' brings to mind Nosoponus, the butt of *Ciceronianus*. He, it will be remembered, devotes his entire energies to the sterile pursuit of a pure Ciceronian style, and also keeps noise to a minimum:

I have a library in the inmost part of my house with thick walls, double doors and windows, and all the cracks stopped carefully with pitch and plaster so that by day scarcely a ray of light can break through or a sound unless it is unusually loud such as that of women's quarrels or of workmen's hammers ...In my house there is not even a fly.[34]

In the interest of his great work he avoids all family cares, eats frugally ('ten small raisins...and three coriander seeds coated with sugar') and uses dry wood in his fire to prevent smoke. It takes him six nights to compose a letter of six sentences which he subjects to ten re-examinations and then lays aside for several days before examining it finally 'when the love of invention has grown cold'. This is a satiric caricature very similar in method to Jonson's, and it has the same end of equating pedantic art with natural disease. Erasmus entrusts his opposite ideal of a living and flexible use of Latin to smart young men who are not averse to baiting the elderly scholar, though their leader, Bulephorus, is more restrained in his wit and less ambiguous than Truewit. Since Barish has conclusively shown that the polarity between Truewit and Morose is displayed by Jonson in terms of their attitudes to language, we should probably allow that *Ciceronianus* casts some shadow on our play.

A character more immediately relevant to Truewit is Eutrapelus in *The New Mother (Puerpera)*. Erasmus uses this name in two colloquies. In the other, *The Fabulous Feast*, it simply denotes a fun-loving host who holds a wit-combat among his guests and shows catholic enjoyment of their various contributions. But *The New Mother* presents *eutrapelia* provocatively, and in a startling context. The lesson of this colloquy is that mothers should breast-feed their infants instead of handing them over to a wet-nurse. Thus the argument is a plea for the importance of 'following nature', but it is paradoxically put into the mouth of Eutrapelus, who is identified as a painter and therefore an exponent of 'art'. Fabulla, the new mother, is visited by this brash and talkative young man. Brazenly interfering in a family matter, he adopts a tone of witty banter and a sophistical method of reasoning that leads them both into remote by-ways of theology. Though the dialogue owes its dramatic vitality to the fact that the girl holds her own in the combat instead of taking offence, its subtler interest lies in the incongruity between an outrageously 'artful' speaker and the 'natural' cause he espouses. At the close of the dialogue we see what Erasmus is doing. Suddenly Eutrapelus calls a halt to sophistry, makes a delicate reference to the girl's full breasts, and appeals, simply and with immediate success, to her maternal instinct. Finally the baby itself is brought in and hailed by Eutrapelus as a masterpiece. Fabulla jokingly objects, 'It's no carven image that stands in need of art', and claims to have produced something better than a painting. But Eutrapelus reminds her that his gift, too, is originally a gift of nature, and that she for her part has not yet completed her work as an artist. By obeying her instinct to suckle her child she, too, would be fulfilling the artist's responsibility to strive to perfect his creation. For

Erasmus the significance of this well-worn topic of debate – and the reason for his odd choice of spokesman – is that it enables him to show that nature and art, despite apparent conflicts, ultimately work together to fulfil God's purpose.

There, it is clear, Erasmus has dramatized the 'cultured insolence' of the *eutrapelos*, and followed Aristotle's suggestion that excesses of wit are to be pardoned in a young man of generous nature and fine perceptions. Did Jonson regard Truewit in the same light? On the surface it might seem that he did, since it would be foolish to deny that Truewit emerges as a charming and likeable figure. We may also admit that it is chiefly through him that Jonson points to the possibility of an alliance between art and nature in the matter of intelligent festivity, since Truewit is successful in combining a high level of sophistication with an instinctual *joie de vivre*. But that is to stop far short of supposing that Truewit was offered as a model of festive behaviour for would-be gentlemen. It begs, like Truewit himself, all questions of morality. We have only to recall Shakespeare's gentleman jesters to note that Truewit does not, like Berowne or Benedick, acknowledge any sort of moral engagement that will curb his intellectual freedom. Instead, despite difference of temperament, he more closely resembles Jaques in displaying a comprehensive wit that is not to be mistaken for wisdom.

In both these characters, Truewit and Jaques, major prerequisites for wisdom are shown to be lacking. The first is 'self-hood', as we see from their inability to do more than adopt a succession of poses. Motley attracts Jaques because it would invest him with a professional identity and shroud his lack of personal convictions, while licensing that continual motion of mind which Overbury attributed to 'the melancholy man'. Truewit is eloquent on the need for self-realization. He calls Daw 'a fellow so utterly nothing, as he knowes not what he would be' (II.iv.154–5). And he ironically urges Morose to 'bee your selfe. It shewes you are a man constant to your own ends' (III.v.17–19). But Jonson means us to test these remarks against the character of the speaker and to ask what Truewit himself 'would be'. And to what ends, if any, is he constant?

Being nothing if not self-assured, he knows well enough what he is. When Morose asks him, 'Whose knave are you?' he replies, 'Mine owne knave, and your compere, sir' (II.ii.11–12), which means not only 'as independent a gentleman as yourself' but also 'as much of a knave as yourself and I know it'. But we have many times seen that, for Jonson, true self-hood can only be realized through an exercise of moral judgement, and of this Truewit gives no evidence at all. Erasmus had been able to admire the *eutrapelia* of More, his adaptability, because he saw it as the reflex of a man whose moral judgement was fundamentally secure. To Jonson's *homo omnium horarum* the same standard has to be applied. When Truewit discourses on how to be all men to all women we remember the prologue's claim that the poet will 'fit' the tastes of every sector in his audience. But the calculated pretence of accommodation by a rooted moralist which we detected in the prologue can hardly be credited to Truewit. Like the rogue-heroes of *Volpone* and *The Alchemist*, he epitomizes the entire comic spirit of the play he appears in with the teasing omission of its moral referent.

The other charge which both Shakespeare and Jonson level against their Lucianic jesters is that they fail to advance from well-knowing to well-doing. Jaques's practical uselessness and lack of charity are clearly criticized in *As You Like It*. By contrast, no such judgement is passed in *Epicoene*, and to criticize Truewit's behaviour is to swim against the tide of the play. But the more we capitulate to his brand of festivity the more we find ourselves cajoled into disregarding the serious ethical issues which the play persistently raises, especially the issues of time-wasting and cruelty. Time-wasting is the speciality of Clerimont, the jaded Epicurean, and cruelty appears most marked in the vindictiveness of the immature Dauphine. But the fact that Truewit can talk very morally about both faults does not acquit him of either. None of his remarks, taken singly, defines his nature. In the first scene he delivers a homily to Clerimont on time-wasting but instantly revokes it. His rebuke to Dauphine, 'How! Maime a man for ever, for a jest: what a conscience hast thou?' (IV.v.135–6), could be proof of good-heartedness, but is matched by phrases like 'heapt, heapt

Ben Jonson

plentie of vexation' or 'I would kill you, sir, I would kill you, if you had', where he relishes the comedy of affliction. The truth is that Jonson no more endows him with a moral identity than with a social one. All his stances and utterances, whatever their validity, have the function of planting, stimulating and confounding possible responses to the action of the play. They cast on the audience the entire burden of deciding at what point wit and high spirits go too far.

Where that point lay for Jonson can perhaps be determined by referring back to the standards of festivity outlined in 'Inviting a Friend to Supper' or the *Leges Convivales*, or by recalling Aristotle's test of 'proper raillery' that 'its jests are never unbecoming to gentlemen', and that it avoids giving pain and may even give pleasure to its object. Certainly we should bear such standards in mind when we echo the consensus of critics that the treatment accorded to Morose and the knights smacks more of the bear-baiting mentality than of satiric correction, and that the 'noise' of the revellers makes a dubious cultural alternative to Morose's reclusiveness. But to repeat that the main source of *Epicoene*'s 'disturbing ironies' lies in the gap between its unstated ideals and the mood it generates in the theatre is to acknowledge that no new view has been advanced in this chapter about what the play actually says. Rather we have been trying to clarify the procedures of *lusus* by which a brittle children's charade was intended to implicate its audience. Better to end, therefore, by recalling the parallel drawn in an earlier chapter with Erasmus's *Exorcism*. There, similarly, in the outline of a five-act drama, *ingenium festivum* had been openly celebrated with laughter while its trivial and punitive tendencies had been silently exposed to question. In the character of Polus, Erasmus had dramatized his awareness of the cliff-hanging morality on which the satiric teasing and practical joking of More's household depended. And instead of moralizing on the subject, he, like Jonson, shared with his public as much of that awareness as it chose or was able to discern.

CHAPTER 9

Comedies of accommodation

1. 'Ollas ostentare': *The Alchemist* and *Bartholomew Fair*

Since Truewit bears a close resemblance to a Lucianist and little
to a Morality Vice, he reminds us that an advantage of our
approach to Jonson is that it sheds light on all of the four major
comedies, linking them as the Morality approach cannot do. In
terms of the latter *Epicoene* must be odd play out, so that Dessen,
for example, in *Jonson's Moral Comedy*, could scarcely take
account of it at all. The rhetorical method which the four plays
share thus strengthens our hypothesis that Jonson's art in all of
them drew much from the techniques of Lucianic satire, and
that his use of the Moralities was a relatively incidental matter
of exploiting, where appropriate, associations of the genre which
were familiar to his public. But in *The Alchemist* (1610) and
Bartholomew Fair (1614) we come to deal with 'citizen' comedies
where Morality allusions were apt and are clearly central. Here,
even more than in *Volpone*, we find Jonson grafting his learned
art on to native stock. It is the purpose of the first three sections
of this chapter to indicate ways in which Lucianism can add
to our understanding of these plays. And since a curious feature
of Jonson's development is that *Catiline* (1611) came between
them, the last section will try to explain why that mastodontic
failure should not, any more than *Epicoene*, be considered in
isolation from the other plays of Jonson's maturity.

Face's appeal at the close of *The Alchemist* provides a classic
example of synthesized traditions:

> I put my selfe
> On you, that are my countrey: and this pelfe,
> Which I have got, if you doe quit me, rests
> To feast you often, and invite new ghests.

The audience-jury will confess by its applause that it has been bribed into passing an erratic verdict, thus owning its share in the conspiracy of greed described by the play. The passage, as Dessen very properly argues, recalls the power of the Vice to bring the worst out of his public,[1] but at the same time, as in the *Volpone* epilogue, we can see that Jonson is playing games with the *plaudite* in the manner of Erasmus's Folly, who had ended by inviting her bemused 'initiates' to clap their hands, live and drink. The pattern of moral delusiveness which Face's words complete needs little explanation, being as obvious to the critical sense as it is difficult to resist in terms of theatrical enjoyment. The two characters expected to 'do justice' in the play have collapsed beneath the strain. Surly, who has seen through alchemy as 'a pretty kind of game, / Somewhat like tricks o'the cards, to cheat a man', is finally heard to grumble 'Must I needs cheate my selfe, / With that same foolish vice of honestie!' His guiding standard has not been 'honestie' but the cardsharp's determination not to be outsharped. He is disabled in his battle with the rogues by the humourless arrogance which his name then implied, an unwarranted sense of superior virtue, so that spectators who accept him as an adequate judge of the action are annihilated along with him by the stronger and truer dynamics of barefaced rascality. Similarly Lovewit, whose return from the country offers a reassuring reminder of how 'order-figures' tended to turn up in the fifth acts of comedy – his name, which might give him away, has never been spoken – quickly confounds expectation by playing on the audience's predisposition to love wit more than justice. A comparable stratagem operates at the close of *Bartholomew Fair*. When Quarlous takes the centre of the stage, he propounds a philosophy which is warmly appealing in terms of the mood established by the play but comes no closer to establishing a reliable verdict on the action than do the valedictory speeches of Volpone or Truewit or Face.

About all his ironic comedies Jonson could have said, as Erasmus said of *Folly*, that they taught the same message as his explicit writings but 'via diversa...oblique...sub specie lusus' (see p. 238, note 26). So seen, *The Alchemist* and *Bartholomew Fair* refuse to belong where many critics have placed them 'on the rising graph of Jonson's geniality'.[2] In the last analysis their author's genial smile is the expression on the face of a tiger who has taken his victims for a ride and taken them in; his Cheshire-cat grin is that of a moralist who only pretends to vanish. Yet the smile and the grin are what give these comedies their life. The earlier play is for many the funniest ever written, and the second is so comprehensively irreverent as to mock all critical solemnity. If they are not genial, they do none the less invite that epithet by their robust humour and disarming permissiveness. Their rhetorical approach is so exceedingly oblique that it can well be taken as direct.

One reason for this is that Jonson, in these plays, becomes a little less concerned with nailing his audience and more with a quizzical contemplation of his comic art. It is true that both *Volpone* and *Epicoene* had been self-conscious demonstrations of what a master-poet could do with farcical matter, combining it with classical form, learned allusion and intricate moral patterning. But in them the joking had been ultimately sanctioned by the threat it posed to the spectator, by the serious questions it forced him to ask or the incriminating reactions it pressed him to betray. The laughter they elicit is nearly always tinged with some form of culpable delight, whether in blasphemy or cruelty, in the wilful perversion of the moral sense or in a simple escape from it. In his next two comedies Jonson continues to let thoughtless spectators hang themselves but gives them more comfortable rope with which to do so. His humour sheds many of its moral barbs and allows us to laugh more freely. Lovable rogues, harmless idiots and ludicrous moralists begin to flourish among his characters, as though propagated by a climate of almost Shakespearean tolerance. But what he does in these plays, very knowingly, is to push to its limits that indulgence of popular taste which he had reluctantly come to accept as an inescapable part of comedy. Compromise of principle increasingly comes to the fore as a central theme, and in his treatment of it Jonson's irony becomes less punitive and more wry as he sees the accommodations of his characters and his audience as unconscious variants of what he consciously practises himself.

The two plays are his masterpieces in combining most fully

the opposite directions which his genius could take toward comic exuberance and moral steadiness, farce and erudition, energy and artistic control. To make high art from the lowest ingredients has always been a potent impulse. 'Tu m'as donné ta boue, et j'en ai fait de l'or' – what Baudelaire wrote of Paris, Jonson might have said of his London underworld. It was an impulse naturally fostered by the humanist concept of *lusus*, and one which is probably indicated by the Lucretian motto on the Folio text of *The Alchemist: 'petere inde coronam / Unde prius nulli velarint tempora Musae'* ('to seek the Muses' garland where no one has won it before'). Before Jonson not even Rabelais, to whom he makes a significantly scatological allusion in *The Alchemist's* opening lines, had stretched the extremes of matter and art so tautly apart, or managed the tension between them with such effortless mastery. 'Lowness' could not be established more emphatically than in the first exchange between Subtle and Face or in the dialogue around Ursula's booth, yet the rogues' republic and the Fair community quickly burgeon with 'high' import as political and social metaphors. As the social level of the action declines in the comedies which follow *Epicoene*, the scope and pressure of metaphoric significance correspondingly increase. Jonson's virtuosity in these plays can also be seen in their structure. Criticism has only recently uncovered the exact principles by which he orders, without seeming to, the apparent chaos of the *Fair*;[3] and although the ingenuity of *The Alchemist's* plot has long been admired, it continues to give the impression in performance of being improvised by the rogues from one moment to the next.[4] A similar delight in concealment of art is apparent in matters of language. If we ask why *The Alchemist* was written in verse, part of the answer must lie in the challenge of distilling poetry from an incongruous variety of schemes and dreams and uniting them unobtrusively through the blank-verse line. In *Bartholomew Fair* it is only after study that one sees how much care and discrimination have gone toward the forming of twenty-odd separate prose-idioms. Both plays, and especially the latter, suggest that Jonson deliberately set himself to permit the maximum of licence and energy to abound within an intricate framework of moral and artistic ordering.

Comedies of accommodation

The epideictic impulse of *lusus*-as-virtuosity also appears in the way these plays exploit the occasions for which they were written. Exactly when and where *The Alchemist* was first acted is uncertain, but whatever the facts may have been, evidence in the text as Jonson printed it suggests that he aimed at a *tour de force* of exact topicality and contemporaneity, probably writing for the Blackfriars Theatre, since his action is set in that district, and probably meaning the play to be staged as soon as the plague receded sufficiently for the theatres to open. Action which purports to be happening next door to the theatre at the time of performance is bound to come across as a demonstration of ingenuity no less than as a warning to home-owners or gullible citizens, and so marks a shift in motivation from the hostile matching of play to audience noted in *Epicoene*. About the first two showings of *Bartholomew Fair* one can speak with more certainty. This had its first performance at the Hope, a disreputable bear-pit theatre, on All Hallows' Eve and its second the following night at court before the King. In no other play was Jonson so conscious of uniting the popular and élitist extremes of his art, parodying and yet not disowning his roles as moral poet and writer of tragedies and masques. Certainly he wrote with an eye wide open to the disparate nature of those first two audiences, and probed the common frailties of their human flesh and blood, but in bringing 'the Smithfield Muses to the Ear of Kings' he realized a triumph of artistic integration which was essentially personal and private.

In interpreting these plays our perception that Jonson has fused *jocus* and *serium* in some private crucible of wit is apt to be daunting. There are times when 'Thy worst. I fart at thee' seems to be his message to academic critics, until we turn back the page and observe that *The Alchemist* was dedicated to Sidney's niece. His approach can best be appreciated by recalling what Erasmus and More understood by erudite joking. Of this we found a clear statement in Erasmus's comment on the adage 'ollas ostentare' ('to parade one's kitchenware'): 'this is to bring forward something which is ridiculous and squalid, but also of great importance'.[5] Erasmus said he had done this in *Folly*, and echoed the opening of

Lucian's *A True Story* in asserting that such *lusus* could be worthwhile, as mental relaxation or exercise, 'provided the joking is erudite' (*modo jocus sit eruditus*). For Erasmus and More 'kitchenware' meant mundane, temporal topics on which they played in Lucianic fashion by weaving around them a learned network of punning etymologies, literary parody and mythical allusion. Earthier spirits such as Rabelais and Jonson carried the notion to more vulgar extremes: it is no accident that real pots and pans play major roles in the plays we are discussing. Everyone would like to turn dross into gold; Jonson, with some help from Sidney, perceived that only the poet can do so, only he can reward with immortality the services which Ursula's utensils render to humanity. This kind of mock-Platonic theorizing was seminal to Jonson's low humour. But we saw also that the early humanists were like Lucian in associating their playful descents with the baffling of ignorant *idiotai*. The nonsense etymologies in *Utopia* were meant to bamboozle readers whose Greek was defective, and Lijster waxed smug about the failure of 'stuffed nostrils' to relish the allusions in *Folly*. So, for Jonson, erudite joking always involved an assertion of intellectual superiority, even, and especially, when it took its materials from the gutter and pretended to be accessible to the meanest intelligence. In that sense it is true to say that the more he appeared to vulgarize his art, the more private and exclusive it became. As he turned his teasing on himself as well as on his public, tentatively in *The Alchemist* and more fully in *Bartholomew Fair*, his irony arrived at an esoteric pitch somewhat difficult to reconcile with the didactic commitment 'to informe men, in the best reason of living' which he had described in the *Volpone* Epistle as 'the principall end of *poesie*'.

2. 'Pseudomantis': *The Alchemist* as rogue-fiction

Few would dispute that Jonson's travesty of alchemic philosophy, and his metaphorical use of it to portray man's escape from the self into dreams of material betterment, was the most elaborately erudite joke he ever penned. The joke itself and its inherent seriousness are well understood, but a few useful bearings on it can be obtained by glancing at some examples of how Lucian and Erasmus approached rogue-fiction. This approach consists, not surprisingly, in maintaining a cool intellectual perspective not only on the rogues but also on their victims, on the morality of the genre, and on the writer's reasons for taking it up.

To look first at one of Jonson's recognized 'sources', Erasmus's *Alchemy* describes how a priest who has acquired a smattering of alchemic terms battens on the weakness of the rich Balbinus and spends his research-grants on drink, dice and whores. As incidental expenses he charges such items as new types of fuel and equipment, votive offerings of gold to the Virgin, and bribes to courtiers who threaten to denounce the operation. He explains his delay in completing the project by citing personal failings ('peccata obstant'): he has omitted to say essential prayers, and has been caught in bed with a courtier's wife. The tale ends with Balbinus being warned by a friend of the priest's reputation. Instead of exposing him, he pays him off with hush-money.

The focus of Erasmus's irony is more on the victim than on the unnamed rogue. In Balbinus, reason and religion are shown as helpless to combat a foolish obsession. As well as being rich, he is said to be learned and virtuous, and shrewd in all matters but one, since 'no mortal is wise at all times or perfect in every respect'.[6] The suggestion that Balbinus would be the pattern of a renaissance patron if his patronage were not misplaced helps to explain that glimpse, often felt to be incongruous, which Surly gives us of Sir Epicure Mammon: 'a grave sir.../ A wise sir, too, at other times' (II.iii.279–80). Mammon, we recall, when on his best behaviour, shows awareness of the proper role of the rich man in a Christian society ('founding of colledges, and *grammer* schooles, / Marrying yong virgins, building hos- pitalls, / And now, and then, a church'), and it is typical of Jonson that he builds on Erasmus's point by referring Mammon also to the pagan prototype of the Christian patron, Aristotle's 'great-souled' and 'magnificent' man described in the *Ethics*. Dol alerts us to this when she describes him approaching, 'slow of his feet, but earnest of his tongue', a comic allusion to Aristotle's remark that 'traits generally attributed to the great-souled man are a slow gait, a deep voice, and a deliberate utterance'.[7] Mammon's role as patron is emphasized by the stress in his early speeches on munificent generosity more than self-indulgence, and in his last scene he is allowed to recall his project of benefiting the Commonwealth, in a finely comic moment of dignity, because Jonson's concern, like Erasmus's, is to show how easily a venerated ideal can collapse into parody of its potential greatness.

That is a small point of contact, but the two writers also share a larger notion of how rogue and victim co-operate to fulfil their natures and bring about the triumph of folly. The sober interlocutor in *Alchemy* counters the flow of the narrator's gossip by expressing the dialogue's 'epiphany': 'I might feel sorry for Balbinus if he himself didn't enjoy being gulled' ('miseresceret me Balbini, nisi ipse gauderet deludi').[8] In *Exorcism*, too, we saw how Erasmus's witty jokers give the 'ghost' they impersonate the same name as its would-be exorcist in order to help their victim to identify with the object of his obsession and so bring his folly to full flower.[9] Jonson's play gives an even stronger impression of fools fulfilled by those who exploit them. The pursuit of pleasure which constitutes Mammon's title to be an Epicure is seen to depend on his enjoyment of being well deceived (thus disqualifying him, incidentally, from the other Epicurean title of Sceptic). Whichever of the dupes in *The Alchemist* one chooses to think of, it is clear that all of them owe to the rogues the benefit of being liberated from the demands of day-to-day living into an ecstasy of dream-fulfilment. Here Jonson's irony, anticipating Swift's, was plainly influenced by Erasmus. Both saw folly as having its necessary place as a solace for the weak in God's fallen world, and rogues as having the necessary function of giving it release as well as punishing it. And for both, too, folly was incurable. Thus their fools respond to disappointment not by contrition or making amends but by covering their traces or changing their fields of operation. The victim of *Exorcism* is cured only by 'exchanging one form of madness for another', much as Mammon is to turn from alchemy to apocalyptic preaching on a turnip-cart.

Comedies of accommodation

For other antecedents of Jonson's rogue-fiction one looks back beyond Erasmus to Lucian's brilliant and seminal *Alexander, or The False Prophet* (*Pseudomantis*), which describes and exposes the career of a charlatan who grew rich and achieved a wide following in Italy and the eastern Mediterranean by posing as an oracle. Lucian in his second paragraph had pin-pointed the moral problem inherent in rogue-fiction for both writer and reader. 'I blush for both of us', he says, '... for you because you want a consummate rascal perpetuated in memory and in writing, and for myself because I am devoting my energy to such an end.' Typically, he no sooner touches that issue than he evades it by citing literary precedent in Arrian's life of the brigand Tilloborus; he himself will tell of a worse brigand who operated not in mountains and forests but in cities. Though he hints at the outset that his muck-raking role may be socially cleansing (fetching, like a minor Hercules, a few basketfuls of filth from the Augaean stable), and though he ends by posing as an Epicurean opponent of mumbo-jumbo, Lucian never seriously tries to conceal that his primary aim is *voluptas*, to have fun with his subject. This was clear to Erasmus when he commended his translation of *Alexander* to the well-blown nose of the Bishop of Chartres, and similarly, when he dedicated *Folly* to More, he made only a conventional apology for the lightness of his theme. In humanist wit-writing the immorality of celebrating an unworthy object was condoned on the assumption that the reader would be clever enough to perceive the anomaly. Jonson, in condoning the triumph of Face, well knew that this was a rash assumption in respect of the audience he wrote for.

The literary art of *Alexander* resembles that of *The Alchemist* by achieving its effects through a process of alternately inflating and deflating the rogue. Lucian begins with a glancing comparison between Alexander and his namesake of Macedon: 'the one was as great in villainy as the other in heroism'. Some tendency to mock-heroic inheres in all sophisticated forms of rogue-fiction in as much as the rogue (Diccon in *Gammer Gurton's Needle*, for example) is comically dignified by his mere presence in a 'literary' work. But Lucian, like Rabelais and Jonson, achieves the double vision of mock-heroic with exceptional force and precision, building up and cutting down at almost the same

moment. Thus, in the midst of a glowing tribute to Alexander's
'god-like' physical appearance, he remarks that his wig deceived
almost everyone. His stupendous intellectual endowments are
generously praised – 'he had the quality of magnificence, of
forming no petty designs' – and are at once bathetically illustrated by the chewing of soap-wort to simulate manic possession, by the rigging-up of a 'divine' serpent's head out of canvas,
and the construction of a tube made of cranes' wind-pipes so
that messages could be passed through the serpent's mouth from
an adjoining room. Built out of sordid materials, and comically
fallible, the oracle none the less grows in repute. Alexander's
countrymen know that his parents were ordinary people like
themselves, yet they swallow his claims to be descended from
Asclepius and Perseus, and finally celebrate with magnificent
funeral-games the death of 'the god' from a gangrenous foot.
There is no evidence that Jonson 'used' *Alexander* in *The
Alchemist*, but even these instances will suggest that the two works
are similar in their humorous treatment of 'pseudomantic'
imposture. Subtle's transmogrification from a raker of dung-hills
into 'sovereign' and high-priest of alchemy is presented by
Jonson on one level as an absurd joke, but on another level the
pretensions of the character are sustained, like those of
Alexander, by the conviction and panache with which he
pursues his roles and exercises power.

This brings us to a less obvious but ultimately more significant
point of resemblance among the writers discussed, that they
meditate a parallel between themselves and the impostors they
describe. Lucian is explicit in including himself in his biography
of Alexander as one who has tricked the oracle on several
occasions and narrowly escaped being murdered on Alexander's
orders. Theirs was a conflict not only of incompatible philosophies, the mystic and the sceptic, but also of travelling performers
on the same circuit. Though opposites, they were two of a kind.
The one thing they agreed on was hostility to the rival
mystery-cult of the early Christians,[10] and it was that point
which intrigued Erasmus, committed as he was to synthesizing
reason and faith. Recommending *Alexander* as 'an object-lesson
for detecting and refuting the impostures of those who even

to-day pull wool over the eyes of the mob with their hocus-pocus miracles, false relics, bogus pardons, and such-like trickery',[11] he could not fail to be aware that the mystical basis of Christianity had encouraged fraud and superstition and made the rational detection of them harder. That is why the deluded victims in *Exorcism* and *Alchemy* are presented as well-meaning Christians who stumble over the treacherous border between faith and credulity. Rogue-fiction gave Erasmus an effective means of dramatizing their problem. But the dualistic habit of mind which led Christian thinkers to dwell on the proximity of virtues to their corresponding vices also led such as Erasmus, who were capable of ironic self-criticism, to see the close relationship between themselves as 'true' prophets and their 'false' counterparts. Folly, among many other things, is a rogue-variant of Erasmus himself, his 'pseudomantic' counterpart, who, in a pseudo-scholarly oration addressed to deluded devotees, subtly perverts or blandly confounds her author's best attempts to bring faith and reason, discipline and nature, God and the world, into some sort of satisfactory accord.

That Subtle is used in a comparable way must be argued more fully. The first sign of deviousness in Jonson's presentation of this character is the uncertainty the audience is made to feel about his pretensions. In the teeth of deflating ridicule from Face, he persists in advancing high claims for his 'great art', claims which the actor must voice with conviction if the quarrel is not to lose point. Here we can see Jonson's irony at work on both the private and the forensic levels.

His forensic purpose was to needle the uncertainties of every sector of society in his day about alchemy and occult sciences in general. Where the modern disbeliever in magic sees in Subtle a cozening rogue and nothing more, the clients of John Dee and Simon Forman could see a rogue and a magician as well. By researching his topic with extreme thoroughness, and giving Subtle a solid mastery of its terms, Jonson was able to subject his audience to impressive and bewildering rhetoric. 'The monster ignorance', he was to write a year later, 'still covets, to enwrap it selfe in darke and obscure tearmes, and betray that way.'[12] He dramatized that betrayal by making Subtle something of an enigma for credulous spectators, queering the pitch of their laughter with undertones of awe. Not until the end of the play are they fully disabused of the visions they have formed of his off-stage laboratory, and even the explosion could be awesome as well as funny, since the fact that it was a put-up job to stall Mammon is concealed until after the event. So Jonson's refusal to make absolutely clear from the outset that Subtle's 'great art' is nothing more mysterious than the art of cheating shows him again using character in the 'Menippean' manner as a tool in his engagement with the audience. Subtle's evasiveness enacts his author's rhetorical strategy, just as the audience-responses which Jonson anticipates are enacted in such features of the play as the 'changeling' behaviour of the Neighbours and the moral collapses of Surly and Lovewit.

But 'Menippean' writing also, as we know, warranted the exploration of subjective interests. Thus, to take a random example, when Subtle declares

> I should be sorry
> To see my labours, now, e'ene at perfection,
> Got by long watching, and large patience,
> Not prosper, where my love, and zeale hath plac'd 'hem
> (II.iii.10–13)

Jonson echoes his own thought, to 'damne his long-watch'd labours to the fire' rather than waste them on an unworthy public.[13] His private reason for building up Subtle's pretensions was to make him a credibly threatening type of the false artist, one of those 'professors' who, in the words of the preface, 'by simple mocking at [imitating] the tearmes, when they understand not the things, thinke to get off wittily with their Ignorance'. Through Subtle he could hint at contrasts, flattering to himself, between the charlatan's parroting of 'tearmes' and the true poet's knowledge of 'things'; between the art of the alchemist which violates Nature and that of the poet which reveals her as she is; between Subtle's failure and his own success in making something precious out of dross. But the analogies pointed in the play do not always appear so simply to Jonson's advantage. They show him beginning to analyse wryly the relation of the poet to his public.

One place where this can be detected is a playful passage at

the mid-point of the action, where the rogues are taking stock
of their success and planning the next round. 'General' Face
employs a startling comparison in reporting to Dol on the state
of their 'campe':

> As, with the few, that had entrench'd themselves
> Safe, by their discipline, against a world, DOL:
> And laugh'd, within those trenches, and grew fat
> With thinking on the booties, DOL, brought in
> Daily, by their small parties.   (III.iii.34–8)

On the basis of a complex theatrical joke,[14] he envisages his
army as an élite who protect their professional status and grow
smugly rich at the expense of the mob: the word 'discipline'
brings to mind the humanists as well as the Puritans. Earlier,
Subtle and Mammon, in answer to Surly, have associated terms
of alchemy and terms of rhetoric in support of the 'closed shop'
principle, naughtily twisting the maxim *ars est celare artem* into
a defence of obscurantism:

SUBTLE.   And all these, nam'd
>   Intending but one thing: which art our writers
>   Us'd to obscure their art.
MAMMON.   Sir, so I told him,
>   Because the simple idiot should not learne it,
>   And make it vulgar.
SUBTLE.   Was not all the knowledge
>   Of the Egyptians writ in mystick *symboles*?
>   Speake not the *Scriptures*, oft, in *parables*?
>   Are not the choicest *fables* of the *Poets*,
>   That were the fountaines, and first springs of wisedome,
>   Wrapt in perplexed *allegories*?
MAMMON.   I urg'd that,
>   And clear'd to him, that SISIPHUS was damn'd
>   To roule the ceaseless stone, onely, because
>   He would have made ours common.
>   *Dol is seene* (III.iii.34–8)

The appearance at that point of Dol, the 'common' woman
masquerading as a 'rare schollar', completes Jonson's wide
evocation of the humanist debate (in its scientific, scriptural and
poetic facets) on how widely knowledge should be shared. Why
serious artists should traditionally conceal their most precious
truths from the understanding of ordinary men was a question
which the writer of popular comedy could well put to the writer

Ben Jonson

of court masques. Jonson had answered it in the latter capacity
by arguing that only the educated could lay hold on 'remov'd
mysteries'.[15] But placed in the mouths of Subtle and Mammon
the argument showed his awareness of how an élitist conspiracy
between artist and patron flattered both parties and was
especially remunerative to the artist.

Subtle, of course, does make his art vulgar, selling horoscopes,
familiar spirits, quarrelling-lessons and so forth, not to mention
the favours of Dol. The picture of a 'learned doctor' hectoring
and cozening simple-minded dupes, while pretending to sell
them what they want, has alarming implications for the
humanist poet who stoops to please a popular audience. It is
in that sense that Jonson projects through Subtle a parodic
vision of himself as *pseudopoietes*, prostituting the commonwealth,
profiting from pleasing the people while sniggering in his sleeve
at their follies.

Those who read between the lines of *The Alchemist* are
regularly charged with a defective sense of humour, so it is worth
insisting that the spectacle of Jonson standing his ideal of the
poet on its head does not make the play less funny. He was
shrewdly and humorously aware that by giving his audience
what it wanted in Act V he was exactly contradicting his
defence of the end of *Volpone*, that 'the office of a *Comick*-POET'
is 'to imitate justice, and instruct to life'. Though he could
defend the Face–Lovewit *débâcle* as an exercise in oblique
teaching and testing of judgement, one suspects that as well as
seeing something of himself disappear over the wall in the
person of Subtle, he was also conscious of reappearing to
collect the spoils in the person of Lovewit. His sardonic
inspection of moral collapses surely included his own.

The vision of *The Alchemist* depicts an orgy of moral accommodations. Tribulation Wholesome's speech is at its heart:

> Good *Brother*, we must bend unto all meanes,
> That may give furtherance, to the *holy cause*.
>
> Beside, we should give somewhat to mans nature...
>
> We must give, I say,
> Unto the motives, and the stirrers up
> Of humours in the bloud.   (III.i.11–12, 17, 27–9)

Jonson's irony gains depth from his perception that he himself seemed to be doing just that. What he criticizes, of course, is not the sacrifice of means to ends but the misuse of judgement in choosing false ends or perverting good ones. He saw alchemy itself as a symbol of man's tendency to bend holy causes, God's purposes in Nature, to the furtherance of his appetites; and he presents us with a series of comic variations on that pattern, from the nervous little challenges to the moral order of Dapper and Drugger to the monstrous casuistry of Mammon and the Puritans. In the crescendo of moral compromise which marks the last act, one of the loudest notes is Lovewit's ridicule of Surly for not having matched the 'pliancy' of his mistress or compromised his moral role wholeheartedly enough. Vision and rhetoric finally come together when the audience is invited by Lovewit and Face to join their conspiracy to 'straine candor' and 'stretch truth'. And since they ask us to consider their proposal in relation to the 'strict canon' and *decorum*' of comedy, Jonson would seem to have included in his vision a consciousness of having bent the cause of the comic poet's art very close to breaking-point.

3. 'Comiter errare': *Bartholomew Fair* and *The Praise of Folly*

He contrived to bend it further, however, in *Bartholomew Fair*, where he 'gives', it would seem, so much to man's nature as to give away the creed of a lifetime. Not the rogue artist but the moralist without warrant is the play's central image, fixing the author in the target-area 'like a stake in *Finsbury* to be shot at' (V.vi.94). At *The Alchemist's* close one can detect his wry sense of complicity in the on-going swindle and yet feel no weakening of the play's authority as a judgement on greed. But when *Bartholomew Fair* ends in similar conspiracy, the satirist seems to be disarmed. Some have inferred that he was surrendering his right to judge altogether.

Judgement is certainly his dominant concern in the play: the word rings like an alarm-bell in the induction and echoes through all that comes after. As the power of moral discrimination, issuing in action and in censure or praise, it had been the lodestar of Jonson's writing since *Every Man In*, and it would remain, he hoped, when strength of body failed, to be 'last...i'the field / With a true Poet'.[16] He inclined to the authoritarian Catholic belief that independent judgement was a right to be earned, and earned not so much by age or experience as by gradations of learning, of intellectual and moral discipline. The induction asserts this parodically. 'It's come to a fine degree in these *spectacles* when such a youth as you pretend to a judgement', says the Book-holder to the elderly and experienced Stage-keeper, adding: 'And yet hee may, i'the most o'this matter i'faith: For, the *Author* hath writ it just to his *Meridian*, and the *Scale* of the grounded Judgements here, his Play-fellowes in wit.' The Articles of Agreement continue to build on the earned right to judge, offering the spectator his 'free-will of censure' according to the price he has paid for admission, so long as 'his place get not above his wit'. And Jonson's ideal of a constant judgement is obliquely invoked through confusion with the *idées fixes* of the ignorant:

Hee that will sweare, *Jeronimo*, or *Andronicus* are the best playes, yet, shall passe unexcepted at, heere, as a man whose Judgement shewes it is constant, and hath stood still, these five and twentie, or thirtie yeeres. Though it be an *Ignorance*, it is a vertuous and stay'd ignorance; and next to *truth*, a confirm'd errour does well; such a one the *Author* knowes where to finde him.

All this is richly sardonic, and suggests Jonson's lasting commitment to a concept about to be murdered by the rhetoric of his play. Every pretence to judgement will be suspect, from the King's disapproval of tobacco downward. All who profess it will founder; even Grace will resort to a lottery. The moments of triumph enjoyed in the action will belong to characters who are hostile or immune to moral discipline, all rogues or imbeciles or shifting opportunists. In Act IV the madman's refrains will echo Lear's idea that, since no man's judgement is warranted, all by human standards are acquitted. And by the time we perceive that the play's festive ending depends on everyone's acknowledging a share in human frailty, judgement as a standard will have been thoroughly discredited and replaced by a plea for humility and forgiveness.

Comedies of accommodation

Undoubtedly this probing of the censorious mentality results in Jonson's most morally complex play, rightly compared with *Measure for Measure* as a comic parable on the text 'Judge not, that ye be not judged'.[17] It is also his most humanly warming play, satisfying those who can at last see the author mellowing like a pear in the dog-days of 1614. But neither of these factors should obscure its teasing intent, or lead us to forget Jonson's promise in the induction that 'his *Ware* is still the same'. Abdication of judgement, which he had flaunted provocatively in *The Alchemist* as an obvious lapse, is here disguised speciously in the garb of related Christian virtues. *Bartholomew Fair* is a work of Christian humanism in being built on a conflict between Christian and classical values: between Christ's injunction not to judge and the Graeco-Roman cult of *krisis/judicium*. But instead of attempting to synthesize the two, it works by indirection, elevating the former, depressing the latter, and implying (from the chaos that will surely ensue) that a synthesis is needed. Not the least of its resemblances to *The Praise of Folly* lies in the fact that Erasmus had ended with a similar tactic. The more rapturously his speaker extolled the madness of Christian unworldliness, the more strongly the mind-based values of classical *sapientia* were implied as a necessary counterpoise.

Jonson's play is so much a product of his fullest maturity that to argue its debt to another man's work is a delicate task. To show how it recalls *The Praise of Folly*, and is illuminated by it, will be a sufficient objective. But if earlier chapters have been persuasive in arguing that Jonson drew creative stimulus from Erasmian irony, we can expect to find this at its height where the two writers' aims and subjects were most alike.

Each was engaged on a light-hearted but radical reassessment of his life's work, the sort of exercise often prompted by a change of occupation and scene. The idea of *Folly* came to Erasmus while travelling on horseback from Italy to England, and much that is basic in *Bartholomew Fair* can reasonably be attributed to Jonson's sojourn in France in 1612/1613 as tutor to young Walter Ralegh – the theme of challenge to moral authority, most obviously ('He that will correct another, must want fault in himselfe'), but also, surely, the play's fresh perspective on London life and on the author in relation to the whole of his public from King to commoner. In each work an underlying question is the relevance of humanist goals to humanity at large. Erasmus had ruefully measured the gulf between a life spent in annotating texts and more ordinary ways in which people seek happiness. Jonson's play opens with the Stage-keeper musing on the 'absurd courses' of 'Master-*Poets*' out of touch with their world.

As their main technique of reassessment both writers use self-parody. Jonson's well-recognized allusions to himself through Justice Overdo's appropriation of Horace and Cicero show him testing his concerns and allegiances by presenting them ridiculously, as Erasmus had done by making Folly pour scorn on his New Testament annotations. But self-parody of another kind can be traced in Jonson's play by analogy with Erasmus's claim that *Folly* had obliquely restated the teachings of the *Enchiridion* (*The Christian's Handbook*) 'in the guise of a game'. An element in the design of *Bartholomew Fair* is its inversion of Jonson's early comedy, *Cynthia's Revels*. This, we recall, had been Lucianic in its witty handling of myth, and Erasmian in its device of measuring man by the quality of his amusements, but it had not (despite the presence in the cast of Moria and Philautia) shown the least infusion of Erasmian irony, leading instead to the most overtly moral of Jonson's conclusions. Contrasts between the two plays are too sharp to be entirely accidental. The one which most emphasizes the shift to obliquity is between Crites the paragon of judgement and Overdo the deluded justice, with both of whom Jonson allows himself to be associated. But there are structural affinities, too, which suggest that the second play was patterned on the first. Both employ an expository first act after which the scene changes to represent self-contained worlds, at opposite ends of the social spectrum, the court and the Fair. In each the plot-movement is circular more than progressive, with groups of characters drifting on and off in search of amusement, or dialogue passing from one group to another on the full stage. Both employ word-games, at tedious length, to show a growing perversion of rational discourse. And in their last acts the masque and the puppet-play, opposite ends of the dramatic spectrum, hold corresponding positions, the one leading 'up' to Cynthia's judgements and the other 'down' to judgement's ignominious collapse. Where the early play had been careful in its handling of allegory and myth, the same techniques are loosely burlesqued in the *Fair* in a spirit of wild indecorum. Ursula, for instance, the pig-woman whose iconology has so stimulated critics, should probably be seen as inverting the 'chaste and fair' queen of the *Revels*, who had been invoked to keep state in her silver chair with her pearl bow and crystal quiver. Ursula's attributes are her bottle of ale and her pipe. 'Pray thee take thy chaire againe, and keep state', Knockhem bids her. 'Sit i'thy chaire, and give directions, and shine *Ursa Major*.' In the court of the pig-booth influences are reversed, and Cynthia's is represented only by Ursula's bullied attendant, the blighted Mooncalf.

Because *Cynthia's Revels* is generally deplored as a dramatic disaster, one might think that Jonson was making fun of it and his high-flown youthful ideals. But that would be wide of the mark. It is likely, indeed, that he was revising and expanding its text for the 1616 Folio at about the same time as he wrote *Bartholomew Fair*. The self-parodic *lusus* of both Jonson and Erasmus, though bristling with comic self-awareness, by no means denies or belittles the ideals which it turns upsidedown. Rather it was a devious means of asserting them. This is why Jonson may have supposed that he was doing to the *Revels* what Erasmus said he had done to the *Enchiridion*. His two plays are ultimately alike in embattling judgement against folly in a time of licence, with triumphant success in one case and challenging failure in the other. The court and the Fair are complementary in the sense of being sectors of society where the same battles have to be fought. But Jonson looked up at one, and down at the other. Crites's desire to reform the court, and draw a world to virtue after it, reflects the upward and positive thrust of humanist idealism; he shows a lofty faith, appropriate to a courtier, in the human potential for goodness; the task of his judgement is to protect an ideal from the encroachment of man's

Ben Jonson

lower nature. Jonson never lost his capacity to think in such terms. In the *Fair*, however, that lower nature is the object of his scrutiny, his eye cast downward on human limitations, on man as animal. Broaching flesh and blood (as Dame Purecraft would say) 'on the weaker side', he can not only lavish uninhibited energy on the 'creeping sport' of the fairground but can also focus on the problems of the would-be reformer, problems impossible to treat on the masque-like plateau of the *Revels* where banishing of vice was effected symbolically at the rising of the moon.

He almost certainly drew on Erasmus for his particular version of the all-fools vision, and the patterning of his characters probably grew from mature familiarity with Erasmus's design. His vision is clarified and unified if we see that his Fair-people, for all their astuteness, are fools of the first kind that Folly admired, those whose welfare derives from animal vitality, nurtured by instinct and the habitual repression of conscience. Thus Ursula, living off the body's needs, and Knockhem, with his vapours, are planned as antithetic to the examined life of the mind. A more predictable group of Folly's adherents were the simple and easily deluded, those in whom 'a cheerful confusion of the mind frees the spirit from care and at the same time anoints it with many-sided delight'.[18] We are here with the persistently happy fools, with Cokes and to some degree Littlewit. She had also patronized Philautia, that infinite capacity for thinking well of oneself which assists in making life bearable. The teasing distinction between self-respect and deluded complacency is a favourite humanist *topos* which Erasmus exploited, and one to which Jonson subjects his audience in the induction (83–4). Within the play, the knife-edge between them is trodden by Winwife and Grace, whose pride in their superior understanding may be proper at times but in the context of the Fair is apt to seem smug.

Whether Dame Purecraft's frenzied devotion to 'madnesse in truth' alludes to Folly's peroration on the madness of Christian piety is rather too contentious a topic to be debated here, though it is worth noting that Jonson's hatred of Puritan inspirationalism could have made him interpret that passage with less

208

Comedies of accommodation

reverence than Erasmus intended. But a more clear coincidence lies in the treatment both authors accord to the moral censors. Folly claimed kin with her professed opponents on account of their foolish severity and blindness to their own true natures. Her ridicule of the Stoic 'wise man' is recalled many times in Overdo, and also in Busy, since Jonson made a practice of transferring to the Puritans criticism traditionally aimed at the Stoics. The blinkered outlook of these characters results in isolation, that loss of touch with reality which Folly had seen as a consequence of Stoic self-sufficiency. And central in both satires is the metaphor of unmasking. In the passage quoted in Chapter 3, Folly had described how the wise man invades the stage of life and insists on unmasking the actors to reveal their true faces, but in doing so spoils the play, which is the only reality we have. It is a likely guess that that passage was in Jonson's mind as he conceived Overdo's intrusion into the Fair, bent on 'discovering' enormity. It applies more literally to Busy's interruption of the puppet-show, his confusion of the stage with reality, and the undressing of the actors which causes his collapse.

Parallels like these cast light on how Jonson designed his gallery of fools but do little to affect our sense of his meaning. More decisively helpful in interpreting the play is to note that Folly's answer to the wise man was to temporize with frailty:

As nothing is more stupid than wisdom out of season, so nothing is less prudent than prudence out of place – which indeed is the result if one refuses to bend to circumstances [*se accommodare rebus praesentibus*] or to use the ethics of the market-place [*foro uti*], if one forgets even the rule of good-fellowship, 'drink or get out,' and insists on stopping the play [*ut fabula iam non sit fabula*]. But true prudence, since you are mortal, consists in not wanting to be wiser than you may be, in winking gladly at what all men do, or straying along with them sociably [*cum universa hominum multitudine vel connivere libenter, vel comiter errare*].[19]

'This', Folly says, 'is to act the play of life' ('vitae fabulam agere'), and so says *Bartholomew Fair*. Erasmus's 'since you are mortal' ('cum sis mortalis') has the same ironic implications as 'remember you are but *Adam*, Flesh, and Blood', similarly urging recognition of frailty as an excuse for doing nothing about it. But Jonson has complicated his pattern by showing

his 'wise men' as expert 'benders' from the start. They bend
to the Fair just by going, and having got there they drink.
Though we see that their true motives are to satisfy frailty in
themselves – Busy to eat pig, Overdo to play God, Wasp to find
an outlet for mindless wrangling – they claim to be making
necessary allowances for the frailty of others. Busy accommod-
ates 'a naturall disease of women'; Wasp 'must give way' to
his master's 'diseases of youth'; and Overdo's 'thus must we
doe...that wake for the publike good' shows him shouldering
the burden of corrupt officers in an imperfect world. Thus the
theme of accommodating frailty is kept prominently in view.
And when all three have made fools of themselves by asserting
their judgement, variously trying to 'stop the play', they are
brought to a state which looks like Christian humility and
charity but closely corresponds to the ultimate accommodation
counselled by Folly, that wholesale rejection of moral concern
expressed in the rich phrase 'comiter errare'. It is in Folly's sense
that all three agree to 'let the Play goe on'.

Descriptions of the end of *Bartholomew Fair* as genial and
forgiving will be true to almost any imaginable theatrical
experience. So again one must argue that the author has worked
to make us feel something different from what he means us to
think. His insight into audience-responses to comedy is nowhere
more keen or sardonic. He knows that a 'Shakespearean'
conclusion will be popular, that an audience will forget the
induction's sarcasm on the '*Jigges* and *Dances*' of '*Tales*' and
'*Tempests*', and will choose to ignore that the puppets are
'entreated to come in' to indict the same taste which Shakespeare indulged. He knows that, in the theatre, when censorious
idiots such as Busy, Wasp and Overdo are forced to climb down,
few will observe that they climb down further than they need
or should. He is aware, above all, that the image of the author
finally relaxing his judicial irony will delight many more
spectators than will notice the parallel with Overdo's ludicrous
picture of himself, genially relaxing over supper at home like
God after a hard day's judging. It is precisely that sentimental
strain in Overdo, and indeed in the audience as well, which
Quarlous so successfully exploits in his plea for general in-

dulgence. With Overdo's response ('This pleasant conceited Gentleman hath wrought upon my Judgement, and prevail'd'), judgement's white flag is run up once again in surrender to wit, as it had been in Lovewit's promise to be ruled by Face, and in Clement's verdict on Brainworm in the Folio *Every Man In* ('Thou hast done, or assisted to nothing, in my judgement, but deserves to bee pardon'd for the wit o' the offence'). Quarlous, however, the law-school drop-out turned gamester, differs from Brainworm and Face in a manner characteristic of the play. He is not so much a rogue as a pragmatist, wholly addicted to 'the play of life'. It is appropriate that he, as the arch-opportunist of the play, its expert in the ethics of the market, should steer it to its ambivalent close in the accents of Erasmus's Folly.

That there are tricks as well as treats in Jonson's Halloween entertainment has been partly inferred from clues in the text and partly from Erasmus's example. Obviously the play does celebrate the multifarious and unquenchable human energies which it makes us enjoy, and obviously it does this with a zest and vigour which many find difficult to reconcile with irony. When Overdo leads his troop from the stage, vowing in sonorous Latin to think positively in future, it is impossible not to admire, as we have done all along, the self-protective resilience of the human animal, however deluded. But to spot such delusions, and to resist the boisterous comic spirit with a part of our minds, is the challenge which is offered to our judgement. Typically, Jonson ends his inquisition with a test of clearheadedness which directly opposes the emotional pull of his finale. Sharing in the warm glow of reconcilation, the audiences which first saw the play on the Eve or the Feast of All Saints were none the less required to resist the Christian connotations of that final supper and see it for what it was, as a Feast of All Fools, where the puppets were to finish their mindless play and the critical faculty at large was to be drowned in a bowl.

We do not know why Jonson wrote an 'apologie' for *Bartholomew Fair* or what its subject was – only that he wrote it in the form of a dialogue ('By Criticus is understood Done') and prefaced it to his translation of the *Ars Poetica*.[20] We do know, however, that the play was one of those which he thought had

Ben Jonson

been misunderstood. He attached to the printed text an epigraph from Horace to the effect that 'if Democritus were alive now, he would find more to laugh at in the audience than in the play; he would think the author was telling his tale to a deaf ass'. It is possible that Jonson was conscious of extending his play's association with *The Praise of Folly* by writing a counterpart to Erasmus's apology. Certainly, if our reading of the play has been correct, he had courted misinterpretation no less dangerously than Erasmus and in an essentially similar way. One is tempted to guess that Donne's role in the dialogue was that of the adversary, and that in the year of his solemn preparation to take Holy Orders he had charged Jonson with writing irresponsibly. Though that is speculation, we have seen how Jonson made it a condition of using the Lucianic mode that the moral commitment which lay behind his use of it should be clear to understanders. The topic on which he found it necessary to defend himself could well have been whether that condition had been fairly met.

One piece of evidence which points in that direction is the epilogue addressed to the King at the court performance:

> *You know the scope of* Writers, *and what store,*
> *of* leave *is given them, if they take not more,*
> *And turn it into* licence: *you can tell*
> *if we have us'd that* leave *you gave us, well:*
> *Or whether wee to* rage, *or licence* break,
> *or be* prophane, *or make* prophane *men speake?*
> *This is your power to judge.*

Editors gloss this by citing *Ars Poetica*, 51 ('dabitur licentia sumpta pudenter'). But in fact a more pertinent gloss on the epilogue is from the dedication of *Folly*, where Erasmus had used Horatian terms in a sense much closer to Jonson's:

Semper haec ingeniis libertas permissa fuit, ut in communem hominum vitam salibus luderent impune, modo ne licentia exiret in rabiem ['this liberty has always been granted to men of wit, that in their jests they may poke fun at the general manners of men with impunity, so long as their licence does not extend to outrage' (Hudson)].

The two passages are linked by the progression from 'leave' to 'licence' to '[out]rage'. 'Libertas'/'leave' is trust freely given; 'licentia'/'licence' is advantage wrongfully taken, and 'rabies'

/'rage' is the madness or frenzy of the morally irresponsible writing that may result. By 'prophane' Jonson surely meant to refer not merely to blasphemous speech but also, more generally, to the behaviour of the uninitiated, those 'outside the temple' of the humanist beliefs which he claimed to share with the King – those who, in fact, call the tune in his play. And in distinguishing between being profane and making profane men speak – a distinction which seems to correspond to that between rage and licence – he raises the issue of *decorum personae* which Erasmus also had gone on to raise in the same passage, insisting that it was Folly who spoke and not he. At what point does an author become responsible for what he makes his characters say? And can a dramatist writing for the stage be allowed the same freedom as a scholar writing for scholars? From his experience in prison after *Eastward Ho* Jonson knew that *decorum personae* was not an argument to which James attached weight. But the question was particularly acute in *Bartholomew Fair*, where 'profaneness' was a matter not of isolated speeches but of the discrediting of judgement apparently upheld by the play as a whole. Whether it was 'rage' to carry obliquity so far, and whether the moralist in the theatre could afford to dispense with a spokesman, seem to be the concerns of the epilogue which Jonson refers to the judgement of the King, and they may also have been the subject of his apology. We can guess that James approved of the play, because Jonson dedicated it to him. Significantly, however, in his next comedy, unlike the four which preceded it, he was careful to express his own judgement on the action with unequivocal clarity.

4. 'In forum descendere': wise men in the market-place

In *The Alchemist* and *Bartholomew Fair* Jonson rationalized his distrust of the audience into something very close to a theory of comedy. The bending of judgement to accommodate frailty is not only what these plays describe in themselves and induce in the spectator; it is also what their author has come to conclude that comedy essentially is. We must consider what

Ben Jonson

bearing that notion may have had on his thinking about tragedy, and especially on the enigmatic relationship of *Catiline* to *Bartholomew Fair*.

When Folly equates moral compromise with acting the play of life we assume that she is thinking of comedy, but in fact in that passage as a whole she had seen the play as Lucian had described it, as an unpredictable mixture of comedy and tragedy. It is More, not Erasmus, who most clearly anticipates Jonson in identifying comedy with concession to weakness. As we saw in the chapter devoted to him, he and his biographers often used the acting metaphor to describe a departure from principle or belief – to mean speaking someone else's lines or contributing to someone else's design – and when used in that way it was always seen as comic, whatever the consequence might be. Thus the guest called upon to add to a chorus of flattery was 'forced... to play a part to accommodate himself somewhat to the players in this foolish, fond stage play' (see above, p. 75). At the rigged election of Richard III the common folk act a miniature comedy of accommodation in accepting the role designed for them – a nice example of 'connivere libenter' and 'comiter errare' – instead of interfering in the 'kings' games' which they see as potentially tragic (see above, p. 74). Conniving, there, is the comic behaviour appropriate to their position; to have insisted on showing that they saw through the fraud would have taken them out of their depth into tragedy. The essential distinction More drew between tragedy and comedy is partly obscured in that example by the issue of the participants' rank – the appropriateness of tragedy to rulers and of comedy of commoners – but is made clearer in *Utopia* (pp. 71–3 above) where 'More' argues that the philosopher statesman must adapt himself to the comedy in hand and not, like Hythloday, introduce alien elements of tragedy by coming on stage in philosopher's attire reciting from Seneca. In such passages, and especially in the contrast between the flexible 'More' and the unbending Hythloday, we can see how More adumbrated a pattern which proves to be relevant to Jonson. Like Erasmus's heroine, like Quarlous for that matter, 'Morus' is the worldly 'fool' who thrives by making allowances for man's lower nature, by accepting and manipulating things as they are, and his posture is seen to be comic. Tragedy, on the other hand, is associated with Hythloday, the Christian fool who obeys to the letter Christ's command to preach high ideals in defiance of worldly consequences.

Before testing that formula on *Sejanus* and *Catiline* we must first face the question of whether More was a figure of significance for Jonson, comparable to Erasmus. The likelihood that he was is supported by very little evidence. We noted in Chapter 3 that Jonson owned a copy of the biography of More by Thomas Stapleton, but beyond a passage in *Discoveries* (899–906) which lists him among early sixteenth-century wits who were admirable for their times and 'began' English eloquence, and the presence in *The English Grammar* of numerous examples drawn from his *Richard III*, we have no proof that Jonson gave More any serious thought. On the other hand, some allowance may be made for the reluctance to discuss More publicly which was normal in Jonson's day. Sensitivity about him was in fact redoubled in the years which chiefly concern us here, those following the Gunpowder Plot when the requirement of oaths of allegiance from Catholics, and the danger of provoking martyrdoms, were centres of a controversy to which Donne, More's kinsman, contributed his *Pseudo-Martyr* in 1610.

The least doubtful guess is that More's international fame as the greatest of early English humanists, and his use of English in much of his work, stirred Jonson's national pride as Erasmus could not. Only slightly less certain is that the bulwark of English Catholicism mattered to Jonson during his twelve-year adherence to that faith from 1598 to 1610. Though his reasons for becoming and remaining a Catholic are veiled in the same discreet silence, they can plausibly be linked to such permanent features of his thought as his respect for authority, his suspicion of compromise, and his deep distrust of mob-judgement. On all these points More could have spoken to him, especially the last. In the *Dialogue Concerning Heresies*, for example, More argues that if the common people had the right to interpret scripture for themselves then should ye have the more blind the more bold, the more ignorant the more busy, the less wit the more inquisitive, the more fool the more talkative of great doubts and high questions of Holy Scripture and of God's great and secret mysteries, and this, not soberly of any good affection, but presumptuously and irreverently at meat and at meal. And there, when the wine were in and the wit out, would they take upon them with foolish words and blasphemy to handle Holy Scripture in more homely manner than a song of Robin Hood.[21]

It would be hard to find a more succinct anticipation of Jonson's attitude to Puritan ignorance in *Bartholomew Fair*. There is no need to suppose that his consciousness of More would be lessened by his return to the Anglican fold. On the contrary, since he seems to have posed as a partisan Protestant during his visit to France, and even to have engaged in theological controversy,[22] one can fairly imagine that what England had done to her most celebrated scholar would have been cast in his teeth. Quite another facet of More which may be relevant here was the tradition of his interest in the theatre, a point on which Jonson needed all the reassurance he could get from the example of serious scholars. Finally, if we were right in thinking that the personal myth underlying *Bartholomew Fair* was that of the humanist poet measuring his concerns against those of the market-place, it is reasonable to assume that Jonson remembered More's reputation as the scholar with the common touch. Erasmus had compared him to

that Pythagorean philosopher who casually strolls through the market and contemplates the tumult of buying and selling. Though no one is less influenced by the judgement of the mob, no one is less lacking in a sense of human community [*sensus communis*].[23]

Jonson would seem to have measured himself by an ideal very similar to that.

But to locate More's presence more precisely in *Bartholomew Fair* means carrying conjecture further and counting him among the numerous figures alluded to in Overdo. The variety of Overdo's parodic roles is sufficiently astonishing to admit such a possibility. Quite apart from the historical and mytho-logical figures to whom he compares himself, he parodies James in his sermon on tobacco, an unidentified chaplain in his unctuous addresses to Ursula in Act II, and at other times variously Jonson's own portraits of Crites, Horace and Cicero.

Comedies of accommodation

There is some reason for adding More to that list. When Nightingale's song alludes to the story of More and the cutpurse, we are reminded that popular tradition placed him at the head of the line of eccentric magistrates to which Overdo belongs: in the tale of the cutpurse, and doubtless many others, Sheriff More in the antic disguise of 'Morus' had indeed been 'Justice in the habit of a foole' (II.i.9). There is also a nest of possible allusions to More in Overdo's soliloquy in Act III.iii. Looking forward to mirth with his family at supper, he reminds us of More's teasing jokes at the expense of his domestic circle, even to the extent of revealing that his wife's name is Alice. He also begins to employ homely metaphor ('To see what bad events may peepe out o'the taile of good purposes!') in a manner reminiscent of More, and reels off six consecutive proverbs which seem to burlesque a well-known feature of More's English prose. Last, and most interestingly, it is in this speech that Overdo begins to relish the prospect of martyrdom, or at least persecution:

I am resolv'd, come what come can, come beating, come imprisonment, come infamy, come banishment, nay, come the rack, come the hurdle, (welcome all) I will not discover who I am, till my due time.

At several points in *Bartholomew Fair* Jonson deftly reminds us of people who really did suffer for refusing to bend their beliefs – the contemporary harrying of Catholics (II.i.33–5) is recalled as well as the Bartholomew Massacre of Protestants (II.vi.145–51) – and he does not allow us to forget that Smithfield was the burning-ground of heretics (IV.ii.73). Overdo's thirst for suffering here, and later when he 'kisses the stockes' like a 'seminary' (IV.i.37–8), ludicrously negates those subtle passages in More's *Dialogue of Comfort* where Anthony explains why tribulation can be welcome but must not be sought.[24] Towards the end of the *Dialogue*, in a celebrated speech, Anthony envisaged being led to execution 'through the broad high street of a great long city', and described the comfort he would take from the approbation of 'wise and worshipful folk', while disregarding the abuse of 'ragged beggars and madmen'.[25] That passage, too, Jonson seems to have turned upsidedown. When Overdo, led to the stocks, observes that 'it

217

is a comfort to a good conscience, to be follow'd with a good fame, in his sufferings', he mistakes the approbation of the ragged madman Troubleall for that of 'a sober and discreet person' (IV.i.27–9).

If parodic allusions to More are present in Overdo, they illustrate again Jonson's practice of hinting at figures who have contributed to his imaginative design. It does seem likely that the design of *Bartholomew Fair* owed something to More's example. As a humanist scholar who had applied his wisdom in the public arena and preserved the *sensus communis*, who had championed the stage and forecast the threat of Puritan ignorance, who had counselled flexibility of judgement and died for a principle – in all these respects he has a relevance to the play and to Jonson's concerns in it which is probably not accidental.

But the main point of these conjectures is to serve as a basis for pursuing the parallel between More and Jonson in their thinking on comedy and tragedy. If we grant that Jonson came to share the ironic view of comedy as essentially a concession to weakness, the question is whether the converse is also true: that maintenance of principle, refusal to concede, was essential to his view of tragedy. In terms of rhetorical approach it obviously was. Whatever he meant to say in *Sejanus* and *Catiline*, everyone agrees that he said it in a relentless and uncompromising manner, giving no quarter to popular taste and appealing absolutely to the 'trying faculty' of a well-informed judgement.[26] But by analogy with the comedies one would expect his rhetoric to be mirrored in the tragic action. This is true of *Sejanus*, where tragedy in the Morean sense can be found in the fearless and constant maintenance of principle by the virtuous characters. They are tragic because they suffer for their beliefs, if not by dying then by having to live where their virtue can achieve no outlet. Jonson looks 'up' at the plight of these characters with the admiration proper to tragedy, while the devious behaviour of his fortune-hunting Machiavels is presented as a sinister but fundamentally comic spectacle of error, the object of a 'downward' vision which is not of course concessive but satiric. In *Catiline*, however, both his vision and his rhetoric are a good deal more complex. Again we are pointed strenuously upward to admire the heroism of a man of conscience, but this time the hero is by no means a martyr to principle. Cicero achieves political success, and does so through the methods of 'More' not of Hythloday. The topic which More had debated – whether the wise man can be politically effective without ceasing to be wise – also turns out to be Jonson's, whose doubts on the matter are not quite resolved by Cicero's triumph.

A reminder of this topic's continuing centrality in Jonson's day is the prominence given it by Bacon near the start of *The Advancement of Learning* (1605). Denying that statesmanship is a merely empirical skill, Bacon argues that the advantages of 'learning' in a statesman outweigh their opposites:

for although men bred in learning are perhaps to seek in points of convenience and accommodating for the present, which the Italians call *Ragioni di stato*...yet on the other side, to recompense that, they are perfect in those same plain grounds of religion, justice, honour, and moral virtue, which if they be well and watchfully pursued, there will be seldom use of those other, no more than of physic in a sound or well dieted body.[27]

Jonson might seem to reinforce that conclusion by choosing as his subject the deliverance of Rome by its most famous orator and moral philosopher. Certainly, to the extent that he attributes Cicero's success to the eloquent expression of moral convictions, Jonson does use the story to assert his long-cherished ideal of the value of the 'poet' in society, 'indirectly glorifying his own art', as J. B. Bamborough puts it.[28] But *Catiline* is not simply a masque-like presentation of vice put to rout by the combination of virtue and eloquence. It is a play which deals squarely with political realities. So far from resembling Bacon's wise man who has no need of *ragioni di stato*, Cicero is shown as one who conscientiously attempts to employ them.

Complementing his triptych analysis of the Machiavellian threat in *Sejanus*, Jonson's focus in *Catiline* is not on the conspiracy but on three different ways of coping with its threat. Cicero obtains evidence for exposing the conspiracy by playing his adversaries' game, exploiting (as Catiline also does) the greed and ambition of worthless tools. His conscious use of politic means to achieve a good end represents the 'middle' response to the threat, the response which is approved in the play and had been sanctioned by 'More'. He is flanked on his right by Cato, the archetypal Hythloday of antiquity who shuns base tactics and half-measures, and on his left by the cynical trimmers, Caesar and Crassus, who are deeper Machiavels than Catiline and thus themselves constitute a more serious long-term threat to the republic. The pattern culminates (IV.523–37) in Cicero's rejection of Cato's advice to expose the complicity of Caesar and Crassus in the plot. This rejection, as Robert Ornstein has noted, is specifically worded in terms of Machiavelli's argument that rulers must temporize with evils which they lack the power to destroy.[29] It is an argument more completely amoral than the nearest approach to it made by 'More', who had merely told Hythloday that the philosopher in politics must handle opposition tactfully ('what you cannot turn to good you must make as little bad as you can'). Cicero's 'leftward' and 'downward' movement at this point to a position associated with Machiavelli appears to be a significant part of Jonson's patterning. It is from that point onward that some doubt is cast on Cicero's political wisdom, as the consul continues to protect Caesar and Crassus through Act V in spite of growing evidence of their guilt.

Perhaps the most necessary thing to see in *Catiline* is that the ultimate reservations which Jonson means us to share with him about Cicero as a political hero are what might be called the 'valid residue' of more obvious reservations which he makes us feel from the start and then means us to overcome. To sort out the ratio of hero and fool in Cicero is in fact the chief test of understanding proposed by the play, which fails as drama because the test is so exclusively cerebral. Unlike the comedies, *Catiline* offers few compensating attractions – little, indeed, but continuous boredom – to those who do not notice or relish its political critique.

Most readers find it hard to admire Cicero as much as the play keeps telling them they should, and conclude themselves hopelessly out of sympathy with the author. To give Jonson his due, however, we should see that he has carefully planted the evidence on which our negative reactions are based, and planted it in accordance with criticisms of Cicero common in his age. We must also remember that Jonson's contemporaries knew Cicero more intimately than any other ancient writer. Those who had been reared on his speeches and letters were forewarned of the obsessive vanity and touchiness so amply displayed in the tragedy, especially with regard to his social rank and the achievement of his consular year. His reputation as orator and sage had been, from his own time onward, of the perilous kind which invites attention to the warts of the man.[30] That he was physically a coward, bullied by his wife, paranoid in imagining dangers, are examples of traditional gibes which in Jonson's day 'every schoolboy knew' and which Jonson takes pains to build into his text. Moreover, in a period which strongly reacted against Cicero's style, it was easy to accuse him of empty rhetoric and to find in him (as Montaigne provocatively did) 'for the most part...nothing but wind and ostentation'.[31] Such charges are laid against him in the play mainly through the jeers of his enemies, but not only so: his brother Quintus, for example, is one of those who suggests that he talks instead of acting and fabricates bogeys, while his own speech of flattery on Fulvia (III.341-55) is an instance of overblown rhetoric which ludicrously exceeds the demands of the occasion. Jonson's aim in alluding to such unheroic traits was not just historical accuracy, and certainly not the provision of a rounded portrait, but was a straightforward challenge to the audience. The deflationary elements are there to be resisted. Just as Cicero rises above his flesh-and-blood weaknesses, so the audience must overcome its petty inclination to mock or be bored by a self-satisfied windbag and judge him by the fact of his achievement. Here we see Jonson's tragic rhetoric running quite counter to that of his comedy. Frailty is subsumed and rendered insignificant by the triumph of a man's better self.

That is the side of *Catiline* which most clearly supports the contention that Jonson thought of tragedy as an assertion of absolutes. Cicero's defeat of the conspiracy is presented as an absolute good, a model of moral and political heroism, from which nothing must be allowed to detract: even Caesar and

Crassus, with apparent sincerity, join in the chorus of praise (V.309–18). The play ends, however, as Bryant first showed,[32] on a much more ambivalent note, by hinting at the consequences, outside the play, of Cicero's subsidiary actions. The heavy stress which is laid on his protection of Caesar and Crassus points forward to the triumvirate and so to the destruction of the republic under Caesar's dictatorship, while the final debate on what to do with the conspirators similarly points forward to Cicero's own future. Swayed by Cato's emotional speech, he orders the death-penalty in violation of the law and against the advice of Caesar, who ominously warns that he will 'repent / This rashnesse' (V.579–80). This is to remind us not only that Cicero will be banished for his illegal act but also of one of the best-known aspects of his life-story: the ignominious futility of his later political career. So the point of the forebodings in Act V is perhaps not so much, as Bryant would have it, to predict the tragedy of the Roman state as to imply a more critical perspective on the hero's statesmanship.

In the last scenes of the play we again find Jonson planting evidence, though this time not obvious baits to be resisted but difficult clues to pick up. They are difficult because the tide is now flowing so strongly in Cicero's favour that everything he does seems right, yet any spectator with a cool head and a basic knowledge of history should detect them without trouble. The two faults for which Cicero the politician was notorious – vacillation and time-serving – are suddenly laid bare. Coolly considered, his moderating role in the final debate, his total and repeated deference to the wishes of the senate, clearly appears as an abdication of his earlier leadership and as an instance of the 'irresolute' behaviour which Bacon said the educated statesman could learn to avoid from Cicero's example.[33] More crucially, when he bends his judgement both to Caesar's influence and to Cato's emotional rhetoric in a single breath ('Caesar, be safe. Leade on: / Where are the publike executioners?') – simultaneously suppressing the evidence of crime and breaking the law of the land – his capacity for expedient compromise, earlier upheld as responsible, blatantly approximates to the 'timorous time-pleasing' for which history condemned him.[34]

Comedies of accommodation

In the *De Officiis*, a philosophical work well known to the Renaissance, Cicero dealt with the problem of moral accommodation and reached, as J. P. V. D. Balsdon puts it, the 'astonishing and convenient conclusion...that the good man might pursue the right (*honestum*) and the expedient (*utile*) indifferently because, in the end, they were the same'.[35] An impression of just such complacent naïveté is what Jonson's character gives at the end of the play, showing no awareness of the precipitous path he is treading and none of the political realism with which his handling of the conspiracy could be credited. Thus Jonson leaves us with an unresolved counterpoint which demands a detached response. The wise man, hailed as saviour of the state, appears none the less as a fool in the political market-place, dangerous as well as vulnerable. His positive achievement, the subject of the play, is not undermined but is finally distanced. By invoking the larger perspective of history, Jonson suggests a conclusion more moral than Machiavelli's and similar to the conclusion we infer from the dialogue between 'More' and Hythloday, that temporizing with evil is short-term wisdom but is apt to prove long-term folly.

Catiline, then, continues to exemplify the theory of tragedy as an assertion of moral absolutes, openly through its praise of Cicero's success and covertly through its hints of his failures. It does this, however, while testing the black-and-white code of political morality which *Sejanus* had assumed. Eight years earlier, Jonson's central figure would not have been the wise man who risked a descent into the forum but the absolutist Cato who spurned it. In the meantime his interests had changed. According to Bacon, the statesman who looks into the errors of Cato 'will never be one of the *Antipodes*, to tread opposite to the present world'.[36] Jonson's concern was with treading between 'the present world' and the world of ideals. Hard as it is to explain how he thought that *Catiline* could be effective in the theatre, the puzzle of why he wrote such a play between *The Alchemist* and *Bartholomew Fair* is to a great degree solved when we note how all three grew out of his absorption with issues of compromise.

It also becomes clear that the parody of *Catiline* which has long been recognized in *Bartholomew Fair* ought not to be seen,

Ben Jonson

as it usually is, as a sudden act of penance and self-ridicule on Jonson's part.[37] As with his parody of *Cynthia's Revels*, his aim was by no means to recant an ideal but rather to restate it *sub specie lusus*, showing what a shambles human folly can make of it, and applauding its collapse with the ironic indulgence appropriate to comedy. In Cicero, however, much more than in Crites, the possibility of ridicule and censure had already been admitted; *Catiline*, as well as *Bartholomew Fair*, was built on Jonson's critical self-awareness. His ambivalence with regard to his public pretensions is reflected in both, and seemingly resolved in opposite directions by his tragic and comic rhetoric. Like Jonson himself, and also like More (whose shade, we have guessed, informs the whole myth), Cicero and Overdo are scholars with a high reputation for judgement in more dignified spheres who descend into the market-place to apply it. The latter's 'speciall day for the detection of...enormities' plainly recalls the great year of Cicero, whose willingness to touch pitch in detecting the conspiracy is paralleled by Overdo's venture to the Fair. What Jonson does in Overdo is to throw wide open for comic derision the same doors which in Cicero had been teasingly indicated and then sternly blocked in the interest of tragic admiration. Faults in the consul which are meant to be discounted are magnified *ad absurdum* in the Justice of Peace. The most obvious of these are self-satisfaction and rhetorical self-intoxication, but we can also see how Overdo's mistaken judgement of Edgeworth repeats the mistake which Cicero seems, during 200 lines, to make about Fulvia. The suspicion that Cicero goes in fear of assault becomes fact in his English disciple, as also does that graver suspicion, voiced by Crassus and Quintus, that the consul has a habit of exaggerating opposition to boost his vanity. But comedy, while it releases the delight in deflation which tragedy suppresses, correspondingly prevents us from recognizing the virtue which tragedy insists on. The idiocy of Overdo blinds us to the fact that he prizes the same values of 'care', 'industrie', and 'vigilance' which Cicero proposes for himself as magistrate (III.32–3). It is as difficult to suppose that Jonson allows any respect for Overdo as to see that in the last act of *Catiline* he criticizes Cicero. Our 'affections' are so swayed by the opposite rhetorics of comedy and tragedy that the virtue of the one and the folly of the other are almost wholly obscured.

But ultimately, as we have seen, Jonson means us to stand against the tide of his rhetoric and especially to note that his final judgement on his two wise men is essentially the same. Neither Cicero, as he moves round the stage dispatching the conspirators to their deaths, nor Overdo, as he ranges the 'weedes of enormitie' before him in a row, guesses that his moment of glory is soon to turn sour – a reversal, again, which the comedy shows and the tragedy can only imply. Both become fools, in the absolute sense, by surrendering their independent judgement and straying along with the herd. Cicero's collapse is disguised as statesmanship and Overdo's as Christian charity, but each, as the willing victim of a Caesar or a Quarlous, stands finally revealed as a convert to the time-serving ethics of the market. To the degree that their descent into the forum is a metaphor for their author's involvement with the public stage, they show Jonson fixed in his distrust of the medium to which his needs and his instincts drew him, paradoxically lavishing his art as a dramatist on the comedy of his own accommodation. 'Tragicomedy', perhaps, would describe his feelings better. Though the treatment of moral compromise by More and Erasmus helped him to the achievement of the plays we have discussed, his attitude to the subject was not the same as theirs. He saw human frailty with none of More's compassion and little of Erasmus's intellectual detachment. He was irked by imperfection always, and by nobody's more than his own. That relentless, nagging indignation – however it may be felt to have limited his wisdom – added to the intentness and urgency of his art as a moral inquisitor.

CHAPTER 10

After the Fair: conclusions

When Jonson rejects the oblique mode of teaching in the fourth act of *The Devil is an Ass* (1616), he makes capital out of the event as a dramatic surprise. The play has promised to be an expression of his irony at its most sardonic, opening with Satan's kataskopic observation of how modern man, emancipated from traditional theology, finds his own ways of riding post-haste to hell, faster than old-fashioned Vices could fetch him. There have also been signs that Jonson's irony of vision was being matched, as before, by his rhetoric. Wittipol and Mrs Fitzdottrel have whetted the audience's erotic expectations more blatantly than Volpone and Celia, because in this case the lady with the unworthy husband has encouraged her admirer's Ovidian wooing and even allowed him to 'playe with her paps', while Manly, his friend, has been similarly complaisant in lending his chamber for their assignation. Jonson appears to be repeating the strategy of his previous comedies, this time by teasing us into accepting adultery. But the dangerous ambivalence of these three characters is suddenly resolved (IV.vi) on the side of virtue. Wittipol decides to be the lady's 'true friend' instead of her 'servant', and is not mocked for losing an opportunity as Surly had been mocked by Lovewit. The lady herself professes to have encouraged him only with a view to putting his talents 'to a right use'. And Manly, coming forward to strengthen their good resolutions, reveals that he has been anxiously watching their conduct from the start, much as Wittipol has shown a corresponding concern to cure Manly's addiction to Lady Tailbush (IV.iv.3–4). From this point in the play onward – for the first time in comedy since *Poetaster* fifteen years earlier – Jonson's audience is clearly told whom it can trust.

In this development one is bound to see the author backing

out from the *impasse* of misunderstanding arrived at in *Bartholomew Fair*. As though scornfully acknowledging that his devious
rhetoric had placed too much strain on his public, he concludes
by making Manly clarify issues which a Quarlous or a Face
would have obscured. 'Sir, you belie her. She is chaste, and
vertuous, / And we are honest' spells out a judgement hard to
misconstrue, and Manly goes on, in stern monosyllables, to issue
a statement which would answer any charge that *Bartholomew
Fair* had been soft on human weakness:

> It is not manly to take joy, or pride
> In humane errours (wee doe all ill things,
> They doe 'hem worst that love 'hem, and dwell there,
> Till the plague comes) The few that have the seeds
> Of goodnesse left, will sooner make their way
> To a true life, by shame, then punishment.

But this return to overt, exemplary teaching was not prompted
solely by the public's failure to apprehend irony. Both *The Devil
is an Ass* and the much later *The Staple of News* (1626) show
Jonson latching on to specific contemporary abuses to protest
against the spirit of the times. Though he retains a firm grip
on many of his old techniques of confrontation, daring his
audience to inspect its world in the light of Morality values,
urgency and impatience appear to be driving him to ram his
points home more strongly. Protest, involving impotent anger
over a world that was running away from him, probably
explains why even the earlier and better of these comedies, when
judged by his own high standards, does show some loss of
control. Jonson's insight is shrewd into the dire implications of
capitalist free-enterprise represented by Meercraft, but he views
them with alarm from a horrified distance and does not handle
them as coolly as the errors of alchemy or the abuses of wit and
judgement in earlier plays. The result is that Meercraft is
portrayed less subtly than those other rogues whom Jonson drew
as intimate perversions of himself and his cherished ideals.

A well-controlled personal involvement in his creations was
a secret of his comedy at its best. *Volpone* and *Epicoene*, *The
Alchemist* and *Bartholomew Fair* are not his best comedies just
because they are his most ironic, but because their irony was

made possible by absolute control of the tensions and excitements which he experienced in writing them. As a 'straight' moralist Jonson always wrote with conviction, and rarely wrote less than well, but he found it too easy to preach, and when he did so in drama, late as well as early, he was apt to 'spoil the play', like Folly's 'wise man'. Thus the effect of the moralizing passages in *The Devil is an Ass* is not to resolve the drama satisfactorily but to short-circuit the currents of excitement which its best moments make us feel. Since Jonson must have known that he had written most successfully in the indirect mode, his difficulty in restraining his moral fervour could be a reason who he wrote no comedy between 1616 and 1626. During that period he found masque-writing more congenial. The conventions of this form, which he himself had done much to establish, allowed moral fervour while at the same time imposing a degree of control. Within the fixed framework of antimasque and masque, and by turning the former into something like comedy, Jonson built up and exploited quite openly the same tensions and oppositions which underlay the ironic comedies: between 'low' actuality and 'high' ideals, coarseness and delicacy, energy and order, wit and judgement, sense and understanding. Convention demanded that the poles should be kept apart, but Jonson did his best to ensure that understanders would bring them together. And though deviousness of approach to a masque-audience was normally unthinkable, it is noteworthy that in the exceptional circumstances of *The Gypsies Metamorphosed* – a private holiday entertainment for the royal circle, which as Orgel says is 'all antimasque'[1] – he achieved his most daring triumph in the art of teasing the Crown.

His last comedies – *The New Inn* (1629) and *The Magnetic Lady* (1632) – show recovery of control but at the cost of creative excitement. They are well-made and relatively gentle fables in which the poet, now crippled and confined to his room, retrospectively analyses and demonstrates his old comic methods. The first point which concerns us is that analysis of the comic poet's role, presented in both plays through the familiar technique of composite portraiture. In *The New Inn* the char-

acters of Lovel and the Host complement each other by representing opposite extremes in Jonson's comic outlook. The latter
is the pragmatic crowd-pleaser whose income depends on
satisfying his customers (I.i.20–4). He is also the Democritan
observer of men and manners, with 'a seat, to sit at ease here,
i' mine Inne, / To see the *Comedy*' (I.iii.132–3) – the sort of
fun-loving, critical, but uncommitted Lucianist whom Pope was
to recognize in one side of Swift, laughing and shaking in
Rabelais's easy chair. But the irresponsibility engrained in the
Host's genial and attractive philosophy is exposed by the
qualities in Lovel which he laughs at: commitment to moral and
artistic ideals and willingness to impart them. Since the Inn is
a metaphor for the comic stage, Lovel's highmindedness is seen
in that context to tremble precariously on the edge of absurdity
and to be constantly subject to disappointment; but it is not in
the last resort mocked. A comparable balance is maintained
between Compass and his brother Ironside in *The Magnetic Lady*,
where the focus is less on the comic poet's outlook than on the
means by which he tries to be effective. Ironside – the Asper or
Hythloday in Jonson – speaks his mind freely, denounces folly,
draws his sword and upsets the company, whereas Compass fits
himself to company and reconciles humours, 'More'-like, by
tactful management. We are told, however, that the happy
final outcome could not have been achieved without Ironside's
blunt intervention; his righteous anger is short-term folly which
turns out to be long-term wisdom. His motive for intervening,
moreover, is wholly disinterested. Compass, on the other hand,
who has claimed, like Quarlous, to be acting 'for the sport: /
For nothing else' (I.ii.51–2), is finally seen, again like Quarlous,
to have manoeuvred the action to win himself a wife and a
comfortable fortune. Both diptychs work out at length, in a
leisurely and almost programmatic fashion, the same consider-
ations about the role of the moralist in the theatre which, as
we saw, gave subliminal force to *The Alchemist* and *Bartholomew
Fair*.

The other point of relevance in the last two comedies is
rhetorical method. *The Magnetic Lady* harks back to *Every Man
Out* by educating the audience to the author's purposes through

the use of *entr'acte* commentators, a procedure the opposite of teasing rhetoric. Yet it is here that Jonson comes closest to acknowledging that temptation to misinterpret was a part of his strategy in writing. He tells us that

a good *Play*, is like a skeene of silke: which, if you take by the right end, you may wind off, at pleasure...But if you light on the wrong end, you will pull all into a knot, or elfe-lock (Induction, 136–40).

– from which we could infer that a not-so-good play will be one where such a choice is not offered. Between the acts of *The Staple of News* Jonson had demonstrated spectators grasping the wrong end of the skein. In *The New Inn*, however, there are no choric intermeans and no critical demonstrations, because here for the last time Jonson is putting the oblique mode into practice, reviving in particular the devious techniques of his earlier 'festive' comedies. Like the Fair, the Inn is a vacation-centre, a *diversorium*, this time attracting the circle of the court, for which the play itself was meant, though it notoriously failed to survive its first public performance. Like *Epicoene*, it is *lusus* the subject of which is *lusus*: the audience is to recognize its modish diversions in the sports and pastimes practised in the Inn and to test them against implied standards of more civilized amusement. Here again Jonson provocatively offers long scenes of mindless below-stairs buffoonery which the audience is dared to enjoy along with Sir Glorious Tipto, but his main challenge lay in the Court of Love scenes at the centre of the play. Lady Frampul institutes these as a sophisticated game in the spirit of her religion of love, a blend of neo-Platonism and *amour courtois* then popular at the court of Charles and Henrietta Maria. Lovel aims to raise the tone of these occasions by restoring the *festivitas* of humanist debates such as the *convivia* of Erasmus or Castiglione. In the first, defining love, he invokes the authentic neo-Platonism of Ficino's commentary on Plato's *Symposium*, leading the amorous courtier Beaufort to reject 'these *philosophical* feasts' in favour of an Ovidian 'banquet o' sense' (III.ii.125–6). In the second he defines valour, not in the swashbuckling and honour-fixated terms of the Cavaliers, but in the internal sense proposed by Seneca's moral essays. Absurdly as Lovel's speeches are at odds with the deflating context in which they are given, the courtly audience is expected to admit their essential validity, and so to acknowledge how it has debased the ideals of an earlier and better age. While some doubt attaches to exactly what Jonson thought he was doing in his last two scenes, with their grotesque revelations of mistaken identity, on the whole it seems best to regard them as a final mirror-image of his audience's diversions, its tastes in comedy itself. As with the puppet-show at the Hope, Jonson's tactic is to end by giving his public what it wants with apparent equanimity, hoping that understanders will detect the flavour of a conscious concession to frailty.[2]

Though carefully built and meticulously furnished, *The New Inn* was bound to collapse. Isolated and sick, the poet had lost touch with his audience and so lost the first essential of successful *lusus*, the power of delighting which compels engagement in his game. To judge by Owen Feltham's account of the play's reception,[3] the 'nominal' jesting of Tipto and his crew merely provoked disgust; no one can have seen or cared that it was offered in the same spirit as Mosca's entertainment or the brawling of the knights in *Epicoene* or the vapours-game at the Fair. The plot was scorned as 'unlikely', and Lovel's discourses, so far from being recognized as criticism of the present, were simply condemned as old-fashioned ('as might have serv'd of old / For Schools'). Jonson's contempt for the audience which had refused the compliment he paid it of testing its intelligence issued in a famous piece of humanist invective. But the tone of the 'Ode to Himselfe' has no parallel in More or Erasmus. Its 'just indignation' was that of a foiled idealist, one who shared Lovel's yearning for perfection and his capacity to express it in fine lyric verse, but could never reconcile it with the fact of human weakness, as his more philosophic predecessors could. 'Quid laedit', Folly asks, 'si totus populus in te sibilet, modo tute tibi plaudas?' ('Why should the cat-calls of the world upset you, if you can be happy applauding yourself?').[4] That thrust of Erasmus's dispassionate mind transfixes Jonson's anger and arrogance. He had complained that in *Bartholomew Fair* he was telling his tale to a deaf ass. Now again he was upset that *The New Inn*'s spectators 'never made piece of their prospect the right way'.[5] He could not perceive, or would not admit, that misunderstanding had resulted inevitably from his offer of a game on very private terms to an audience which had forgotten the rules. Erasmus, we recall, had made a similar mistake in *Ciceronianus*, where readers promptly recognized the Lucianic game but were reluctant to play it.[6] Also written late in life, it was another example of what happens to the art of teasing when an author's wit loses its flexibility and stiffens into an instrument of his vanity and dogma. But that Jonson should have sought to revive the art, as he fought his battles over again in his bedridden years, is not at all surprising. By doing so he showed his lasting respect for the mode of his most brilliant plays.

Before he died, the future of the mode in a less easily mistakeable form would be forecast by the appearance of the first of Milton's great tempters:

> I under fair pretence of friendly ends,
> And well plac't words of glozing courtesie
> Baited with reasons not unplausible
> Wind me into the easie-hearted man,
> And hugg him into snares.[7]

Even Milton's God, not many years later, would 'try' the judgement of new-created man with a little light-hearted teasing.[8] Our assumption that Jonson himself played that part is not, we must remember, warranted by any of his numerous statements on comedy. Since he never quite admitted to thrusting the wrong end of the skein on his public, the argument that he did stands or falls by our view of his practice. To accept it, however, does not isolate Jonson but links him with many other writers in our literature, from Chaucer onward, who variously assumed the tempter's role and rarely saw fit, as Erasmus did, to justify their practice in theory. In the relationship of Jonson to Erasmus and More, and of all three to Lucian, we have singled out a branch of a much wider literary growth. With one set of roots in the Christian concept of training the spirit to withstand the flesh, and another in the Greek educational practice of training the reason to resist false logic and emotive rhetoric, what we have called the art of teasing – and what Stanley E. Fish called the art of 'intanglement' –

was a natural extension of literary didacticism, from teaching by example to teaching through involvement. When Erasmus wrote that children could learn about folly better from his *Colloquies* than from 'experience, which trains up fools', or Sidney claimed that we gain from comedy 'as it were an experience' of 'the filthiness of evil', they distinguished literary from actual experience not only on the score that its conflicts were exemplary in outcome but also on the assumption that the writer projects life's battles, with pointed significance, into the mind and soul of the reader.

Most of the writers who used devious rhetoric to achieve that end did so when writing for a 'fit' audience, or at least when writing in literary kinds which encouraged meditation and reflection; so too did Jonson to the extent that he published his comedies to be examined and weighed in print by understanders. But the theatre as an arena of temptation was a case apart. It offered unique advantages, which religious drama had made use of from the start, in the direct confrontation of actor and audience and in the sensual immediacy with which all kinds of bait and dangerous doctrine could be pitted against standards of orthodox morality. On that basis Marlowe created an influential rhetoric of tragedy, but it was in comedy, with its traditional stress on man's lower nature, that the advantages could best be exploited. There, the old Christian view of wrongdoing as a laughably foolish rejection of God's will interacted in the Renaissance with Aristotle's prescription that comedy should deal with men worse than the average. The playwright could feel justified in extending his comic world to embrace the spectators by playing on their corresponding imperfections. Such irony became something of a norm in Jacobean comedy, where morally dubious endings are often held up for applause, but it was not always practised in a hostile or critical spirit. More commonly, then as now, the audience was implicated through a species of flattery, invited by the author with a leer or a wink to show that it could share his sophisticated knowingness about the way of the world. Jonson's practice was unique, and in line with the *lusus* of Erasmus and More, in being based at every turn on his belief in the moral responsibility of the writer; it was not only his contemptuous

Ben Jonson

distance from spectators but also his sense of obligation to teach them which led him to calculate his rhetorical approaches so intently. Thus the writer of some of the funniest comedies of his time could yet honestly endorse the theorist's view that 'moving of laughter' was an insufficient end in itself. But the same moral consciousness made him increasingly aware of how easily his ends could be thwarted. His victims might decline to notice his probing, might laugh regardless and refuse to be shamed. In *Volpone* and *Epicoene* he discounted that danger, harrying his audiences with the vindictiveness that Drummond was to find in his character. In *The Alchemist*, however, and much more in *Bartholomew Fair*, he showed (as Drummond was also to observe) that he could turn his vindictiveness on himself.[9] His pretensions as artist and as public censor, though by no means denied, are subjected to scrutiny. Did not the very success of his comedies seem to prove that he had pandered to the ignorance he meant to examine? If these plays and *Catiline* are united by his obsession with the accommodations forced on the poet in the market-place, they may have owed something to the insights of More on the 'comedy' of compromise and the 'tragedy' of holding to principle. And if *Bartholomew Fair* is his most complex statement, this could be because it reflects the comprehensiveness of Erasmus's concept of folly. But Jonson achieved his finest complexity at the cost of misleading his public. His inquisition had become too subtle and too subjective to achieve its didactic aims. Thereafter, except in a single late play, he abandoned obliquity and resorted to teaching by example.

Whether this study has overstated the case for associating Jonson with Erasmus and More is now open to debate. Clearly it is only within strict limits that the link between them can hold; it threatens to dissolve as soon as one considers the nature of the men themselves. Jonson, 'passionately kynde and angry', differed *toto caelo* from the solitary and cool Erasmus, still more from the man whom Roper perceived 'never...as much as once in a fume'. To compare them for quality of mind or spirit is equally fruitless. Such a comparison, like the famous one with Shakespeare, mainly serves in the end to remind us of Dryden's remark that Jonson was great by managing his strength, by forcing us through sheer power of art and conviction to accept his terms and forget how constricting they are. Some points of contact can be found in their humour, particularly in their enjoyment of farce and 'erudite joking', and we have found more coincidence than might have been expected in their ironic vision. But there, too, the divergences are obvious. The ultimate object of Christian irony is the wrong choice of road made by man when faced with the signpost clearly marked Heaven and Hell. More lays his stress on the blindness which keeps man from reading the sign, the weakness which robs him of his sense of direction. The Erasmian vision focusses most memorably on the comforts we administer to ourselves and each other as we set out serenely on the broad downward path. Jonson, harshest and most sardonic of the three, typically sees man as wilfully perverse, embarking on a 'bold adventure for hell', eager to find a short route to his goal and arrive there sooner than expected.

The essential link proposed here is narrower and relates to the motives and methods of their irony, not to its substance. Near the start we noted how Lucian, by spicing the philosophical dialogue with comic appeal, claimed to have found a way of disseminating culture to a wider public, continually (through his use of the 'Menippean' method) requiring emotional response to be controlled by the detached intelligence. The revival of his practice by Erasmus and More through their fictional *lusus*, addressed to the growing circle of readers of Latin, was extended by Jonson with characteristic boldness to embrace the whole range of his English audience. Infusing his doctrine into farcical comedy, he exploited his distrust of the Delilahs of the stage by exaggerating their appeal (not unlike his namesake, Ionesco, in this) and by challenging his public to resist them, much as Erasmus had required his readers to resist the 'imposture' of fiction. Jonson sought to validate the theatre by making it a proving-ground of virtue, a testing-place of judgement, worthy of the belief in the function of literature which he shared with other humanists, after him as well as before. 'That which purifies us is trial.' In Milton's call to arms we can recognize the same concept of a *katharsis* through moral and spiritual exercise by which *The Praise of Folly* and Jonson's ironic comedies sought their deepest justification.

Notes

Introduction

1 *The Staple of News*, first prologue, 21–7. Throughout this book, citations of Jonson's work refer to *Ben Jonson*, ed. C. H. Herford, P. and E. Simpson (11 vols., Oxford, 1925–52), designated *HS*. In quotations 'i' for 'j' and 'u' for 'v' have been normalized.

2 *Bartholomew Fair*, induction, 84.

3 *Drama & Society in the Age of Jonson* (London, 1937), p. 187.

4 *Jonson's Moral Comedy* (Evanston, 1971), pp. 249–50.

5 *Paradoxia Epidemica: the Renaissance Tradition of Paradox* (Princeton, 1966).

6 John Donne, *Selected Prose*, chosen by E. Simpson, ed. H. Gardner and T. Healy (Oxford, 1967), p. 111.

7 *Surprised by Sin: The Reader in 'Paradise Lost'* (London and New York, 1967).

8 *Humanism and Poetry in the Early Tudor Period: an Essay* (London, 1959).

9 *Selected Prose*, p. 111.

1 Lucian

1 *Lucian: Satirical Sketches*, trans. P. Turner, Penguin Books (Harmondsworth, 1961); *Lucian: Selected Works*, trans. B. P. Reardon, Library of Liberal Arts (Indianapolis and New York, 1965). The complete four-volume translation of *The Works of Lucian* (Oxford, 1905) by H. W. and F. G. Fowler remains very readable.

2 Cicero, *Academica* (Loeb ed.), I.2.8.

3 *Discourse concerning...Satire* (1693) in *Essays of John Dryden*, ed. W. P. Ker (Oxford, 1900), II, 84.

4 *Prose Works of John Dryden*, ed. E. Malone (London, 1800), III, 374.

5 *Ibid.*, p. 371.

6 *Anatomy of Criticism* ([Princeton, 1957] New York, 1965), pp. 308–12.

7 The term will be used, with misgivings, on the authority of J. Bompaire, *Lucien Ecrivain: Imitation et Création* (Paris, 1958), p. 327: 'le rôle de κατάσκοπος qui du haut d'une montagne ou d'un astre observe (et méprise) les humains est conforme à l'affabulation cynique'. But its usual literal meaning of 'spy' or 'scout' (because troop-movements were observed from high ground) is retained metaphorically by Epictetus (Loeb ed., III.22.24) where the philosopher observes good and evil and reports his findings to humanity. For the outlook of the detached observer Greek used the prefix ἐπι. Julian uses ἐπιβλέπειν of the Cynic looking down from Olympus (Loeb ed., VII.226B) and Lucian himself subtitles *Charon*

οἱ ἐπισκοποῦντες (cf. *The Dream, or Lucian's Career*, 15; *Nigrinus*, 18). Thus the proper term here would be *episkopos*, but its metaphoric associations have been pre-empted.

8 *Icaromenippus, or the Sky-Man*, 19. English titles of Lucian's works, references to and quotations from them, are taken from the Loeb translation (8 vols., London and Harvard, 1913–67), trans. A. M. Harmon (vols. 1–5), K. Kilburn (vol. 6), M. D. Macleod (vols. 7 and 8).

9 The term means originally 'private citizen', hence 'layman', hence 'unskilled', hence its modern sense. The opposite term in Lucian (*The Dance*, 84) is οἱ ἀστειότεροι συνιέντες, 'the politer sort who understand'.

10 *Lucien Ecrivain*, p. 742.

11 *To one who said 'You're a Prometheus in Words'*, 2ff.

12 Cicero, *Tusculan Disputations* (Loeb ed.), v.4.10.

13 ἀνὴρ σπουδαῖος ἐς τὸ γελασθῆναι (cited by Reardon, p. xxxi).

2 Erasmus

1 See C. R. Thompson, *The Translations of Lucian by Erasmus and St. Thomas More* (Ithaca, New York, 1940) and (ed.) *Translations of Lucian, Complete Works of St. Thomas More*, vol. III, Part 1 (New Haven, 1974).

2 Letter to John Claymond, quoted in translation by P. S. Allen, *Erasmus* (Oxford, 1934), p. 153.

3 Evidence from school curricula in T. W. Baldwin, *William Shakspere's 'Small Latin & Lesse Greeke'* (Urbana, 1944). See esp. I, 355.

4 *Desiderii Erasmi Roterodami Opera Omnia*, ed. J. Leclerc (Leiden, 1703–6), I, 213–14. Here, as traditionally, this edition will be cited as *LB*.

5 *LB*, I, 229–30. Translations mine in this and subsequent chapters, unless otherwise stated.

6 *LB*, I, 183–4.

7 *LB*, I, 243–6.

8 *Opus Epistolarum Des. Erasmi Roterodami*, ed. P. S. Allen, H. M. Allen and H. W. Garrod (Oxford, 1906–58), IV, 16, 118–19. This edition will be cited as *EE*.

9 Introductions to translations by H. H. Hudson (Princeton, 1941) and L. F. Dean (New York, 1946), the latter reprinted in *Essential Works of Erasmus*, ed. W. T. H. Jackson, Bantam Books (New York, London, Toronto, 1965); introduction by A. H. T. Levi to translation by Betty Radice, Penguin Books (Harmondsworth, 1971). See also the useful collection of criticism in *Twentieth-Century Interpretations of 'The Praise of Folly'*, ed. K. Williams (Englewood Cliffs, 1969).

10 Dean (Bantam ed.), pp. 346–50.

11 *Rhetoric* (Loeb ed.), 1.3.2.

12 *LB*, II, 460E.

13 *LB*, IV, 399–40.

14 Preface to *Folly*, *LB*, IV, 403–4 ('maxime si nugae seria ducant').

15 *Ibid.*

16 *Volpone*, 'The Epistle'; *Bartholomew Fair*, epilogue (see below, pp. 145 and 212).
17 Preface to *Folly* (Hudson's translation).
18 *Ollas ostentare*, *LB*, II, 461B.
19 Preface to *Folly*.
20 *Ollas ostentare*, *LB*, II, 461A.
21 Preface to *Folly*.
22 *LB*, IV, 401–2, note 13.
23 M. M. Phillips, *The 'Adages' of Erasmus: A Study with Translations* (Cambridge, 1964), p. 269.
24 *Ibid.*, p. 270.
25 *Ibid.*, p. 275.
26 *LB*, IX, 2–3:
    'Nec aliud omnino spectavimus in *Moria*, quam quod in caeteris lucubrationibus, tametsi via diversa. In *Enchiridio* simpliciter Christianae vitae formam tradidimus. In libello de Principis institutione palam admonemus, quibus rebus Principem oporteat esse instructum. In *Panegyrico* sub laudis praetextu, hoc ipsum tamen agimus oblique, quod illic egimus aperta fronte. Nec aliud agitur in *Moria* sub specie lusus, quam actum est in *Enchiridio*.'
27 *The Works of Lucian*, I, xxviii.
28 *Ollas ostentare*, trans. Phillips, p. 357.
29 *EE*, I, 520, 20.
30 Wilbur S. Howell glosses what Aristotle in the *Topics* calls 'contentious' (eristic) arguments as 'misreasonings employed in seminar or theater or academic chair to test hypotheses or display wit or develop skill in the processes of debate and controversy' (*Logic and Rhetoric in England, 1500–1700* (Princeton, 1956, New York, 1961), p. 43). Possibly this description should rather be given to what Aristotle calls 'training' (gymnastic) arguments. See also 'Additional Note', p. 246 below.
31 See the vivid record of a disputation in William T. Costello, S.J., *The Scholastic Curriculum at Early Seventeenth-Century Cambridge* (Cambridge, Mass., 1958), pp. 14–31. I am indebted to Professor Peter Dyson for this reference.
32 Preface to *Folly*.
33 *Ibid.*
34 This is to discount the *Julius Exclusus*, an example of *lusus* which does not seek to implicate the reader. See Sister Geraldine Thompson, *Under Pretext of Praise: Satiric Mode in Erasmus' Fiction* (Toronto, 1973), p. 96: 'The reader has no more perplexities than has Julius: to him it is obvious that thinking as Julius thinks and acting as Julius acts are bad ways to think and act.'
35 But see Sister Geraldine Thompson, *ibid.*, pp. 137–48. Her careful and balanced study of Erasmus's satire is a corrective to the one-pronged thrust of the present chapter.
36 Translation of *Ciceronianus* in Izora Scott, *Controversies over the Imitation of Cicero* (New York, 1910), Part 2, p. 101.
37 To Germain de Brie, quoted Scott, *ibid.*, Part 1, p. 33.
38 *Ibid.*, Part 1, p. 40 (my italics).

39 See below, p. 79.
40 Baldwin, *Shakspere's 'Small Latin & Lesse Greeke'*, I, 150, 165, 217, 310–11, 355, 725.
41 Preface (1636) to the *Colloquies* in *LB*, I, 895–6.
42 'The Usefulness of the *Colloquies*' in *The Colloquies of Erasmus*, trans. Craig R. Thompson (Chicago and London, 1965), p. 630. English titles of the *Colloquies* refer to this translation.
43 Jackson (ed.), *Essential Works of Erasmus*, p. 33.
44 Thompson, *The Colloquies*, p. 623.
45 *LB*, I, 901F.
46 *Ibid.* 901D–E: 'hoc genus illecebris inescare teneram aetatem...velut irrepens in animos adolescentium'.
47 *Ibid.*, 901E.
48 Jackson (ed.) *Essential Works of Erasmus*, p. 224.
49 Thompson, *The Colloquies*, p. 217.
50 *Ibid.*, p. 65.
51 Preface to *Luciani Samosatensis Opera* (Basel, 1563).
52 *The Fictions of Satire* (Baltimore, 1967), p. 41.

3 More

1 *Lives of Saint Thomas More*, ed. E. E. Reynolds, Everyman's Library (London and New York, 1963), pp. 50, 167. Later cited as *Lives*. In this chapter quotations from English works are generally taken from modernized texts. In some cases old-spelling texts have been modernized silently.
2 D. McPherson, 'Ben Jonson's Library and Marginalia: an annotated catalogue', *SP*, 71 (1974), 91.
3 Line-references to edition by W. W. Greg, Malone Society Reprints (London, 1911).
4 *Bartholomew Fair*, III.v.102–5.
5 *Lives*, p. 3.
6 *Acts and Monuments of John Foxe*, ed. J. Pratt (London, 1877), V, 100.
7 *Hall's Chronicle*, ed. H. Ellis (London, 1809), p. 818.
8 David Bevington, *Tudor Drama and Politics: A Critical Approach to Topical Meaning* (Cambridge, Mass., 1968), esp. Chapter 16.
9 *Acts and Monuments*, IV, 652.
10 *Tudor Drama and Politics*, p. 256.
11 *A Dialogue of Comfort Against Tribulation*, ed. L. Miles, Midland Books (Bloomington and London, 1965), Book 2, Chapter 1, pp. 69–71. In the first extract the word εὐτραπελία is introduced on the authority of *The Complete Works of St. Thomas More*, vol. 12, ed. L. Martz and F. Manley (New Haven and London, 1976), p. 82.
12 E. R. Curtius, *European Literature and the Latin Middle Ages*, trans. W. R. Trask, Harper Torchbooks (New York and Evanston, 1963), pp. 417–35 (Excursus IV: 'Jest and Earnest in Medieval Literature').

13 Almost but not quite. Lady Philosophy is at times the Menippean *kataskopos*, surveying the follies of mankind and finding them laughable. She even tells one joke (Book 2, Prose 7).

14 *A Hundred Merry Tales and Other English Jestbooks of the Fifteenth and Sixteenth Centuries*, ed. P. M. Zall (Lincoln, Nebraska, 1963), p. 156.

15 Facsimile reprint (Gainsville, Florida, 1962), p. 170.

16 *English Works* (London, 1557), p. 127B.

17 *The Life and Illustrious Martyrdom of Sir Thomas More*, trans. P. E. Hallett (London, 1928), p. 139.

18 *Ibid.*, p. 137.

19 *EE*, IV, 16, 113–27.

20 *Ibid.*, 21, 254–6.

21 *LB*, I, 265–6.

22 Dedicatory Letter to Thomas Ruthall in *The Correspondence of Sir Thomas More*, ed. E. F. Rogers (Princeton, 1947), p. 11.

23 See C. R. Thompson, *The Colloquies of Erasmus*, p. 230.

24 Letter to Ruthall (note 22 above).

25 *LB*, I, 749B; 751C.

26 *Ibid.*, 749C.

27 *Ibid.*, 750A.

28 *Ibid.*, 752E.

29 *St. Thomas More: Selected Letters*, ed. E. F. Rogers, rev. ed. (New Haven and London, 1967), pp. 11–12.

30 *Lives*, p. 110.

31 Letter to Willibald Pirckheimer prefaced to More's *Epigrammata* (Basel, 1518), quoted in translation by L. Bradner and C. A. Lynch, *The Latin Epigrams of Thomas More* (Chicago, 1953), pp. 127–8.

32 *A Defence of Poetry*, ed. J. A. Van Dorsten (London, 1966), pp. 33–4.

33 *Utopia*, ed. E. Surtz, S.J., *Selected Works of St. Thomas More* (New Haven and London, 1964), p. xiii. (Subsequent quotations are from this edition, cited as *Utopia*). See also the Yale *Complete Works*, vol. 4 (1965), pp. clxi–ii. And see also 'Additional Note', p. 246 below.

34 *More's Utopia: The Biography of an Idea* (Princeton, 1952).

35 T. S. Dorsch, 'Sir Thomas More and Lucian: An Interpretation of *Utopia*', *Archiv*, 203 (1966–7), 345–63.

36 *Ibid.*, p. 357.

37 *English Literature in the Sixteenth Century excluding Drama* (Oxford, 1954), p. 169.

38 Dean's translation, *Essential Works of Erasmus*, pp. 381–2.

39 *Utopia*, pp. 48–50.

40 *LB*, IV, 401–2: 'cum omnibus omnium horarum hominem agere, et potes et gaudes'.

41 *Utopia*, p. 151.

42 *The History of King Richard III*, ed. R. S. Sylvester, *Selected Works of St. Thomas More* (New Haven and London, 1976), p. 83.

43 *A Dialogue of Comfort*, p. 165.

44 *Lives*, p. 74.

45 *A Dialogue of Comfort*, p. 44.

4 Images of Lucian

1 *Luciani Samosatensis Deorum Dialogi* (Strasbourg, 1515), n.p.
2 More, *Correspondence*, ed. Rogers, p. 12.
3 *Certaine Select Dialogues* [of Lucian], trans. F. Hickes, ed. T. Hickes (Oxford, 1634), 'To the Reader'.
4 Trans. Conrad Wackers (Goclenius) (Louvain, 1522), preface.
5 *EE*, VIII, 128, note; P. Smith, *The Life and Letters of Martin Luther* (New York, 1911), p. 211.
6 Smith, *ibid.*, p. 212.
7 *Dialogus de Imitatione Ciceroniana adversus Erasmum* [1535], quoted and translated by Izora Scott, *Controversies*, Part 1, p. 67.
8 *Oratio pro M. T. Cicerone contra Desiderium Erasmum* [1531], quoted and translated by Scott, *ibid.*, p. 50.
9 *De Tradendis Disciplinis*, trans. Foster Watson as *Vives: On Education* (Cambridge, 1913), p. 143; *The Book named the Governor*, ed. S. E. Lehmberg, Everyman's Library (London and New York, 1962), p. 30.
10 Watson (trans.), *Vives*, p. 148.
11 *Ibid.*, p. 185.
12 Phillips, *'Adages' of Erasmus*, p. 217.
13 Watson (trans.), *Vives*, pp. 272–304.
14 *An Answer unto Sir Thomas More's Dialogue* [1530], in *The Works of the English Reformers*, ed. T. Russell, II (London, 1831), 202.
15 *Acts and Monuments*, IV, 198, 679.
16 *Works of the English Reformers*, II, 15–16 (my italics).
17 *A Confutation of Tyndale's Answer* [1532], in *The Essential Thomas More*, ed. J. J. Greene and J. P. Dolan, Mentor-Omega Books (Toronto, 1967), p. 223.
18 Baldwin, *Shakspere's 'Small Latin & Lesse Greeke'*, I, 215–17.
19 *Ibid.*, I, 109.
20 *De Vita et Scriptis Luciani Narratio.*
21 *Gabriel Harvey's Marginalia*, ed. G. C. Moore Smith (Stratford upon Avon, 1913), p. 23.
22 [George Puttenham] *The Arte of English Poesie* (London, 1589), p. 218.
23 *Marginalia*, p. 149.
24 *Ibid.*, p. 147.
25 Quoted R. Gottfried, *Spenser's Prose Works*, Variorum edition of the Works of Spenser, x (Baltimore, 1949), 460.
26 *Ibid.*, p. 471.
27 *Foure Letters...* [1592], ed. G. B. Harrison, Bodley Head Quartos (London, 1922), p. 50.
28 *Foure Letters Confuted* [1592], in *The Works of Thomas Nashe*, ed. R. B. McKerrow, rev. F. P. Wilson (Oxford, 1958), I, 283.
29 *Ibid.*, I, 285.
30 *A Defence of Poetry*, p. 49–50.
31 [Innocent Gentillet] *A Discourse upon the Meanes of Wel Governing...against*

Nicholas Machiavell, trans. Simon Patericke (London, 1602), Epistle Dedicatorie, n.p.

32 *Workes* (London, 1629), p. 167.

33 *Abuses Stript, and Whipt, or Satirical Essayes* (London, 1613), n.p., 'Of Man'.

34 *Foure Letters...*, p. 101 (sonnet dated 1586).

35 'Then cease fond satyres, quipping epigrammatists, / Sly scoffing critics, jeering Lucianists' (John Weever, 'A Prophecy of this Present Year 1600', lines 1–2). Printed in *Tudor Verse Satire*, ed. K. W. Gransden, Athlone Renaissance Library (London, 1970), p. 137.

36 *The Scourge of Villainy*, Proemium to Book 3, lines 1–2 (*Tudor Verse Satire*, p. 116).

37 *A Defence of Poetry*, p. 49.

38 *Timon, or the Misanthrope*, 8.

39 *A Defence of Poetry*, pp. 28–9.

5 Teasing Drama: Medwall to Marlowe

1 *A Confutation of Tyndale's Answer* in *The Essential Thomas More*, p. 223.

2 F. S. Boas, *University Drama in the Tudor Age* (Oxford, 1914), Chapter 1.

3 *Ibid.*, p. 8.

4 R. J. Schoeck, 'More and Lincoln's Inn Revels', *PQ*, 29 (1950), 426–30.

5 See E. K. Chambers, *The Mediaeval Stage* (Oxford, 1903), I, 336–71.

6 *OED*, 'disour'.

7 *Tudor Drama and Politics*, p. 46. Recurring debts to Bevington's book will be apparent in this chapter.

8 Line-references and quotations are from the edition by F. S. Boas in *Five Pre-Shakespearean Comedies*, The World's Classics (London, 1934).

9 *Tudor Drama and Politics*, p. 78.

10 *The Dramatic Writings of John Heywood*, ed. J. S. Farmer, Early English Drama Society (London, 1905), p. 135.

11 Bevington, *Tudor Drama and Politics*, pp. 64–70.

12 Farmer's edition, p. 97.

13 *Tudor Drama and Politics*, p. 224.

14 See Howell, *Logic and Rhetoric in England*, pp. 160–83.

15 *The Logike of the Moste Excellent Philosopher P. Ramus Martyr* [London, 1574], Scolar Press facsimile (Menston, 1970), p. 100.

16 'Was this the face that launch'd a thousand ships...?' Cf. *Dialogues of the Gods*, 409 ('Menippus and Hermes').

17 C. Leech, 'Marlowe's Humor', in *Marlowe: A Collection of Critical Essays*, ed. C. Leech (Englewood Cliffs, 1964), pp. 169–72.

18 J. D. Jump's text, The Revels Plays (London, 1962), VIII.71–5.

19 For an Erasmian approach to Marlowe see J. Weil, *Christopher Marlowe: Merlin's Prophet* (Cambridge, 1977).

20 R. Levin, *The Multiple Plot in English Renaissance Drama* (Chicago and London, 1971), p. 121.

21 C. F. Tucker Brooke, *The Life of Marlowe* (London, 1930), p. 98.

6 Before *Volpone*

1 *HS*, I, 150.
2 Quoted B. Crick (ed.), Niccolò Machiavelli, *The Discourses*, Penguin Books (Harmondsworth, 1970), pp. 68–9.
3 *Discoveries*, 2468–9.
4 Prologue (1616), 14.
5 *Ben Jonson* (London, 1970), p. 26.
6 Introduction to edition, Regents Renaissance Drama Series (Lincoln, Nebraska, 1971), p. xvii.
7 *A Defence of Poetry*, p. 29.
8 *Ibid.*, p. 44.
9 See J. A. Barish, 'Jonson and the Loathèd Stage', in *A Celebration of Ben Jonson*, ed. W. Blissett, J. Patrick, R. W. Van Fossen (Toronto, 1973), p. 42.
10 *HS*, IX, 425–7.
11 *Ibid.*, pp. 492–3.
12 *Ibid.*, p. 567.
13 *The Colloquies*, p. 630.
14 Dedication (1616).
15 Prologue, 3.
16 For further discussion of Jonson's tragic criteria in relation to *Sejanus* and *Catiline*, see below, pp. 213–15, 218–23.

7 *Volpone*

1 See *HS*, note to I.ii.66–81; Hudson's translation of *Folly*, pp. 47–50.
2 *HS*, notes to I. ii. 98–109, 112.
3 Evidence of Jonson's use of Lucian and Erasmus in *Volpone* was first collected by J. D. Rea in his edition (New Haven, 1919). Since he interpreted the evidence rashly ('the sources are almost the play itself'), he received acid treatment in *HS*, IX, 678–81. But the Oxford editors endorse most of his sources, unhelpfully transcribing the Lucian passages in Greek where Rea was right to see that Jonson had almost certainly used Erasmus's Latin.
4 See above, pp. 28–9.
5 'Jonson's Metempsychosis', *PQ*, 22 (1943), 231–9.
6 A. B. Kernan (ed.), *Volpone*, The Yale Ben Jonson (New Haven, 1962), p. 21.
7 *Discoveries*, 786–93 (my italics), following Quintilian.
8 II.ii.13, 68, 117; IV.iv.22.
9 'The Argument', 7.
10 See Bamborough, *Ben Jonson*, p. 84.
11 *HS*, note to I.i.16–20; Seneca, *Epistles*, cxv.15, trans. R. M. Gummere (Loeb).

12 *Defence of Poetry*, pp. 68–9.
13 K. Varty, *Reynard the Fox: A Study of the Fox in Medieval English Art* (Leicester, 1967), p. 51 and *passim*.
14 A. B. Kernan, *The Cankered Muse* (New Haven, 1959), pp. 167–8.
15 J. Benedict (ed.), *Luciani Samosatensis Opera* (Saumur, 1619), *Praefatio*.
16 J. A. Barish, 'The Double Plot in *Volpone*', *MP*, 51 (1953), 84.
17 I. Donaldson, 'Jonson's Tortoise', *RES*, 19 (1968), 162–8.
18 *LB*, II, 790–1: 'Domus amica, domus optima'.
19 *Every Man in his Humour*, prologue (1616), 24–6.
20 On this point, and for a view of Jonson's rhetoric which anticipates much in this chapter, see S. L. Goldberg, 'Folly into Crime: The Catastrophe of *Volpone*', *MLQ*, 20 (1959), 233–42.

8 *Epicoene*

1 *Volpone*, V.xi.1–5.
2 *Discoveries*, 2629–31, following Daniel Heinsius. Some modernized texts accept the 1692 Folio reading 'fooling' for 'fowling', but Heinsius wrote 'movere risum...aucupium est plebis, et abusus' (see *HS*, note).
3 *The World Upside-Down: Comedy from Jonson to Fielding* (Oxford, 1970), p. 32.
4 *Ben Jonson*, p. 94.
5 L. A. Beaurline, Regents Renaissance Drama Series (Lincoln, Nebraska, 1966), p. xviii; E. Partridge, The Yale Ben Jonson (New Haven and London, 1971), p. 1.
6 A. Harbage, *Shakespeare and the Rival Traditions* (New York, 1952), p. 54.
7 Second prologue, 10.
8 One, Nathan Field, was twenty-two. See A. Leggatt in *The Revels History of Drama in English*, vol. III '1576–1613', ed. C. Leech and T. W. Craik (London, 1975), p. 112, citing R. A. Foakes.
9 See Harbage, *Rival Traditions*, esp. pp. 76–80, 210–14.
10 *The World Upside-Down*, pp. 26–7.
11 *Ibid.*, p. 44.
12 *Ibid.*, p. 43.
13 *Ben Jonson's Poems: A Study of the Plain Style* (Stanford, 1962), pp. 186–7.
14 *Epigrams*, x.48.21–4, trans. W. C. A. Ker (Loeb).
15 *Libanii Sophistae Clarissimi Declamatio Lepidissima* (Paris, 1597).
16 See O. J. Campbell, 'The Relation of *Epicoene* to Aretino's *Il Marescalco*', *PMLA*, 46 (1931), 752–62.
17 *The Carousal, or the Lapiths*, 45.
18 *Ibid.*, 34–5.
19 *Essay of Dramatic Poesy* in *Essays*, ed. Ker, I, 86.
20 Preface to *An Evening's Love, or The Mock Astrologer* (Ker, I, 142).
21 Defence of the epilogue to *The Conquest of Granada* (Ker, I, 174).
22 J. A. Barish, *Ben Jonson and the Language of Prose Comedy* (Cambridge, Mass., 1960), p. 176.

23 Perhaps derived from a romance by DesEscuteaux, *Les Chastes et Heureuses Amours de Clarimond et Antonide* (Paris, 1601).
24 The following discussion takes hints from *The Idea of Comedy*, ed. W. K. Wimsatt (Englewood Cliffs, 1969), pp. 9–11.
25 *The Schoole of Abuse* [1579], ed. E. Arber (London, 1906), p. 31.
26 *Nichomachean Ethics*, IV.8.1–7, trans. H. Rackham (Loeb).
27 *Rhetoric*, II.12.16, trans. J. H. Freese (Loeb).
28 *Ibid.*, 13.15.
29 Liddell and Scott, *Greek-English Lexicon*.
30 'A speech at Eton', in *Irish Essays, and others* (London, 1882).
31 Preface to *An Evening's Love* (Ker, I, 142–3).
32 *Ben Jonson and the Language of Prose Comedy*, pp. 156–7.
33 N. Perrot D'Ablancourt, *Lucien* (Paris, 1654), 'Epistre'.
34 Scott, *Controversies*, Part 2, pp. 28–9.

9 Comedies of Accommodation

1 *Jonson's Moral Comedy*, p. 135.
2 F. H. Mares (ed.), *The Alchemist*, The Revels Plays (London, 1967), p. xlii.
3 See R. Levin, 'The Structure of *Bartholomew Fair*', *PMLA*, 80 (1965), 172–9.
4 Bamborough, *Ben Jonson*, p. 99.
5 Phillips, *The 'Adages' of Erasmus*, p. 357.
6 Thompson, *The Colloquies of Erasmus*, p. 239.
7 *Nichomachean Ethics*, IV.3.34, trans. H. Rackham (Loeb).
8 Thompson, *The Colloquies of Erasmus*, p. 245.
9 See above, p. 63.
10 *Alexander*, 25, 38 (Loeb).
11 See above, p. 28.
12 Note to *Love Freed from Ignorance and Folly*, 98.
13 *Poetaster*, 'Apologeticall Dialogue', 205–21.
14 The joke can be tentatively reconstructed. Face answers Dol's 'say lord *Generall*, how fares our campe?' (cf. *The Spanish Tragedy*, I.ii.1). Kyd's play, with its account of the capture and ransom of a Don, underlies Face's advice to Dol on how to treat her Spanish client. His reference here to 'the few' recalls the reply of Kyd's General: 'All well, my sovereign liege, except some few / That are deceas'd by fortune of the war.' The absurdity – all the troops are well except for those who are dead – is magnified when the General insists on marching the survivors across the stage, 'whereby by demonstration shall appear / That all (except three hundred or few more) / Are safe return'd and by their foes enrich'd' (107–9). After such a build-up the appearance of three or four extras with rusty swords would have struck Jonson as funny.
15 *Hymenaei*, 19.
16 *The New Inn*, first epilogue, 11–13.
17 See Donaldson, *The World Upside-Down*, pp. 76–7.
18 Dean's translation, *Essential Works of Erasmus*, p. 390.

19 *LB*, IV, 429C (my translation); cf. Dean's version quoted above, p. 71.
20 *Conversations with Drummond*, 82–5, 416–17.
21 *The Essential Thomas More*, p. 203.
22 *HS*, I, 65–7.
23 *EE*, IV, 16, 126–30.
24 *A Dialogue of Comfort*, ed. Miles, Part I, *passim*.
25 *Ibid.*, pp. 214–15.
26 *Catiline*, 'To the Reader in Ordinairie'.
27 *The Advancement of Learning*, ed. G. W. Kitchin, Everyman's Library (London and New York, 1915), p. 11.
28 *Ben Jonson*, p. 53.
29 *The Moral Vision of Jacobean Tragedy* (Madison, 1960), p. 101.
30 See J. P. V. D. Balsdon, 'Cicero the Man', in *Cicero*, ed. T. A. Dorey (London, 1964), esp. pp. 204–5.
31 *Essayes*, trans. Florio (1603), 'Of Bookes'.
32 J. A. Bryant, jr, 'Catiline and the Nature of Jonson's Tragic Fable', *PMLA*, 69 (1954), 265–77.
33 *The Advancement of Learning*, p. 12.
34 *Works of Thomas Nashe*, ed. McKerrow I, 284.
35 'Cicero the Man', p. 184.
36 *The Advancement of Learning*, p. 12.
37 Barish, *Ben Jonson and the Language of Prose Comedy*, pp. 212–13.

10 After the Fair: Conclusions

1 S. Orgel, *The Jonsonian Masque* (Cambridge, Mass., 1965), p. 99.
2 For a fuller discussion of the play see my 'A Guide to *The New Inn*', *Essays in Criticism*, 20.3 (1970), 311–26; also objections by R. Levin in 'The New New Inn and the Proliferation of Good Bad Drama', *ibid.*, 22.1 (1972), 41–7. Levin's main point – if Jonson's intention was ironic, why didn't he acknowledge it when his play came under attack? – cannot be answered except by recalling that Jonson never did acknowledge ironic intention, so far as we know. The present book offers a rich harvest for Levin's sickle.
3 *HS*, XI, 339–40.
4 *LB*, IV, 433B.
5 Dedication, To the Reader.
6 See above, p. 44.
7 *Comus* (1634), 160–4.
8 *Paradise Lost*, VIII, 367–471.
9 *Conversations with Drummond*, 688–9.

Additional Note (pp. 39–40, 67). In Chapters 2 and 3 my account of the mischievous rhetoric of Erasmus and More should be supplemented by Arthur F. Kinney's 'Rhetoric as Poetic: Humanist Fiction in the Renaissance', *ELH*, 43 (1976), 413–43. See also his *Rhetoric and Poetic in Thomas More's 'Utopia'* (Los Angeles, 1979).

Index

Index

Index

Index

Characteristics – *continued*

15–21; evasive personality, 11–14; defender of *lusus*, 24–5; 'Menippean' method, 14–15; educator of the public, 23, 46, 235; self-dramatization, 11–12, 135, 198; social satirist, 23–4; stylist, 9, 10, 27; variety, 10–11; virtuosity, 31–2

REPUTATION AND INFLUENCE, 9–15, 77–96 (*see also under* Erasmus; Jonson; More)

attacked: as atheistic and blasphemous, 77, 78, 82–3, 85–6; as irresponsible and uncommitted, 88, 90; as scoffer, 79, 83, 90; as sophistic, 79–80; as bad for the young, 79, 82

defended: as *bel esprit*, 183; on Erasmian grounds, 82–3, 86; on pagan grounds, 77, 84; as author of merry tales, 84

influence: on relativist thinking, 51, 89; on sceptical thinking, 90–1; on Shakespeare, 91–4

linked: with Aretino, 78, 85, 86; with Machiavelli, 86, 88

popular at Cambridge, 84, 86, 111

translations and editions, 26, 77, 78, 82–3

used in schools, 27, 44, 79, 82, 91

WORKS: *Alexander, or The False Prophet*, 16, 24, 28, 39, 197–8; *The Carousal, or The Lapiths*, 132–3, 176–7; *Charon, or The Inspectors*, 14, 17–18, 19; *The Cock*, see *The Dream, or The Cock*; *The Cynic*, 13, 16; *The Dance*, 18–19; *The Dead Come to Life, or The Fisherman*, 11, 17, 22; *Dialogues of the Courtesans*, 14, 86; *Dialogues of the Dead*, 14, 147; *Dialogues of the Gods*, 14, 77, 111, 130, 242 (n. 16); *Dialogues of the Sea-gods*, 14; *The Double Indictment*, 11; *The Dream, or The Cock*, 21, 28, 144–5; *The Dream, or Lucian's Career*, 11, 16; *The Fly*, 30;

Hermotimus, 11, 17, 78–9, 90; *Icaromenippus, or The Sky-Man*, 15–16, 17, 19, 91, 92, 105, 112; *Lexiphanes*, 23–4, 130; *The Lover of Lies*, 13, 62; *Menippus, or The Descent into Hades*, 13, 62; *Nigrinus*, 11, 16, 20–1, 70; *The Parasite*, 13–14, 30, 39, 152; *The Passing of Peregrinus*, 24, 78; *Philosophies for Sale*, 17, 90; *A Professor of Public Speaking*, 24; *To one who said 'You're a Prometheus in words'*, 11, 23; *On Salaried Posts in Great Houses*, 13, 17; *Timon, or The Misanthrope*, 79, 83, 91, 93; *A True Story*, 11, 13, 21, 24–5, 32, 39, 194; *The Tyrannicide*, 61

Lucretius, 192

lusus, 24–5 and *passim*; interpreted and defended by Erasmus, 31–9, 46–7

Luther, Martin, 51, 61, 79

Lyly, John, 130

Machiavelli, Niccolò, 84, 86–8, 111, 119, 138–40, 220

MacIlmaine, Roland, 110–11

Marlowe, Christopher, 108–15, 142, 149, 233; deceptive rhetoric, 109–11, 113–15

Marston, John, 90, 136

Martial, 172, 174

Martianus Capella, 11

Mason, H. A., 6

Medwall, Henry, 99–104, 114

'Menippean' fiction, 6; in Erasmus, 38, 50; in Jonson, *see under* Jonson; in Lucian, 14–15; in Marlowe, 114; in *Utopia*, 67–9

Menippus, 6, 10–11, 57

Milton, John, 58–9, 95–6, 232, 235

Miracle plays, 99

Moltzer, Jakob, (Micyllus), 82

Montaigne, Michel de, 109, 135, 221

Morality plays, 4–5, 98–9, 106–7, 110, 113–14, 227; *see also under* Jonson